P9-CFD-766

Harry Potter
and
History

PURCHASED FROM
MULTNOMAH COUNTY LIBRARY
TITLE WAVE BOOKSTORE

Wiley Pop Culture and History Series

Series Editor: Nancy Reagin

Twilight and History
Edited by Nancy Reagin

Harry Potter
and
History

Edited by
NANCY R. REAGIN

WILEY

John Wiley & Sons, Inc.

This book is printed on acid-free paper. ∞

Copyright © 2011 by John Wiley & Sons, Inc. All rights reserved

Published by John Wiley & Sons, Inc., Hoboken, New Jersey
Published simultaneously in Canada

Chapter opener design by Forty-Five Degree Design LLC

Illustration credits: p.3, from the 1681 edition of *Saducismus Triumphatus*, London, by Joseph Glanvill; p. 11, Kunsthistorisches Museum Wien, KK 1001; pp. 17, 20, Library of the University of Salzburg, Special Collections, W II 251 (*Hortus Sanitatis*, Strasbourg, Johann Prüss, 1497); p. 75, from Paul Lacroix, *Manners, Customs, and Dress during the Middle Ages, and during the Renaissance Period* (London: Chapman & Hall, 1876); p. 93, Zentralbibliothek Luzern, Hs. S. 23, fol. 60r

No part of this publication may be reproduced, stored in a retrieval system, or transmitted in any form or by any means, electronic, mechanical, photocopying, recording, scanning, or otherwise, except as permitted under Section 107 or 108 of the 1976 United States Copyright Act, without either the prior written permission of the Publisher, or authorization through payment of the appropriate per-copy fee to the Copyright Clearance Center, 222 Rosewood Drive, Danvers, MA 01923, (978) 750-8400, fax (978) 646-8600, or on the web at www.copyright.com. Requests to the Publisher for permission should be addressed to the Permissions Department, John Wiley & Sons, Inc., 111 River Street, Hoboken, NJ 07030, (201) 748-6011, fax (201) 748-6008, or online at http://www.wiley.com/go/permissions.

Limit of Liability/Disclaimer of Warranty: While the publisher and the author have used their best efforts in preparing this book, they make no representations or warranties with respect to the accuracy or completeness of the contents of this book and specifically disclaim any implied warranties of merchantability or fitness for a particular purpose. No warranty may be created or extended by sales representatives or written sales materials. The advice and strategies contained herein may not be suitable for your situation. You should consult with a professional where appropriate. Neither the publisher nor the author shall be liable for any loss of profit or any other commercial damages, including but not limited to special, incidental, consequential, or other damages.

For general information about our other products and services, please contact our Customer Care Department within the United States at (800) 762-2974, outside the United States at (317) 572-3993 or fax (317) 572-4002.

Wiley also publishes its books in a variety of electronic formats. Some content that appears in print may not be available in electronic books. For more information about Wiley products, visit our web site at www.wiley.com.

Library of Congress Cataloging-in-Publication Data:

Reagin, Nancy Ruth, date.
    Harry Potter and history / Nancy Reagin.
      p. cm.
    Includes bibliographical references and index.
    ISBN 978-0-470-57472-0 (paper : alk. paper); ISBN 978-1-118-00324-4 (ebk.); ISBN 978-1-118-00325-1 (ebk.); ISBN 978-1-118-00326-8 (ebk.)
    1. Rowling, J. K.—Characters. 2. Literature and history. 3. Potter, Harry (Fictitious character) 4. Children's stories, English—History and criicism. 5. Fantasy fiction, English—History and criticism. I. Title.
  PR6068.093Z846   2011
  823'.914—dc22

2011010968

Printed in the United States of America
10 9 8 7 6 5 4 3 2

For Mary,
the first magic that ever happened to me

Contents

Acknowledgments
Writing Magical History

"That was far easier than I thought it would be," said Hermione as they joined the crowds flocking out onto the sunny grounds [after their History of Magic exam]. "I needn't have learned about the 1637 Werewolf Code of Conduct or the uprising of Elfric the Eager."

—*Sorcerer's Stone*, 203

Like Hermione Granger, I found my task—editing this book—much easier than I thought it would be. But unlike Hermione, it was precisely because I *wanted* to learn all about things like the Werewolf Code of Conduct: my fellow contributors obliged splendidly, creating chapters that are full of clever insights and interesting nuggets of research regarding magical history. They were a joy to work with, and I want to thank all of them for bringing their passion for the wizarding world to the job of writing about it.

The editors at Wiley continue to be a godsend. Connie Santisteban, Eric Nelson, and Ellen Wright could probably write their own book about working with academic authors who are also fans—a challenging group to manage—and they made it all seem simple, squeezing in late-arriving photos of bezoars and woodcuts of mandrakes with good humor. Lisa Burstiner, who managed the book's production, brought both her attention to detail and her expertise in the series to working with me; having her assigned to the project could only be attributed to Felix Felicis.

I owe the most to the Harry Potter fandom, however, which originally drew me into the Potterverse. Waiting for each new book in the series together, imagining what would happen next and arguing about each clue: my fellow fans made the experience of J. K. Rowling's marvelous story and characters much better for me than the books ever could have been if experienced alone. The wizarding world is endlessly absorbing, especially when you have such friends to explore, discuss, and debate it with, and my companions (and co-conspirators) in HP have enriched my life enormously. In return, I offer them this book, which I hope will give them (and all Potter fans) a little bit more of Harry's fascinating world.

Harry Potter's Timeline

MUGGLE HISTORY	WIZARDING HISTORY*
753 B.C. (B.C.E.): According to legend, Romulus founds Rome after killing his brother, Remus	
551: Birth of Confucius	
ca. 400: Birth of Gautama Buddha, founder of Buddhism	
384: Birth of Aristotle	**382 B.C. (B.C.E.):** Ollivander's Fine Wands established
55: Julius Caesar invades Britain, beginning process of Roman conquest and occupation	
ca. 30 A.D. (C.E.): Jesus of Nazareth crucified	
ca. 600: First recorded meeting of an English Witenagemot, forerunner of the wizarding Wizengamot	
632: Death of Muhammad, prophet of Islam	
	ca. 990 A.D. (C.E.): Hogwarts School of Witchcraft and Wizardry established
1066: Battle of Hastings, Norman conquest of Britain	**ca. 1000:** The Chamber of Secrets created by Salazar Slytherin
1095: First Crusade preached at Clermont	**1000–1100:** Emergence and development of the game of Quidditch
	1203: Holyhead Harpies founded
	1294: Triwizard Tournament established
	ca. 1300: During this century, Wedelin the Weird allowed herself to be burned at the stake 47 times, in various disguises

*Most of the dates on the wizarding side of the timeline are derived from the seven books of the Harry Potter series. Some dates are taken from Rowling's ancillary wizarding works, *Quidditch through the Ages*, *Fantastic Beasts and Where to Find Them*, and *Tales of Beedle the Bard*. Dates were checked against the "official timeline" included at the end of the DVD version of the film version of *Chamber of Secrets* and also against the Harry Potter Lexicon, located at www.hp-lexicon.org/timelines/timeline.php.

Harry Potter's Timeline *(continued)*

MUGGLE HISTORY	WIZARDING HISTORY
ca. 1330: Birth of Nicolas Flamel, alchemist	
1347: Black Plague reaches Europe	
	1368: The Wizards' Council bans all Quidditch within 100 miles of a Muggle town or village
1436: Johannes Gutenberg develops the printing press	
	1473: First Quidditch World Cup played
1492: Christopher Columbus reaches the New World, beginning European conquest	**1492:** Sir Nicholas de Mimsy-Porpington (Nearly Headless Nick) is executed and becomes a ghost
ca. 1502: Beginning of Atlantic slave trade	
1517: Martin Luther launches Protestant Reformation	
1533: Birth of Elizabeth I, Queen of England	
1564: Birth of William Shakespeare	
	ca. 1600: St. Mungo's Hospital for Magical Maladies and Injuries founded
1640–1649: English Civil War	
	1674: The British and Irish Quidditch League formed
1692: Salem witchcraft trials held in Massachusetts	**1692:** Statute of Secrecy enacted; the wizarding world separates itself from Muggles*
ca. 1750: Beginning of Industrial Revolution; Muggles begin to invent a flood of interesting mechanical devices	

---

*Albus Dumbledore asserted in *The Tales of Beedle the Bard* that the statute was passed in 1689, but the 1692 date (offered by wizarding historian Newt Scamander in *Fantastic Beasts*) seems more plausible for reasons explored in chapter 5.

MUGGLE HISTORY	WIZARDING HISTORY
1789: Beginning of the French Revolution	
1836: Samuel Colt patents his revolver	
	1847: Phineas Nigellus Black born
1848: Karl Marx and Friedrich Engels publish the *Communist Manifesto*	
1861–1865: U.S. Civil War	
ca. 1875: Alexander Graham Bell develops the telephone	1888: Albus Dumbledore born
	1899: Dumbledore finishes at Hogwarts, meets Gellert Grindelwald
	Dumbledore's sister, Ariana, accidentally killed in a domestic dispute
1900: L. Frank Baum publishes *The Wonderful Wizard of Oz*	
	1907: Merope Gaunt (mother of Tom Riddle) born
1914–1918: World War I; United States joins war in 1917	
1917: Russian Revolution	
	1925: Minerva McGonagall born
	1926: Tom Riddle born
1928: Alexander Fleming discovers penicillin	1928: Rubeus Hagrid born
1929: Beginning of Great Depression	
1933: Adolf Hitler and the National Socialists gain control over German government	
1939–1945: World War II	1945: Albus Dumbledore defeats Gellert Grindelwald, who is then imprisoned at Nurmengard
1949: Chinese Revolution	
	1951: Bellatrix Black born
	1954: Lucius Malfoy born

Harry Potter's Timeline *(continued)*

MUGGLE HISTORY	WIZARDING HISTORY
	ca. 1955: Albus Dumbledore becomes Headmaster of Hogwarts School of Witchcraft and Wizardry
1960: Birth control pill becomes available	1959–1960: Birth of James Potter, Sirius Black, Remus Lupin, Peter Pettigrew, Lily Evans, and Severus Snape
1965: Birth of J. K. Rowling	1965: Lucius Malfoy starts at Hogwarts
1968: Political upheaval throughout Western Europe and the United States due to race riots, anti–Vietnam War protests, and youth rebellions	
The Prague Spring	
	1969: Marriage of Arthur Weasley and Molly Prewett
1974: Richard Nixon resigns as U.S. president	1976: James Potter publicly humiliates Severus Snape after their O.W.L.s; Sirius Black plays an almost fatal prank on Snape, luring him to the Whomping Willow
	ca. 1978: Marriage of Lily and James Potter
ca. 1980: Rapid development of the Internet	
	1980: Birth of Harry Potter
	1981: In September, Severus Snape begins teaching at Hogwarts and becomes a spy for Albus Dumbledore around this time
	On October 31, Voldemort murders Lily and James Potter; Harry Potter becomes the Boy Who Lived.
1991: Collapse of the Soviet Union, end of Cold War	1991: Harry Potter enters Hogwarts

Introduction

A Half-Blood World?

Nancy R. Reagin

"Welcome," said Hagrid, "to Diagon Alley." [. . .]

The sun shone brightly on a stack of cauldrons outside the nearest shop.

Cauldrons—All Sizes—Copper, Brass, Pewter, Silver— Self-Stirring—Collapsible, said a sign hanging over them. [. . .]

Harry wished he had about eight more eyes. He turned his head in every direction as they walked up the street, trying to look at everything at once.

—*Sorcerer's Stone*, 71[1]

Harry Potter is magical, as everyone knows. He flies on a broomstick, he talks to snakes and an owl that brings him his mail. His world is magical, too. At his school, paintings talk, staircases move about, and suits of armor defend the castle. In Diagon Alley, the shops sell silver unicorn's horn, dragon's liver, and books that bite—as well as ice cream cones. Even the government is magical: at the Ministry of Magic, memos fly about with little wings, while the Ministry's Department of Magical Maintenance can control underground rainstorms.

Yet Harry Potter is also an ordinary British kid. He has steak and kidney pie and Yorkshire pudding for dinner in *Goblet of Fire*, followed by treacle tart for dessert (his favorite). He takes tea with Rubeus Hagrid and Professor Remus Lupin. Before he goes to Hogwarts, he lives with the Dursleys in a perfectly normal English suburb. Like many Hogwarts students and most of the adults in Harry's world, he is of mixed ancestry, with some Muggle grandparents and other relatives.

Like Harry, the wizarding world mixes magical and Muggle influences. Almost all of the places, the people, and the institutions we see in the Potterverse are not only magical but profoundly British, with roots in earlier Muggle history. The wizarding world is a "half-blooded" one: its people, culture, and institutions are descended from Muggles.

The fact that our modern world and the wizarding world have common roots shouldn't surprise us. For many centuries, author J. K. Rowling tells us, wizards and witches lived side by side with Muggles in villages and towns across Europe, often intermarrying or socializing. They must have often shared knowledge and values, because they were—in most respects—part of the same culture. The highest judicial authority in wizarding Britain, for example— the Wizengamot—stems from the real Witenagemots (councils) established by Muggle kings of England a thousand years earlier, around the time that Hogwarts was founded.

Even before Hogwarts was established, people who practiced magic were common throughout Europe, using charms, potions, and spells to get the results they wanted. Mandrakes were commonly sold in markets across medieval Europe, for example, and very wealthy people might even have bought a powder made from the Sorcerer's Stone. Bezoars were prized by Muggle princes, kings, and queens for centuries: even today, gold or silver-encrusted bezoars from their collections can be seen in European museums, and one of the largest bezoars ever discovered (in South America) was sent to the Pope, in Rome. Almost all of the magical techniques and objects Harry sees at Hogwarts were well-known to medieval and Renaissance Europeans, in fact.

Even after the Statute of Secrecy forced wizarding families to separate themselves from Muggles in the late seventeenth century, there was still a constant flow of Muggle-born students into Hogwarts, which no doubt accelerated after the nineteenth century. The expansion of public education during that period meant that magically gifted children born to Muggle families—even poor ones—would be taught to read and write and thus be given the basic primary education needed to attend Hogwarts.

The constant infusion of new Muggle-borns into wizarding society via Hogwarts meant that the magical world was never truly separated from developments in the Muggle world, although pureblood

A pupil is the apparent victim of an early version of the Levicorpus jinx, as shown in this seventeenth-century English woodcut illustration by William Faithor.

families looked down on those—such as the Weasleys—who liked Muggle gadgets and socialized with the Muggle-born. Yet despite the pureblood elites' disdain of Muggle influences, those influences continued to enter the wizarding world, and Muggle-born wizards and witches might even have carried back wizarding ideas and models to their families of origin, when they went to visit Muggle relatives.

As a result, we see many parallel developments in both worlds long after the Statute of Secrecy was passed. The Malfoys may have looked down on Muggle aristocrats, but they lived very much like Muggle gentry, on a manor with house elves in place of human butlers, maids, and footmen. Like the great Muggle boarding schools it resembled (and perhaps foreshadowed), Hogwarts also divided its pupils into Houses, had them wear house ties and school robes, and hosted an annual competition for a House Cup; in these and in many other respects, Hogwarts was very much like other British boarding schools.

Ideas flowed back and forth between the wizarding and Muggle worlds, along with institutions and lifestyles. Tom Riddle—like Harry, a half-blood raised in the Muggle world—grew up in a Muggle orphanage during a period when fascist political movements were reaching their high-water mark across Muggle Europe. He entered Hogwarts in September 1938, a little more than a month before the Nazis mounted the Kristallnacht attacks against German Jews; the parallels between Nazi ideology and the Death Eaters' ideas are easy to identify even for nonhistorians. Rowling herself acknowledged these similarities in interviews, but given the time and place that Riddle himself grew up, we could have anticipated this.[2]

Like Harry, Severus Snape, and Lord Voldemort—all of Hogwarts' "lost boys"—the wizarding world is a half-blooded one. Its roots go deep into Muggle history, the history that Professor Binns does not teach his pupils. Rowling's world is a rich and dazzling creation, a world built of magic and history. Exploring that history, and seeing how the wizarding world grew from our own, helps us to enjoy it all the more.

Notes

1. J. K. Rowling, *Harry Potter and the Sorcerer's Stone* (New York: A.A. Levine Books, 1998).

2. For a discussion of how Rowling sees the parallels between Voldemort's Death Eaters and the Nazis, see chapter 6 of this book.

PART ONE

"The Burrow Is Just Outside Ottery St. Catchpole"

When Muggles and Wizards Lived Side by Side

The villages of Tinworthin Cornwald, Upper Flagley in Yorkshire, and Ottery St. Catchpole on the south coast of England were notable homes to knots of Wizarding families who lived alongside tolerant and sometimes Confunded Muggles. Most celebrated of these half-magical dwelling places is, perhaps, Godric's Hollow, the West Country village where the great wizard Godric Gryffindor was born.

—Bathilda Bagshot, *A History of Magic,* quoted in *Deathly Hallows,* 319

Magic for Daily Use and Profit

Mandrakes, Charms, Bezoars, and Love Potions in the Muggle and Wizarding Worlds

Birgit Wiedl

When someone harms people or brings them trouble by magic, one should punish them with death, and one should use the punishment of death by fire. When, however, someone uses magic and yet does no one any harm with it, he should be punished otherwise, according to the custom of the case.

—*Constitutio Criminalis Carolina*, 1532[1]

"I'm a *what?*" gasped Harry.

—*Sorcerer's Stone*, 51[2]

When eleven-year-old Harry Potter learns from Rubeus Hagrid about his magical abilities, he is completely stunned and incredulous, despite the signs of magic he had already shown earlier in his life before anyone had taught him how to perform magic. The question of whether magical abilities are inherited through the wizarding family or are a spontaneous occurrence in an otherwise Muggle family notwithstanding, a person in the wizarding world either has magical abilities or doesn't; no school could ever teach magical skills to a Muggle (or a Squib) and succeed. This concept is the exact opposite of what the Muggle world of the Middle Ages and Early Modern Times believed magic to be: those cultures thought that magic was something that could be acquired by studying or passed down in oral tradition. Unlike the wizards of Harry's world, Muggles in medieval and Early Modern Europe thus believed that anyone who chose to be a sorcerer, a magician, a warlock, or a witch could become so, provided that he or she got the right education and training.

Examining the practice of magic in earlier times poses, first and foremost, the problem of how we define *magic*: while to Severus Snape, Lucius Malfoy, Albus Dumbledore, and their lot, it is quite self-explanatory as to *what* magic is (or is it?), the fields of ancient, medieval, and Early Modern magic were categories that varied and changed from one time and place to another. Usually defined by authorities who often took either a condescending or even hostile stance—and narrowed down to concrete examples of specific practices only when accusations were made—magic was (from a historical perspective) seldom categorized as such by those who, allegedly or not, performed it. Indeed, many who performed what others perceive as magic would not have labeled it as such.[3] Magic could be found everywhere and was practiced by a broad spectrum of people from all parts of the social strata, from the stereotypical village witch or the itinerant soothsayer performing at fairs, to the magician at a nobleman's court or the highly educated Renaissance *magi*, to the practitioner of the occult sciences.[4] All sorts of people performed magic in earlier centuries, in other words.

Yet any attempt to strictly separate "elite" or "learned" magic from popular magical practices inevitably leads to similar

A bezoar in a rich gold setting, from the last quarter of the seventeenth century; the height is 4.5 inches. Bezoars like this were prestigious and expensive status symbols and were often part of the accumulated treasures of European aristocrats and royalty.

problems when differentiating between "pagan" (from whichever roots) and Christian magic, particularly as far as the early and high Middle Ages are concerned.[5] Although ancient and Christian authorities defined magic quite differently, the incorporation of pagan magical beliefs, rites, and practices into the early medieval church practices and rituals was, even if some church authorities perceived it as pagan, often inevitable. Sometimes, this kind of "magical transfer" was accepted quite deliberately and even encouraged to avoid clashes with existing traditions and to make it easier for the local population to connect with the new faith, leading to fusions of Christianity with older belief systems on a broad scale.[6]

Pagan charms can be found scribbled in local languages in the margins of medieval manuscripts that were devoted to Latin liturgical prayers. When we track down the roots of these charms to their pre-Christian origins, they are drawn from a broad array of pre-Christian sources, including Egyptian, Graeco-Roman, Celtic, Slavic, Jewish, and Germanic, perhaps with some later Arabic influences as well.[7] Yet the medieval understanding of magic did not depend on the original sources of the charms so much as it did on the intermingling and adaptation of a variety of both practices and concepts of magic.[8]

Particularly the use of spells and charms, bordering closely on prayer, and the administration of herbal treatments might not have been regarded as magical by those who performed them perhaps on an almost daily basis. Magic is, after all, in the eyes of the beholder: what some might call *magic* another might call *religion*. The blessings, the invocations of the saints, and the transformation of bread and wine into the body and blood of Christ in the Eucharist performed by a barely literate parish priest might have seemed to the common people quite similar in their "magical" qualities to the ointments that someone else in their village brewed using herbs, plants, and roots that merely needed a quick spell to work properly.[9] Similarly, a pagan priest would not perceive his (or her) actions as "magical," but instead as religious, and would only appear as a "sorcerer," rather than as a "priest," to Christian authorities. By the same token, the actions of, and stories about, Jesus came across as extremely "magical" to non-Christians, and the cross itself was often associated with malevolent magic in Roman tradition. As in the wizarding world, practical magic was used on an everyday scale in the ancient and medieval worlds.

Even Augustinus of Hippo (St. Augustine), who denounced magic and superstition, relied on the aid of the soothsayer and sorcerer Albicerius at Carthage to find a spoon he had lost.[10] Magic was always a controversial issue within the Christian church, and the discussion of complex theories of magic was important enough to medieval theologians that some church councils (for example, the Council of Basel, held between 1431 and 1449) engaged in quite heated discussions about magic; even church authorities weren't always sure about where religion ended and magic began.[11]

"One Who Is Said to Carry a Brass Cauldron in which Witches Brew": Severus Strioportius Snape, or What the Potions Master and Professor Sprout Are Really Enthusiastic About

And shrieks like mandrakes' torn out of the earth,
That living mortals, hearing them, run mad.

—William Shakespeare, *Romeo and Juliet*, act IV, scene iii

"To bottle fame, brew glory, even stopper death": with the correct administration of Severus Snape's potions, so it seems, everything can be achieved (SS, 137). In his cauldron, potions are brewed that indeed have a broad range of effects on both mind and body: potions that make people think more clearly (Wit-Sharpening Potion); the huge assortment of antidotes and healing potions (such as Skele-Gro and Wound-Healing Potion, both administered to Harry); potions that befuddle the mind of the one who drinks them, persuading them into loving, hating, or being the best friend of the one who gave the potion; potions with self-explanatory names such as Veritaserum or Wolfsbane; potions that have a comical effect (a specialty of the Weasley twins) or a cosmetic use, such as Hermione Granger's Sleekeazy's Hair Potion; and potions—although Snape does not teach these—that are used in sports, such as the solution that is used in Quodpot to prevent the Quod from exploding.

The cauldron is not only Snape's identifying feature. In the wizarding world, cauldrons are of immanent importance: their manufacture is standardized; they are used as devices to carry items, as we see when Ginny uses hers to carry her books in *Chamber of Secrets*; and some of them seem to have magical abilities on their own, like the self-stirring or collapsible ones that are sold at Diagon Alley. Indeed, they are such basic items for wizards and witches that the most famous wizarding pub is named after them: the Leaky Cauldron.

Muggles of earlier historical periods would probably have agreed that the cauldron made the witch (or the wizard). According to the sixth-century *Pactus Legis Salicae*, the (mostly) Germanic law of the Salian Franks (who lived in today's Belgium and the Netherlands), calling someone a *strioportius*, or a "carrier of a witch's cauldron," was a punishable crime if the accusation could not be proved: a mistaken accuser was fined the same amount that someone who killed another person with a spell or a potion would have had to pay.[12] Severus Strioportius Snape, then? The concoction of potions, balms, and salves and their application (for whatever purpose) became central to Europeans' definitions of witchcraft.

Alice Kyteler and her "sect," who lived in fourteenth-century Kilkenny in southeast Ireland, were accused of concocting powders, pills, and ointments from herbs, animal parts such as intestines, nails from corpses, and swaddling-clothes from babies who had died unbaptized, using the skull of a decapitated robber as their cauldron. Kyteler lacked a N.E.W.T. in Potions, but her concoctions were nonetheless said to induce love or hate or to bring sickness or death.[13] In one of the earliest descriptions of a Witches' Sabbath, given in the fifth section of Johannes Nider's *Formicarius* (The Anthill), a handbook for preachers written in 1435–1437, the author claimed that Swiss witches boiled the bodies of children in huge cauldrons, using them to create ointments and potions that were put to various uses inside their "sect," as part of their servitude to the demons.[14] Early modern illustrations of witches and sorcerers, such as Hans Baldung Grien's *Witches' Sabbath* (1510), show witches concocting their potions in a cauldron, although this is mostly connected with the (visual) key element of drawings of early modern witchcraft: the witches' ability to fly through the air, as Lord Voldemort and Snape do.[15]

The ingredients in Professor Snape's potions are a peculiar mixture of local plants that could be gathered right outside of Hogwarts' gates, like belladonna, with plants the Potions Master must have at least Apparated to collect, such as asphodel, which grows in abundance only in the South of Europe. Snape also uses ghastly items, like the dead cockroaches he keeps in a jar in his office, and mythological objects, such as the bezoar. Many of the plants that Professors Snape and Sprout use could also be found in medieval and Early Modern Muggles' herbal magic, albeit with sometimes different qualities attributed to them.

Medieval Muggles' herbal magic, both "learned" and "popular" (and its many mixed forms), was first and foremost medical magic, combining plants with parts of animals or even stones (although the moonstone that Snape advises Harry to add in powdered form to his attempt at a concoction of the Draught of Peace was not commonly used by Muggle brewers).[16] The use of natural ingredients in magical concoctions has an ancient pedigree, deriving from both local European traditions and manuscripts on herbs that combined Greek, Roman, and Arabic knowledge: the idea that herbs, plants, and animal parts could—in skilled hands—wield magical power was common to both pagan and Christian worlds, as was an awareness of the danger they could pose.

"Charmed herbs" (perhaps a concoction of poisonous herbs) were not allowed while fighting a duel, according to the *Edictum Rothari* of 643, the law of the Lombards, a Germanic tribe that invaded Northern Italy in the sixth century.[17] On the other hand, a recipe for skin disease from the "leechbook of Bald," an Anglo-Saxon manual from the mid-tenth century, could have been invented by Snape himself. Readers were told to combine goose fat, a piece of Horse-heal (a plant also known as elecampane), viper's bugloss (a species of the Echium plant), bishop's wort, and goosegrass and pound them together well before squeezing them out and mixing them with a spoonful of soap. The mixture had to be applied to the skin overnight. The affected skin should then be scratched, and blood from the scratch poured into running water. After spitting into the running water three times, the patient should say, "Take this disease and depart with it," and he or she would be healed.[18] Neville Longbottom (and Harry, without the help of the Half-Blood Prince) might not have been able to follow the recipe perfectly, but Hermione and Draco Malfoy would have had no problem with it, while the Weasley twins would have sought a way to turn it into something funny (and profitable), and Snape would probably have scribbled an improvement to the recipe in the margins of his textbook.

The choice of materials in brewing was often determined by what each ingredient symbolized, particularly as far as animals and their parts were concerned. Parts from animals known for their speed, strength, or ferocity (such as dragons) were likely to be chosen for potions or balms that were meant to pass on these traits to the patient, following the common *pars pro toto* principle of sympathetic magic, which asserted that a part could serve as a replacement of the whole.[19] This concept can be found in many aspects of medieval and Early Modern magic, from the potions and the balms mentioned previously to image magic (magic that made use of images of the targeted person, for example, wax figures), or in the casting of spells and curses where some hair or fingernails of the person who was being targeted served as a "stand-in" for the person himself. This sort of sympathetic magic is apparently common in the wizarding world as well, because the potion brewed to restore Voldemort to his body in *Goblet of Fire* consisted of bone of his father, blood of his enemy, and flesh of his servant; each ingredient clearly symbolizes or stands in for a different person or trait.

The Mandrake's Fatal Attractions

"Mandrake, or Mandragora, is a powerful restorative," said Hermione, sounding as usual as though she had swallowed the textbook. "It is used to return people who have been transfigured or cursed to their original state."

—*Chamber of Secrets*, 92

In their second year, Hogwarts students are introduced to a plant that is even more alive than you would expect a magical plant to be: the Mandrake, or Mandragora, which kills with its shriek. Its roots look like a human baby, and it seems to struggle against being used in magical concoctions, even as Hogwarts students are pulling it out of its pot. Used mainly "to return people who have been transfigured or cursed to their original state," the Mandrake is a powerful restorative and, as such, an essential ingredient to most antidotes in the wizarding world. The powers of the mandrake, a poisonous member of the nightshade family, had been recognized by Muggles thousands of years before Harry was born, and people in the ancient world had long attributed magical properties to the mandrake. Its poison made it a deadly weapon, yet at the same time, Muggles saw the mandrake as a powerful love plant, which could also ensure the conception of children.

Two thousand years ago, Muggle writers such as Flavius Josephus described methods to evade the mandrake's fatal cry. He was a Roman historian and writer who suggested having a (doomed) dog pull the mandrake out of the ground. This idea was repeated in many medieval manuscripts that, later on, added ideas about how to protect the dog from the plant's deadly cry, too.

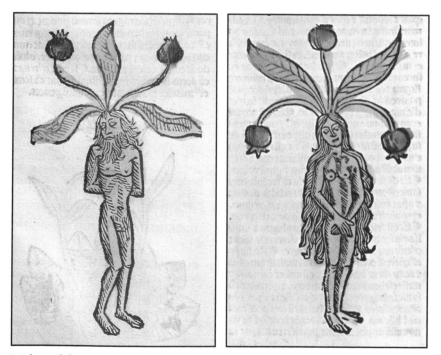

Male and female mandragora, depiction from the *Hortus Sanitatis* (The Garden of Health, 1497), which encourages the use of the roots as an anesthetic as well as an aphrodisiac.

Professor Sprout was not the only practitioner to have special procedures for handling mandrakes: many Muggle legends and rituals surround its planting, growing, and harvesting as well—these included traditions about places where it grows best and times when it should be harvested to fully unfold its magical qualities. Hildegard von Bingen, the renowned twelfth-century abbess and a gifted writer, theologian, visionary, and composer, dedicated an entire chapter of her famous medical treatise *Causae et Curae* (Causes and Cures) to the mandrake, listing not only its medical purposes, such as curing melancholy, but also a series of rituals that were necessary to exorcise the devil that she assumed inhabited the plant.[20]

In the course of the Early Modern period, the mandrake became an integral part of popular medicine and magic, even if it was difficult to come by in the northern parts of Europe, where it did not grow; many of the mandrakes sold at market stalls across northern Europe were indeed fakes.[21] Recipes for what Muggles called "witch salves"—ointments that caused hallucinogenic effects—usually listed mandrake as an essential ingredient. It was also used as an anaesthetic, "in order that one whose limb is being amputated does not feel anything," as the *Hortus Sanitatis* (The Garden of Health) from the late fifteenth century put it. In addition, mandrake was harvested in order to create sedatives, as well as aphrodisiacs, while its unprocessed human-shaped roots were widely used in imitative magic.[22]

What Madam Sprout does not reveal to her—perhaps too young?—students is that there are male and female mandrake roots, and their anatomy was graphically illustrated in most of the Early Modern Muggle herbals and medical treatises.[23] The mandrake's popularity knew no limits and transcended both political and geographical boundaries, as well as social strata: it was brought on stage by the Italian politician, diplomat, and philosopher Niccolò Machiavelli in his play *La Mandragola* (1518), where it serves as the device for the protagonist to trick his love interest into bed with him, but also became an ingredient in a quarrel between neighboring women in seventeenth-century Württemberg, in southern Germany, where the widow of a swineherd was accused of causing the death of her wealthy neighbor's cow because the neighbor had refused to buy something she didn't need—mandrakes—from the poor widow.[24]

Building a Better Bezoar Collection

And there it was, scrawled right across a long list of antidotes: Just shove a bezoar down their throats.

—*Half-Blood Prince*, 377

Long before Harry was introduced to Mandrakes, he had learned of another magical item, one that he would later use to save Ron Weasley's life: "Where would you look if I told you to find me a bezoar?" the intimidating Potions Master asks Harry during his first Potions lesson (SS, 137–138). Harry, who was taken aback at the idea of being expected to remember everything from *One Thousand Magical Herbs and Fungi*, would not have found an entry on bezoars in such a book anyway, because it is neither an herb nor a fungus. In reality, a bezoar isn't a stone—although it rather looks like one—and (despite what Snape tells Harry) it is not found exclusively in the stomach of a goat: it is a lump of indigestible material that forms in the stomach of several sorts of animals. Even in the ancient world, Muggles prized bezoars as very valuable (and thus pricey) commodities. Like wizards, Muggles credited bezoars with magical and healing powers, and their ability to cure poisoning was but one among many abilities these substances allegedly possessed.

The use of bezoars in Europe seems to have begun during the twelfth century, most likely introduced by Arab physicians who knew of their healing powers from both Greek and Persian sources. Medieval bezoars were collected from goats but also from deer and monkeys, which were of the best quality and were reported to derive from the animals' heads, livers, and even—in repeating an Arabic myth—the eyes.[25] When Harry, following the instructions gained from the textbook of Severus "Half-Blood Prince" Snape, presents the bezoar to Horace Slughorn as the epitome of all antidotes,

"The miraculous stone *bezoar*": a sick man is
cured by swallowing a bezoar; *Hortus Sanitatis*
(The Garden of Health, 1497).

a woodcut illustration from *Hortus Sanitatis* might have served as
the model for Snape's notes. In this fifteenth-century drawing, a
bezoar is, exactly as Snape describes it rather curtly, simply shoved
down the poisoned person's throat (*HBP*, 377).[26]

Yet the bezoar's high-water mark as a status symbol among
European Muggles came during the Early Modern period. Despite
the doubts about its healing powers that were raised as early as the
sixteenth century by some authorities, such as the French surgeon
Ambroise Paré, noblemen and rulers spent ridiculous amounts of
money to get hold of the famous "stone." Bezoars helped soothe
their constant fear of being poisoned and were also added to their
treasuries, often encased in gold and jewels, as objects whose possession greatly enhanced the owners' prestige.[27] Bezoars were brought

to Europe from all over the (then known) world, including the Americas—such as the three-and-a-half-pound bezoar from Peru that was sent as a gift from Spain to Pope Gregory XIII in 1534. The pope displayed the enormous bezoar to an awe-struck public in Rome.[28]

Had Snape witnessed this incident, he would have had more to regret than simply the ban on the use of Veritaserum on students. During the reign of the Holy Roman Emperor Rudolph II (1552–1612), at the emperor's residence in Prague, a mixture of wine and a few grains of a bezoar were given to a prisoner who had been poisoned with aconite (also known as wolfsbane or monk's hood), the deadly poisonous plant that Professor Snape quizzes little ignorant Harry about on his first day at Hogwarts. Snape would have been proved right about the power of the bezoar: the prisoner recovered after a quite unpleasant night (most likely due to his heavy vomiting), and the delighted emperor, himself an avid collector of bezoars, not only set him free but bestowed a considerable reward on him.[29] Even as the trust in its healing powers waned among Muggles, bezoars remained valuable objects up until the eighteenth century and were often worked into amulets.

"He Who Must Not Be Named": Charms, Spells, Curses, and the Power of Words

"Saying the magic words properly is very important."
—Professor Filius Flitwick, *Sorcerer's Stone*, 171

"The word alone is not enough."
—Professor Remus Lupin, *Prisoner of Azkaban*, 134

Nearly every sorcerer, magician, and witch of medieval and Early Modern Europe would have agreed with Professor Flitwick, whether he or she was a learned magician educated at a university or a practitioner of popular magic that had been passed down by word of mouth (or, quite likely, both). They might have placed even more emphasis on the use of the precisely *correct* words—whether an incantation accompanying a ritual, an invocation of demons, a spell mumbled while administering a salve on the neighbor's sickly pig's leg, or a curse hurled against the wealthy merchant's haughty wife; this forms the basis for every type of magic to work properly. The formal structure of the spell and its precise word-by-word incantation were essential to both pagan and Christian magic, and its incorrect performance could lead to disastrous results, even if (as Ron is bound to find out) the only mistake is in the pronunciation of "levi-o-sa."

Although Christian authorities tried to establish clear distinctions between religious prayers and magical spells, verbal magic—such as charms, spells, and incantations—was often even more indistinguishable from its religious counterpart than was magic performed with or through tangible objects, such as potion ingredients. Prayers, blessings, and (in extreme cases) admonishments and exorcisms are nothing else but verbal invocations of some sort of higher power, with charms and spells being but one variation, even if they have older roots.[30]

The magic of words and names even extended beyond their verbal utterance: to exorcise a demon, a late-thirteenth-century English manuscript on medicine instructs, a cross and the opening words of the Gospel of St. John should be written on a parchment, then scraped off into a bowl and mixed with holy water. The patient should drink the potion, the effectiveness of which was guaranteed by its original source, because the manuscript contained an assurance that a demon had revealed the secret.[31] Biblical verses were used as spells, both spoken aloud and in written form. To protect newborns and guarantee a long and happy life for them, for example, the prologue to the Gospel of St. John was written out and put into a capsule that was then inserted under the baby's pillow. At the Siege of Dijon in 1513, the combatants tried to foretell the outcome of the battle by opening bibles to random pages, a method of divination called bibliomancy that went back not only to the early Middle Ages, but even had roots in the ancient world, where the works of poets had been used as oracles.[32] No doubt, it worked at least as well as Professor Sibyll Trelawney's methods.

Yet there is much evidence to support Professor Lupin's statement as well: even if the spell is pronounced correctly, such as Neville's "up" when he tries to mount his broom during Harry's first lesson with Madam Hooch, this is no guarantee that the magic will work properly. Muggle reports of magical experiments gone wrong were numerous, most of which were blamed on the evil spirit of the demon, who (although he was correctly conjured) did not do as he was commanded or requested.

Spells and their correct performance were often only part of the entire magical ritual. Liturgical manuals that were assembled in monasteries contained regulations for how to properly collect herbs or slaughter animals and how to prepare balms, ointments, or potions (and their correct applications), along with the appropriate words that go with these actions. Burchard of Worms, the tenth/eleventh-century compiler of the *Canon Episcopi*, a collection of ecclesiastical laws that condemned superstition, nonetheless approved of prayers that accompanied the collecting of medical herbs. Apocryphal legends that were popular in medieval Europe included stories about how young Jesus had collected and blessed herbs for his mother or how he had healed Peter of a toothache; such tales reflect the close intertwining of classical knowledge of herbs, Christian formulas, and Germanic medical lore.[33]

"The Most Difficult of All Magical Arts": Divination, Necromancy, and Astrology, or Are Muggles the Better Wizards?

"I see," said Professor McGonagall, fixing Harry with her beady eyes. "Then you should know, Potter, that Sibyll Trelawney has predicted the death of one student a year since she arrived at this school. None of them has died yet. Seeing death omens is her favorite way of greeting a new class. [. . .] Divination is one of the most imprecise branches of magic. I shall not conceal from you that I have very little patience with it. True Seers are very rare."

—*Prisoner of Azkaban,* 109

On July 23, 1441, Master Roger Bolingbroke, a member of the household of the duke of Gloucester and a personal clerk to the duchess, Eleanor Cobham, was forced to sit on a painted chair on a scaffold at St. Paul's Cross in London, a paper crown on his head. A large crowd of both laypeople and clerics, among them the archbishop of Canterbury, came to witness his confession of having performed harmful magic, and a multitude of instruments, including images of wax and metal, provided evidence to support the charge that he had been in league with the devil, whom Roger (as of that moment) claimed to renounce. It didn't do him any good: only four months later, Bolingbroke was convicted of witchcraft, heresy, and treason and was hanged, drawn, and quartered at Tyburn.[34]

What had happened to Bolingbroke, the Oxford scholar who had been described as a "gret and konnyng [great and knowing] man in astronomye" and "renowned in all the world"?[35] About three hundred years earlier, John of Salisbury, the secretary to Thomas Becket and later the bishop of Chartres, had recounted in his *Policraticus* an episode from his own youth. Had Hermione ever happened to stumble across this story in her reading, it would have sounded familiar to her ears: John's teacher (a priest), instead of instructing his two pupils in Latin, had anointed the boys' fingernails with some sort of sacred chrism that would serve as a reflecting surface for figures to appear. After performing preliminary magical rites, the priest began to mutter names that, to the horror of the young John, sounded like those of demons. Yet unlike his classmate, who saw certain misty figures appear, John saw nothing, and (just as Professor Trelawney told Hermione, dismissively) his teacher declared that he did not possess what was required for the art of necromancy, the main method of divination in the Middle Ages.[36]

Although John added a somewhat gleeful observation that everyone he'd ever known to engage in such rituals was eventually punished by contracting some illness, necromancy nonetheless enjoyed the ambiguous reputation of being both explicitly demonic magic and a complex and prestigious science. Divination, the art of predicting the future and of reading signs in order to make the right decisions, was bound up with necromancy. It was one of the most common magical practices, yet also one of the most emphatically rejected by Christian authorities, who nevertheless engaged in this very art.[37] Even so, learned necromancers who practiced divination were much sought after at the courts of royals and noblemen, and the majority of them were members of the clergy, scholars who possessed at least a basic knowledge of exorcism, demonology, and astrology.[38]

However much Hermione might turn up her nose at Trelawney's somewhat eccentric ways of teaching and forecasting the future, medieval and Early Modern soothsayers would not have gotten their medieval equivalent of knickers in a twist over things as harmless and mundane as tea leaves that formed the shape of a dog: those who foretold the future were, first and foremost, necromancers. They conjured either demons or the dead, although in the case of the dead, this was not done in order to bring them back to life, but rather to milk them for information about the diviner's own future or that of a client.[39] Like John's teacher, Bolingbroke, too, had, allegedly, conjured a demon that had foretold the future for Duchess Eleanor.[40]

Soothsaying by necromancy had been present in the Gracco-Roman tradition much earlier, where a mythical figure such as Circe was the epitome of a necromancer, and also in Norse sagas. Yet the medieval Muggle concepts drew mainly from Judaeo-Christian roots, such as the biblical Witch of Endor, who invoked the ghost of Samuel by using a magical amulet. "The most difficult of all magical arts," Trelawney calls her subject, and scholars from the twelfth up to the eighteenth centuries might have agreed.

Bolingbroke might have added "most dangerous," because it was first and foremost the divination aspect of his practices that earned him the accusation of treason. In trying to foresee whether Eleanor, his mistress, would ever become queen, he was also asking about when the king was to die. For the most part, he was condemned not merely for the practice of necromancy and divination itself, but rather because of the goal he had pursued (finding out when the king would die) in using these skills. By contrast, an unnamed necromancer who assisted a medieval bishop to defeat heretics by forcing the demons he invoked to reveal information about local heresy ran no such risk.[41]

The preferred techniques of Trelawney and Cassandra Vablatsky, the author of *Unfogging the Future* (used as a schoolbook at Hogwarts), were of mixed origins and largely undemonic: palm reading, which traces its roots to ancient India and China; the Roman practice of haruspicy, the reading of bird entrails; the reading of tea leaves, allegedly an old Chinese practice but perhaps invented only when tea arrived in Europe during the seventeenth century; and fire omens, the antique practice of pyromancy.

Their Muggle counterparts were playing a much riskier game, however. Medieval and Early Modern diviners worked with demons, whom they invoked by use of their secret names. Reflecting surfaces—including, as in the previously mentioned story, fingernails, but also the traditional crystal balls—and devices such as brazen heads were used to predict the future. These last items hint at the thin (and indeed, for Muggles of this period, practically nonexistent) line between magic and science: scholars such as Albertus Magnus, Roger Bacon, Robert Grosseteste, and Arnoldus de Villa Nova, whose findings in many fields of science are still used today, were said to have owned such brazen heads or even constructed one for themselves.

Ancient practices that were used to predict the future, such as letter oracles and the drawing of lots, survived through the Middle Ages into the seventeenth century and were influenced by Arabic geomancy (interpreting patterns formed by rocks or soil tossed on the ground), fortune-telling with cards, and numerology (assigning numerical values to letters of the alphabet), and Jewish gematria (assigning numerical values to Hebrew words or phrases), to name but a few.[42] Wizards and witches must have known of these methods of divination, but only numerology (aka Arithmancy) is mentioned as being a regular part of the Hogwarts curriculum.

Harry's culture clearly does recognize the magic inherent in numbers that Muggles had been drawing on for centuries. "Isn't seven the most powerfully magical number?" Tom Riddle asks Horace Slughorn when prying for information on Horcruxes (*HBP*, 498). Coincidence or not, this is the number of years that students usually spend at Hogwarts and the number of players who make up a Quidditch team. Yet Bridget Wenlock, the thirteenth-century arithmancer who discovered this number's magical qualities, was a tad late for the party (Famous Wizards Cards, 22). Numerology, Arithmancy, and related sciences had mostly entered Muggle Europe via the Iberian peninsula back when Spain and Portugal were under Arabic rule hundreds of years earlier. These sciences had been received, translated, and developed already from the eleventh century onward by people such as Gerbert of Aurillac (later Pope Sylvester II), Gerard of Cremona, and Michael Scot. Due to their studies at the "magical" University of Toledo, these men had shared the reputation of being magicians themselves, and because this was centuries before the Statute of Secrecy, which mandated the separation of the wizarding and Muggle worlds, perhaps the rumors were true. Despite this ancient wizarding pedigree, Arithmancy doesn't seem to have enjoyed a particularly great popularity among Hogwarts students: bookish Hermione is the only student of her year who opts for taking the O.W.L. in what she labels her favorite subject (in contrast to "woolly Divination"). The only use the wizarding world seems to have for Arithmancy is to protect Gringotts: an O.W.L. in Arithmancy is a prerequisite for becoming a curse-breaker.

"Lie back upon the floor [. . .] and observe the heavens. Here is written, for those who can see, the fortune of our races," the Centaur Firenze instructs his students, introducing them to a science that covered much more than mere divination in the Middle Ages and Early Modern Europe: astrology (OOTP, 602). Actually, the figure of the Centaur, an enigmatic being of Greek mythology, connects to one of the major roots of medieval astronomy, the Greek and Hellenistic astronomers who not only adapted elder teachings of the Egyptian and Mesopotamian regions, but developed them further and acted as a transmitter for the later Islamic and Christian scientists; whereas the town of Florence (Firenze in Italian) was one of the centers of the Renaissance, thus home to many of the most learned scholars of this time. Far from ever being a mere star-gazing superstition, Islamic and Christian medieval astrology was a highly complex science that was (for both Muggles and wizards of this time) often indistinguishable from astronomy. Astronomia, as one of the original seven liberal arts, included astronomic observation and theory, as well as astrological interpretation, and well-known Muggle astronomers such as Johannes Kepler and Galileo Galilei engaged in astrology as well, because they would not have perceived astrology to be a superstition.

Christian theologians stressed that neither stars nor the moon could possibly influence human fate and will. For example, Paschasius Radbertus, the abbot of the prominent monastery of Corbie, complained that the ninth-century court of Louis the Pious, the king of the Franks, was full of "lot casters, seers, interpreters of omens, mimers, dream mediums, consulters of entrails." Yet church scholars also made use of astronomy, such as in setting the dates for Easter, and they gradually adapted astrology/astronomy into the Christian worldview.[43] Astrology/astronomy ultimately became *the* court science among Muggles, with rulers all over Europe seeking the advice of astronomers such as Frederick II's Michael Scot, Elizabeth I's John Dee, and Rudolf II's Tycho Brahe. All of these men were not only highly educated scientists but also well-paid courtiers—a position that Firenze clearly lacks.

For the Love of Magic: Love Potions, Entranchement Charms, and Wax Images

"Can you not think of any measure Merope could have taken to make Tom Riddle forget his Muggle companion, and fall in love with her instead?"

"The Imperius Curse?" Harry suggested. "Or a love potion?"

—*Half-Blood Prince*, 213

It was during this time, [. . .] that Iseult, the wily queen, set about compounding in a small glass vessel a virulent love-potion, designed and intended with exacting artifice to have this certain power—with whomever one should share it, that person, involuntarily, must one desire above all else, and so the other in return.

—Gottfried of Strassburg, *Tristan*

"It would have seemed more romantic to her," Dumbledore responds to Harry, explaining why he thinks that Merope Gaunt, the awkward, plain, pureblood girl, would have used a love potion to change the mind of Tom Riddle senior, whom she so decidedly fancied. It seems odd that to achieve a change of heart in the man she adored, the smitten Merope seems to have the choice between two rather different means: one a curse that would have assured her a cell in Azkaban (or even a kiss from an entirely different creature); and the other a potion that was, although Dumbledore concedes that Merope was "enslaving [her husband] by magical means," generally presented in the Harry Potter series as a tool the Weasley twins sell for jokes and pranks, with the worst outcome of its use in Harry's circle usually being embarrassment (or, in Merope's case, the birth of Lord Voldemort) (*HBP*, 120).

These "neither dark nor dangerous" potions are rather the subject of idle chat and something a mother, like Mrs. Weasley, would admit to having used long ago in a casual breakfast talk with her daughter, causing the women to break into giggles (*HBP*, 307). The Muggle compiler of a fifteenth-century necromancy handbook showed a similar disregard for the manipulative qualities of the love/ sex magic he described in one chapter. He gave no signs of a guilty conscience, no matter how conniving or even abusive the rituals he recommended in the handbook were, nor did he seem to find any incongruity in evoking demons to achieve an outcome that, in his idea, would appeal to "divine majesty."[44]

Gilderoy Lockhart promoted love potions as well. Unlike his reliance on memory charms, such potions could even be joked about in public:

> "Happy Valentine's Day!" Lockhart shouted. "And may I thank the forty-six people who have so far sent me cards! . . . My friendly, card-carrying cupids . . . will be roving around the school today delivering your valentines! And the fun doesn't stop here! I'm sure my colleagues will want to enter into the spirit of the occasion! Why not ask Professor Snape to show you how to whip up a Love Potion!" . . . Snape was looking as though the first person to ask him for a Love Potion would be force-fed poison. (*COS*, 236)

Perhaps it was the low status apparently assigned to such potions and love magic in the wizarding world that makes Severus Snape look even more sour than usual, when he is asked to instruct the students in brewing a love potion. But then, who wouldn't put on a sour face after having been exposed to a disgustingly cheery Gilderoy Lockhart, clad in lurid pink Valentine's Day robes?

Whatever the reasons for Snape's sour face might have been, it seems that administering love potions does not result in dire consequences in the wizarding world. Romilda Vane's potion-spiked chocolate merely results in embarrassment for Ron, while Slughorn's only concern seems to be that his master scholar has no idea how to whip up an antidote. To many Hogwarts girls, buying the Weasleys' love potion apparently seems like a proper, and not overly illegal, way to get Harry to take them to Slughorn's party. Even rule-obeying Hermione seems more put out at her fellow schoolmates' silliness than by the fact that a love potion was being smuggled into Hogwarts past Filch's eyes. Even when Pansy Parkinson accuses Hermione of having used love potions to ensnare Viktor Krum (according to Rita Skeeter), Ron, too, isn't overly shocked at the idea, only at her choice of victim.

We can assume that the target of Mrs. Weasley's love potion was not her future husband, however. Love that has been induced by magic, it seems, is bound to fail in both the Muggle and the wizarding world: Merope is abandoned by Riddle before her child is born. The Irish princess Iseult, the heroine of a popular medieval Muggle story, had a mother who concocted a love potion for her daughter and her future son-in-law, King Mark (to ensure the newlyweds' happiness). But Iseult, ignorant of the liquid's properties, satisfied her thirst together with the knight Tristan and was henceforth doomed to yearn for him forever (and to betray her husband).[45]

"Sorcerers and magicians [. . .] make a covenant with the devil, in order that he may give them plenty of money or help them in their love-affairs, preserve their cattle, restore to them lost possessions, etc.," none other than Martin Luther (who started the Protestant Reformation) wrote in his small catechism in 1529. Yet love magic, be it by means of potion, spells, or magical devices such as tarot cards or amulets, was not among the magical practices that people were often put on trial for, unless they had practiced darker magic as well.[46] As in the wizarding world, love magic was neither unknown nor uncommon among Muggles of earlier periods. Quite the contrary.

Women who rose to a higher social status through marriage or concubinage were particularly vulnerable to this accusation, perhaps the most famous being Françoise-Athénaïs de Rochechouart de Mortemart, the Marquise de Montespan (1640–1707), the chief mistress of King Louis XIV of France. When the king's affection for her waned, she resorted to drastic measures: the infamous Catherine Monvoisin (who was later burned for witchcraft and murder in 1680) concocted potions for the marquise, which she then added to the king's meals in order to make his affection for her last.[47] At the other end of the social scale, we find young Margaretha Wagner from Marbach, who in 1740 was accused of a variety of magical practices, among them love magic she had learned (she confessed) from her grandmother, along with other occult arts.

Although her case began with the accusation of illicit sexual relationships with several young men, it soon turned into an investigation of the use of more extensive magic. Margaretha readily admitted not only to using love magic, but also to flying to witch dances with the aid of magical salves, causing sicknesses, knowing spells that were carried out in the name of the devil to make cows give extra milk and change the weather, and "pushing people in their sleep," who, in return, reported that they had felt the pressure. The magistrate, however, was doubtful of this long list of claims. "One does not want to believe everything the girl says," he noted, even if she was in league with the devil. When Margaretha later withdrew her confessions, claiming that she had made everything up because she had been afraid, the officials were only too happy to let the case drop.[48]

Accusations were taken more seriously if other people were involved—such as the target's spouse, in cases of "separation magic"—or if love magic was done for purposes other than simply to ensure the targeted person's affection and/or to persuade the victim to engage in sexual intercourse.[49] The trials that the town government of Florence conducted between 1375 and 1450 included many accusations of love magic that were not done for romantic reasons, but rather for material gain. About 250 years later, in late-seventeenth- and early-eighteenth-century Paris, magical practitioners offered their customers manipulative love magic and poisons.[50]

The means that were used to bend the mind and the will of another person toward love were manifold, and love potions *not* taught by Snape fared quite poorly on the popularity scale. Many rituals, spells, and potions required body parts of the "target person" as ingredients, because the *pars pro toto* principle (that a part stood in for the whole) that was common in magical practices also applied in love magic.[51] The complex of love and erotic magic was vast and could include many practices: herbs found under a man's mattress in Germany, simple rituals (such as washing your face in a specific way and then throwing the water toward the couple you wanted to separate), more complicated spells (for example, reciting charms and conjuring demons over a black egg, and then feeding a female cat and a male dog each one half of the egg), and prayers (one prayer we know of required invoking a series of demons, along with the Holy Trinity).[52] All of these were used, combined with a huge number of plants, herbs, and animal parts that were considered aphrodisiacs.

Image magic was especially popular, particularly when it involved wax images. For example, a Carmelite monk at Carcassonne was accused in 1329 of offering wax puppets mixed with his own saliva and the blood of toads to the devil. He had then allegedly placed the puppets under the thresholds of the houses of the women he desired, so that they would either have to yield to him or else be tormented by a demon.[53] Usually, male perpetrators were tried for using love magic in order to debauch women. Accused women were more likely to have used magic to restore a lover's or a husband's affection, although Alice Kyteler, the Irish widow who was tried in 1324 for heresy and witchcraft that included erotic magic, was an exception to this rule.[54] To protect against such exploitative love magic, amulets were particularly popular. In addition, people affected by love magic could burn items belonging to the perpetrator to counteract the effects, which was a sort of reverse application of the *pars pro toto* principle.[55]

Forgetting about Magic: A European-wide Memory Charm?

Astonishing though it may seem to many wizards, Muggles have not always been ignorant of the magical and monstrous creatures that we have worked so long and so hard to hide. A glance through Muggle art and literature of the Middle Ages reveals that many of the creatures they now believe to be imaginary were then known to be real.

—*Fantastic Beasts and Where to Find Them*, xiv

By Harry's day, the situation had clearly changed a great deal. As Arthur Weasley explains to his son George in *Chamber of Secrets*,

"Why would anyone bother making door keys shrink?" said George.

"Just Muggle-baiting," sighed Mr. Weasley. "Sell them a key that keeps shrinking to nothing so they can never find it when they need it . . . Of course, it's very hard to convict anyone because no Muggle would admit their key keeps shrinking—they'll insist they just keep losing it. Bless them, they'll go to any lengths to ignore magic, even if it's staring them in the face." (*COS*, 38)

As the quotation from *Fantastic Beasts* demonstrates, Muggles during the medieval and Early Modern periods wouldn't have been so hard to convince: after all, many of them were aware that magic existed, although (as Muggle stories about love potions show) they knew it didn't always cure everything. J. K. Rowling observes in her introduction to *The Tales of Beedle the Bard* that even though the heroes and the heroines of the tales told to young witches and wizards might be able to perform magic themselves, they still find it just as hard to solve their problems as their counterparts in Muggle fairy tales do.

Given the general disregard for Muggles in the wizarding world—from Voldemort's hatred of them to Lucius Malfoy's contempt for them (and fear of them?), to Arthur Weasley's fascination with them, and Albus Dumbledore's patronizing attitude—the complexity and effectiveness of Muggle magic might take modern wizards by surprise. Yet had the young witches and wizards not slept during Professor Binns's lectures (assuming that he touched on the subject at all), they'd perhaps have learned about the inevitable mingling and mixing of ideas, concepts, and recipes that make up what historians call "cultural transfer": exchanges between adjoining cultures like the wizarding and the Muggle worlds.

Individuals such as Nicolas Flamel could have taught them a lesson about the cultural transfer of magic: not only had he sought out contact with Muggles, but he even reveled in the glory of being a sought-after artist and scientist in both worlds. Whether Dumbledore was aware of it or not, many of the skills that made Flamel famous had been acquired from Muggles. Perhaps Flamel himself had leaked information about his alchemical studies to Muggles in the centuries after his supposed "death," thus creating his own legend among Muggles (explored by Don DuPree in a later chapter in this book).

Given the relatively late date that the Statute of Secrecy was enacted—and we do not know how carefully it is obeyed by witches and wizards in other countries—it should not surprise us that very little of the wizarding world's magic is, in fact, exclusive to that culture. Muggles knew about most of it (and even developed some of it themselves) long before the Statute of Secrecy was passed, thus rendering the wizarding law a case of too little, too late. Although actual magical practices might differ in concept and execution between the wizarding and the Muggle worlds, both ideas and "ingredients"—items used for magical practices—seem strikingly similar in both worlds. And little wonder, because (as the wizarding author of *Fantastic Beasts* acknowledges), Muggles in earlier periods had been aware of magic all along.

Notes

1. Quoted after Edward Bever, *The Realities of Witchcraft and Popular Magic in Early Modern Europe: Culture, Cognition, and Everyday Life* (Basingstoke and New York: Palgrave Macmillan, 2008), 2.

2. All book quotes are taken from the American editions by J. K. Rowling as follows: *Sorcerer's Stone*, A.A. Levine Books, 1998; *Chamber of Secrets*, New York: Scholastic, 2000; *Prisoner of Azkaban*, New York: A.A. Levine Books, 1999; *Order of the Phoenix*, New York: A.A. Levine Books, 2003; *Half-Blood Prince*, New York: A.A. Levine Books, 2005; *Deathly Hallows*, New York: A.A. Levine Books, 2007; *Fantastic Beasts*, New York: A.A. Levine Books, 2001.

3. On the problems of modern and (different) contemporary definitions of magic, see Michael David Bailey, "The Meanings of Magic," in *Magic, Ritual, and Witchcraft* 1, no. 1 (2006): 1–23.

4. Christa Habinger-Tucsay, *Magie und Magier im Mittelalter* (Munich: dtv, 1992, 2003), 177; Margaret Murray's argument, expressed mainly in her book *The Witch Cult in Western Europe*, that witchcraft was a "folk religion," even the true religion of people up until or even after the Reformation, not only reflects a "staggering disregard of the requirements of proof" but also blends together in its assumption of "one" folk religion the great variety of pre-Christian religions that, although influencing one another, lacked any sort of uniformity (quote from Geoffrey Scarre and John Callow, *Witchcraft and Magic in Sixteenth- and Seventeenth-Century Europe* (Basingstoke: Palgrave, 1987 rev. ed., 2001), 39. For a basic critique of both Murray's findings and her methods, see Norman Cohn, *Europe's Inner Demons: The Demonization of Christians in Medieval Christiandom* (Chicago: University of Chicago Press, 1975, rev. ed., 2000), 152–160; Darren Oldridge, "General Introduction," in *The Witchcraft Reader,* ed., Routledge Readers in History (New York and London: Routledge, 2002, 2008), 7–8.

5. Richard Kieckhefer, *Magic in the Middle Ages*, Cambridge Medieval Textbooks (Cambridge: Cambridge University Press, 1990), (throughout the book); Michael David Bailey, *Magic and Superstition in Europe: A Concise History from Antiquity to the Present* (New York: Rowman & Littlefield, 2007), 80; Bailey, "The Meanings of Magic," 12.

6. Valerie I. J. Flint, *The Rise of Magic in Early Medieval Europe* (Oxford: Clarendon Press, 1991), 394–395; Richard Kieckhefer, "The Specific Rationality of Medieval Magic," in *American Historical Review* 99, no. 3 (1994): 813–836, on Flint particularly 822–830.

7. See Claire Fanger, Richard Kieckhefer, and Nicholas Watson, eds., *Conjuring Spirits: Texts and Traditions of Medieval Ritual Magic* (University Park: University of Pennsylvania Press, 1998).

8. Karen Louise Jolly, Catharina Raudvere, and Edward Peters, *The Athlone History of Witchcraft and Magic in Europe*, vol. 3: *The Middle Ages* (London: Athlone Press, 2002), 28.

9. Bailey, *Magic and Superstition*, 46–49; see also "The Disenchantment of Magic: Spells, Charms, and Superstition in Early European Witchcraft Literature" in *American Historical Review* 111, no. 2 (2006), 386.

10. Bailey, *Magic and Superstition*, 28–29.

11. Michael David Bailey and Edward Peters, "A Sabbat of Demonologists: Basel 1431–1440," in *The Historian* 65, no. 6 (2003): 1375–1396.

12. Jolly, Raudvere, and Peters, *The Athlone History of Witchcraft and Magic*, vol. 3, 189–190.

13. Cohn, *Europe's Inner Demons*, 199.

14. Michael David Bailey, "The Medieval Concept of the Witches' Sabbath," in *Exemplaria* 8, no. 2 (1996): 430–431.

15. See image at Web Gallery of Art, www.wga.hu/art/b/baldung/4/2sabbath.jpg.

16. Habinger-Tucsay, *Magie und Magier*, 317–318; Bever, *Realities of Witchcraft*, 280–284.

17. Jolly, Raudvere, and Peters, *The Athlone History of Witchcraft and Magic*, vol. 3, 191.

18. Kieckhefer, *Magic in the Middle Ages*, 65.

19. Ibid., 67.

20. Margret Berger, *Hildegard of Bingen: On Natural Philosophy and Medicine* (Cambridge: Brewer, 1999).

21. Habinger-Tucsay, *Magie und Magier*, 217.

22. Claus Priesner, "Phantastische Reisen: Über Hexenkräuter und Flugsalben," *Kultur und Technik* 17, no. 3/4 (1993): 22–27, 34–39 (two parts), 38; Bever, *Realities of Witchcraft*, 130–131.

23. As depicted in the *Hortus Sanitatis*, www.ubs.sbg.ac.at/sosa/inkunabeln/WII251 (276).jpg (male), and www.ubs.sbg.ac.at/sosa/bdm/hortus02.jpg (female).

24. Bever, *Realities of Witchcraft*, 45 and 306.

25. George Frederick Kunz, *The Magic of Jewels and Charms* (Philadelphia and London: J. B. Lippincott Company, 1915, several reprints), 203.

26. See image at www.ubs.sbg.ac.at/sosa/bdm/hortus07.jpg.

27. Bezoars even made it into English common law, in the case of *Chandelor v. Lopus* (1603), 79 ER 3, dealing with the selling of a bezoar, whose authenticity the seller made clear that he could not guarantee.

28. Reported in Michele Mercati's *Methallotheca Vaticana*; see for the reference Alix Cooper, "The Museum and the Book: The 'Metallotheca' and the History of an Encyclopaedic Natural History in Early Modern Italy," *Journal of the History of Collections* 7 (1995): 1–23. On bezoars from the Americas, see also Miguel de Asúa and Roger French, *A New World of Animals: Early Modern Europeans on the Creatures of Iberian America* (Burlington: Ashgate, 2005), 92, 105–107.

29. The story is told by the Italian physician Andrea Bacci in his *De gemmis et lapidibus pretiosis*, Latin trans. by Wolfgang Gabelchover (Frankfurt a. M.: Becker, 1603), 193; Kunz, *Magic of Jewels and Charms*, 208–209.

30. Kieckhefer, *Magic in the Middle Ages*, 69–75; Jolly, Raudvere, and Peters, *The Athlone History of Witchcraft and Magic*, vol. 3, 35–37. The oldest spells passed down from German-speaking Europe, the Merseburger Zaubersprüche, also give evidence of the adaption of pagan ritual spells into the Christian religious/magic sphere; see Habinger-Tucsay, *Magie und Magier*, 255.

31. Kieckhefer, *Magic in the Middle Ages*, 74.

32. Habinger-Tucsay, *Magie und Magier*, 85.

33. Jolly, Raudvere, and Peters, *The Athlone History of Witchcraft and Magic*, vol. 3, 33, 37.

34. Jessica Freeman, "Sorcery at Court and Manor: Margery Jourdemayne, the Witch of Eye Next Westminster," *Journal of Medieval History* 30 (2004), 349, 351.

35. Freeman, "Sorcery at Court and Manor," 355.

36. Kiekhefer, *Magic in the Middle Ages*, 151; Bailey, *Magic and Superstition*, 101.

37. Jolly, Raudvere, and Peters, *The Athlone History of Witchcraft and Magic*, vol. 3, 53.

38. Bailey, *Magic and Superstition*, 96–101.

39. Ibid., 102.

40. Freeman, "Sorcery at Court and Manor," 347–348.

41. The story is told by the twelfth/thirteenth-century Cistercian Caesarius von Heisterbach, *Dialogus miraculorum V: de daemonibus, XVIII*; see Jolly, Raudvere, and Peters, *The Athlone History of Witchcraft and Magic*, vol. 3, 28.

42. Elizabeth I. Wade, "A Fragmentary German Divination Device: Medieval Analogues and Pseudo-Lullian Tradition," in *Conjuring Spirits*, 90–93.

43. Kieckhefer, *Magic in the Middle Ages*, 127; see also Jolly, Raudvere, and Peters, *The Athlone History of Witchcraft and Magic*, vol. 3, 54; and Flint, *Rise of Magic*, 63 and 101.

44. Kieckhefer, *Forbidden Rituals*, 91.

45. On the aspect of the love potion as a mere symbol of the already existing love between Tristan and Iseult, see Helen Cooper, "Magic That Does Not Work," in *Medievalia et Humanistica* n.s. 7 (1976), 131–146; and Habinger-Tucsay, *Magie und Magier*, 252.

46. Bever, *Realities of Witchcraft*, 272, table 7.1, and 359 (on Luther).

47. For a basic biography, see Jean-Christian Petitfils, *Madame de Montespan* (Paris: Fayard, 1988), and Catherine Decours, *Aimée du Roi: mémoires de Françoise de Rochechouart de Mortemart, marquise de Montespan* (Paris: Plon, 2001).

48. Bever, *Realities of Witchcraft*, 33–35, 135–136, 166, 173, 416–418.

49. For examples, see Jolly, Raudvere, and Peters, *The Athlone History of Witchcraft and Magic*, vol. 3, 60–62.

50. Bever, *Realities of Witchcraft*, 153, 180.

51. Habinger-Tucsay, *Magie und Magier*, 248–253, particularly 251.

52. Bever, *Realities of Witchcraft*, 155; Kieckhefer, *Forbidden Rites*, 69, 74, 79–91, with a survey of examples; see also Mary O'Neil, "Magical Healing, Love Magic and the Inquisition in Late Sixteenth-century Modena" in Brian P. Levack, ed., *New Perspectives on Witchcraft, Magic and Demonology*, vol. 5: *Witchcraft, Healing, and Popular Diseases* (New York and London: Routledge, 2001), 172–199, particularly 185–189.

53. Cohn, *Europe's Inner Demons*, 194.

54. Kieckhefer, *Forbidden Rites*, 79.

55. Habinger-Tucsay, *Magie und Magier*, 251.

Severus Snape and the
Standard Book of Spells
Ancient Tongues in the Wizarding World

M. G. DuPree

"Never used an Unforgivable Curse before, have you, boy? You need to *mean* them, Potter!"

— Bellatrix Lestrange, *Order of the Phoenix*, 810[1]

L anguage is the foundation of magic. All magic—intended, directed magic, that is, magic of ferocious power and energy— depends on the word, even if that word is only in the speaker's head. Words are the vehicles of intention, and intention, as Bellatrix Lestrange reminds us, is everything. But what are all of these words that Harry is supposed to mean, and where do they come from?

Counts of the exact number of spells in the Harry Potter books vary, and they depend on whether you count spells whose effects are mentioned without a name applied to them, such as Dumbledore's age-line spell in *Goblet of Fire*. Counting conservatively, there are about 140 spells in all seven books. Of those, 72 are either Latin, Latin-derived, or Latin in part.

But why Latin? If you need to mean your spell, why on earth would you want half of them to be in a language you don't even speak and that no one has spoken for thousands of years?

The answer lies in the history of Western religion—which is to say, the history of magic, because they are one and the same. Christianity was a religion born among people who spoke Aramaic and wrote Greek. Why and how did Latin come to be so important in Western religion? The answer is not a theological one, but a political one.

Hocus Pocus

The Roman Empire was the ruling power for several centuries before and after the birth of Jesus of Nazareth, and as the empire became Christian, it translated the sacred texts of its newly adopted religion into its own language: Latin. Originally, Latin was used to help people understand their religion better, not to place a barrier of mystery between them and the words of their religious rituals and texts. Yet as time went on and the various provinces of the old empire broke away into feudal kingdoms, their dialects drifted further and further from the Latin original and became what we know today as French, Spanish, Italian, Portuguese, and so on. Latin was still the language of the church but increasingly was a language understood only by those with an education—it became the language of the powerful, the language of scholars, wise men, and clerics. The people understood what was said in church less and less. "What's that the priest is saying?" one farmer might say to another. "Dunno," his friend might shrug. "Just the same old hocus pocus."

Hocus pocus—our catchphrase for magical gibberish, for a nonsensical wave of the wand, a fakery. Yet it's actually a corruption of that old magic at the root of Western civilization: the magic of the Latin Mass, at which bread and wine are "transfigured" (the theological term is *transubstantiation*, but no matter, Minerva McGonagall would know what they meant) into flesh and blood.

Hoc est enim corpus meum, the priest intoned at the high point of the Latin Mass, his back to his flock, his arms upraised to heaven, a wafer held delicately in his fingers as he offered unto God God's own body. *This is my body*. The farmer in the pew, however, what did he understand of that? Say it ten times fast, and you end up with something like "hocus pocus." There's an old psychiatrist's saying that anger turned inward is depression, and anger turned sideways is humor. Thus, religion turned inward might be superstition, but religion turned sideways? Easy: that's magic.

For us who dwell in the hollowed-out shell of the old Roman Empire or in any of Rome's cultural inheritors, the foundation stone of any magical universe is Latin. Latin means power: the power of the empire, the power of the church. And Latin means mystery: the province of the educated, who huddle in their monastic libraries learning ancient secrets and communing with the long-dead. It also means formal speech.

There's a linguist's saying about English speakers that we go to work in Latin and come home in Anglo-Saxon, meaning that much of our professional language (words like *office, supervisor, colleague*—even *computer* and *telephone*) comes from the Latin-derived French, while the language of home (*house, hearth, fire*) comes to us from the German-derived Anglo-Saxon. To use Latin is to ally yourself with all of these powerful connotations at once: mystery, power, and formalism.

Thus, it is interesting to note that the wizarding world falls into the same patterns of speech, with many lower-level hexes and household charms in English, such as Scourgify. It's in the higher-order spells that one sees the shift to Latin and Latinate phrases: Expecto Patronum, Cave Inimicum, Fidelius, Expelliarmus, Finite Incantatem.

Much of Rowling's Latin is grammatically correct, and much is not. Expecto Patronum falls into the former category, because it literally means "I await a protector," although undoubtedly there's also a nudge at the *patr* root because Harry's protector turns out literally to be his father, and Cave Inimicum means "beware of an intruder" in Latin that Julius Caesar would have recognized.

Finite Incantatem is a grammatically exact command meaning "end the spell," but what's of interest in this spell is the verb form. The imperative (command form of a verb) here is plural, which implies that one is telling more than one person to end a spell; thus, the very form of this spell implies that it can put a stop to multiple spells at once, from multiple sources. Verbs such as *tergeo*,[2] *defodio*,[3] *confundo*,[4] and *descendo*[5] become instant spells matching their dictionary meaning.

Other spell creations take more liberties; Severus Snape's sadistically creative invention, the Sectumsempra Curse, combines the participle *sectum*, meaning "cut," with *semper*, meaning "always," to create a wholly new word. Combination words abound in the magic that Harry and his friends learn (Densaugeo,[6] Liberacorpus[7]), as do spells that are almost but not quite correct Latin: Homenum Revelio,[8] which misses actual Latin by only two vowels, as well as Meteolojinx Recanto,[9] which wins the prize for "most languages in a single spell" for combining Greek, English, and Latin in only two words.

Rarest of all spell language in the British wizarding world is Greek, which makes surprisingly few appearances. In pure form, there are only two Greek-based spells mentioned in all of the seven books: Anapneo and Episkey. Anapneo is used on a choking Marcus Belby by Horace Slughorn in *Half-Blood Prince* and is simply a Greek verb meaning "I draw breath." Episkey is clearly a corruption of the Greek verb *episkeuo*, meaning "I repair," and is used by Nymphadora Tonks on Harry's unfortunate nose in *Half-Blood Prince*.[10]

The interesting thing to note is that both of these are spells with medical uses, which should not be surprising: in the ancient world, Greek was the language of physicians.[11] Presumably, if Harry had decided to study Healing, readers would have seen a great deal more Greek spells, but while that might have been fascinating from a linguist's point of view, readers are probably grateful that Harry's adventures were rather more exciting than the examination of sputum.

The Empire Strikes Back

"Now . . . those three curses—*Avada Kedavra*, Imperius, and Cruciatus—are known as the Unforgivable Curses. The use of any one of them on a fellow human being is enough to earn a life sentence in Azkaban."

—Barty Crouch Jr., *Goblet of Fire*, 217

Barty Crouch Jr.—disguised as Mad-Eye Moody—is the first to offer instruction in the serious Dark Arts to a suitably impressed Harry, after a graphic (and spider-hating) display of all three Unforgivables. It's not an accident that two of these curses are in formal, exact Latin, while the third—and most dangerous of all—is in a far older and more secret language.

One says "Imperio" to gain control over the body of another human. Although the action itself is sinister, Harry, when placed under the Imperius Curse by Crouch, describes it as "the most wonderful feeling . . . as every thought and worry in his head was wiped gently away." (*GOF*, 231) Of course, those thoughts and worries are being wiped away in order to be replaced by the will of the spell caster, who can use the victim for any purpose.

That one word, *imperio*, contains millennia of historical baggage. For *imperium* is the Latin word for "power," but it was also the word the Roman state used to refer to itself and is the root of our word *empire*. For hundreds of years, the Imperium Romanum ruled the Mediterranean world and beyond with an iron fist that crushed rebellion mercilessly and bled smaller states of tribute until they crumbled before the inexorable advance of the Imperium.

All of our later understandings of the evils of empire—from cold war rhetoric to George Lucas's creation—are deep memories of this original empire that shaped the history, the speech, the thought, and the religion of the Western world. To cast this curse is to exercise that kind of total dominion over another human being and thus to violate human autonomy in the worst possible way. The verb *impero* itself is a perfectly serviceable Latin word that simply means "to command," but the addition of that "*i*" invokes the far more powerful noun *imperium*—in much the same way that the curse itself crosses the line of ordinary magic into the realm of the Unforgivable.

Even more interesting is the Cruciatus Curse. To cast it, one says the Latin verb *crucio*, meaning "I torture." Yet *crucio* is itself a derivative of another, older Latin word: *crux*. A crux, properly speaking, is any two lengths of wood or any other material overlaid in perpendicular fashion to form an X. Sounds harmless enough, but like the old legend about the Eskimos having a hundred words for snow, the Romans had infinite (and infinitely creative) ways to inflict pain and infinite words for pain itself. Somewhere in the mists of history—no one knows exactly when or where—Romans conceived the idea that human beings could be tied, or even nailed, to lengths of wood like this.

The elegance of this form of torture is that the person does not, of course, die at once. Even with nailing in the joints or the extremities, blood loss was unlikely to be severe enough to cause death. Instead, one simply sat back and waited for nature to take its literally excruciating course. The victim, if hardy, would most likely die of asphyxiation as the torso struggled to inhale and exhale without sufficient support. The lucky died of exhaustion; the fortunate perished after only a few hours of agony.

Roman citizens were never subjected to this form of execution; citizens whose treason was judged severe enough for execution got off with a quick sword to the neck. Crucifixion was a form of butchery the Romans perfected in the provinces, against the non-Romans, although once it came home to the Italian peninsula in unforgettable fashion.

In 71 B.C., after putting down Spartacus's bloody slave revolt, the Roman general Crassus crucified six thousand of Spartacus's followers in a line of crosses that stretched along the Appian Way for miles.[12] The stench and the screams were said to be unbearable, and the Roman populace was repulsed; Crassus's bid to look like the hero made Roman citizens shrink from him in distaste. (Not for nothing does his name give us the adjective *crass*.) Thus, for Romans the crux, whether in the form of an X or the more familiar (and easier to stick in the ground) T shape, was an instrument of the most exquisite torture.

This awareness of the crux as source of pain appears in Roman literature as well. The Roman poet Catullus penned two terse lines that resonate with emotional torture today:

> Odi et amo. Quare id faciam, fortasse requiris.
> Nescio, sed fieri sentio et excrucior.
> [I hate and I love. Perhaps you ask me why I do this.
> I know not, but I feel it happening, and I am cruciated.][13]

Not only does the poet end with the verb *crucifixion*, but the poem itself is constructed in the shape of the crux the poet hangs on. The two verbs in the beginning (*odi et amo*) are echoed by the verb pair at the end (*sentio et excrucior*). The verb of questioning at the end of line one (*requiris*) is echoed by the verb of answer at the beginning of line two (*nescio*). Draw lines connecting these, and you have the crux, the X on which the poet feels himself to be tortured. Finally, draw a more-or-less vertical line connecting *faciam* and *fieri* (two forms of the same verb) to represent the poet himself, torn apart and stretched in two different directions, like the opposition of hate and love in his opening line.

Catullus's imagery is a fair description of what the Cruciatus Curse feels like, according to *Goblet of Fire*, when, at the hands of Lord Voldemort, Harry experiences for the first time what it feels like to be on the receiving end of this curse: "The pain was so intense, so all-consuming, that he no longer knew where he was . . . White-hot knives were piercing every inch of his skin, his head was surely going to burst with pain, he was screaming more loudly than he'd ever screamed in his life." (*GOF*, 661)

One can almost hear the echo of Harry's open-mouthed scream in the final lengthened syllable of Catullus's poem, in the drawn-out moan of the *or* that ends *excrucior*. It's a sound that travelers on the Appian Way would have been familiar with, listening to the screams of the crucified Spartacan rebels, and it's a sound that hums with history.

So when wizards aim their wands and hiss "Crucio" or "Imperio," a powerful weight of Roman baggage comes with them. It's a baggage that reaches back to a brutal world of emperors and bloodthirsty generals, a world in which sensitive poets resorted to images of the torture they saw around them. It is not the hallowed, liturgical world of medieval Latin that oozes from these curses, but the darker and older one of imperial Rome.

Yet for the most dangerous curse of all, Rowling turned to a language older than Rome's. The empire stood for five hundred years (closer to a thousand, if you count its Greek-speaking successor state, the Byzantine Empire), and before there was an empire, there was a Roman Republic that had lasted for five hundred years before that. Rome's history was a long one, but it didn't begin in glory: at first, Rome was nothing more than a squalid, marshy crossroads of minor significance on the Italian salt trade route.

Centuries earlier, while Latin speakers were still clustered in wattle-and-daub mud huts beside the Tiber River, the real center of civilization lay far to the East. What we today call the Middle East had been a center of civilization, literacy, and urban sophistication for millennia before anyone ever knew the word *Rome*. And it's to the Middle East's Semitic language family that we turn for the origin of the most fearsome Unforgivable Curse: Avada Kedavra.

The Killing Curse

"Does anyone know where avada kedavra came from? It is an ancient spell in Aramaic, and it is the original of abracadabra, which means 'let the thing be destroyed.' Originally, it was used to cure illness and the 'thing' was the illness, but I decided to make it the 'thing' as in the person standing in front of me. I take a lot of liberties with things like that. I twist them round and make them mine."

—J. K. Rowling[14]

The story of Avada Kedavra, for readers of Rowling's books, climaxes with the fearful scene on the Astronomy Tower at the end of *Half-Blood Prince*, when Snape uses the curse to kill Albus Dumbledore:

> Snape gazed for a moment at Dumbledore, and there was revulsion and hatred etched in the harsh lines of his face.
>
> "Severus . . . please . . ."
>
> Snape raised his wand and pointed it directly at Dumbledore.
>
> "Avada Kedavra!"
>
> A jet of green light shot from the end of Snape's wand and hit Dumbledore squarely in the chest. Harry's scream of horror never left him; silent and unmoving, he was forced to watch as Dumbledore was blasted into the air. (*HBP*, 595–596)

Yet for linguists and historians of the strange and unusual, the story of Avada Kedavra actually begins with one of the ancient world's most fascinating and little-known figures: Quintus Serenus Sammonicus, a physician, a philologist, a poet, and—it is just possible—a magician.[15] He was the tutor and confidant of Emperor Geta, who ruled the Roman Empire along with his brother Caracalla in the year 211, for a total of only eleven months until Caracalla ordered the Praetorian Guard to murder him in their mother's apartments. Sammonicus himself was killed in the bloodbath that ensued, paying for his closeness to the hated Geta with a sword in the gut at a dinner party Caracalla had invited him to. (Although Sammonicus was a learned man, he was possibly not the best judge of dinner invitations.)

Before his inauspicious death, Sammonicus was the author of a five-volume tome called *Res Reconditae*, or "Hidden Things." Although much quoted in the ancient world, this work survives only in fragments, due possibly to Caracalla's fury with its author's patron: in the year 212 the emperor ordered a *damnatio memoriae*, or an official erasing of Geta's memory from all public records and monuments. Geta was known as a patron of the arts and letters, and in the ensuing persecution of Geta's followers and family, it is not hard to believe that the books of someone so closely associated with Geta might have suffered as well.

From the wreckage, what we have left is the *De Medicina Praecepta*, a medical treatise. (Sammonicus was a noted doctor, as well as a writer, a fact that the delicate Geta probably appreciated.) The *De Medicina* repeats some remedies borrowed from the ancient Greeks, but also includes varied bits of folklore and any number of magical formulae. And buried among all the odd magical formulae that he lists, we find this, history's first recorded mention of the powerful incantation Rowling would make her own and introduce to the world as the Avada Kedavra:[16]

```
A—B—R—A—C—A—D—A—B—R—A
A—B—R—A—C—A—D—A—B—R
A—B—R—A—C—A—D—A—B
A—B—R—A—C—A—D—A
A—B—R—A—C—A—D
A—B—R—A—C—A
A—B—R—A—C
A—B—R—A
A—B—R
A—B
A
```

"Abracadabra," it reads, in an inverted pyramid of nine rows. In each row, one letter is removed, leading to the pinnacle A. The pyramid reads the same along its right and upper sides, although not along its left, which is simply a stack of A's.

What could it mean? Whatever it meant, the ancient and medieval world *loved* it: during the medieval period, *abracadabra* appeared on amulets, in magical incantations, in love potion formulas, and in arcane treatises. The word went viral and survived to become what we know as the word magicians shriek when pulling reluctant rabbits out of hats—or what you and I say when we've miraculously dug our car keys from out of the crack in the sofa. But what on earth is it, and what language is it?

As to the language, there are two possibilities: Aramaic and Hebrew. Both would have powerful incantational meanings to the medieval mind. The simplest possibility is that it is Aramaic, a language Sammonicus could easily have come into contact with in his vast reading (his library is reputed to have held sixty thousand volumes) and in his travels.

Aramaic is a Semitic language closely related to Hebrew, and it functioned for most of its history as the common tongue of ancient Israel, as well as of the entire ancient Middle East. Certain portions of the Jewish scriptures were written in Aramaic, which was also a Jewish liturgical language; indeed, certain portions of the Jewish liturgy today, such as the kaddish prayer, remain in Aramaic. Some scattered quotations in the New Testament are Aramaic as well: Jesus' command of *"Talitha cumi,"* which summons a young girl back from death, is possibly the most famous.[17]

Although Aramaic survives today in increasingly isolated pockets in Syria, Israel, and Lebanon, it was once the language of the street, spoken by nearly everyone in the ancient Middle East from about a thousand years before the birth of Jesus to about the year 200. Around the time of Alexander the Great, from about 200 B.C. onward, Greek became more widely used, but for most of this period, Aramaic was the language everyone in the Middle East could be counted on to speak, even if their formal writing was in Greek. As the "common tongue," Aramaic was the natural language used by most people for intimate communication and private conversations—including conversations with the supernatural.

According to the theory that Sammonicus's "abracadabra" is a transliteration of an Aramaic phrase, the incantation is a representation of *avra k'davra*. In both Hebrew and Aramaic, "*b*" and "*v*" are the same letter, and it's reasonable to assume that a Greek speaker, hearing the phrase, would write down Aramaic *v*'s as *b*'s, because ancient Greek had no such sound.[18] *Avra k'davra* means something like "I will make as I say" and could be understood as a word that strengthens the wish of the supplicant, much as *amen* might for Jews and Christians.

Thus, someone might pray that an illness or an affliction or a demon would be driven off, and the magician assisting in the rite would say the *avra k'davra*, a sort of ancient "make it so." The connection between saying and making is an ancient one and a deeply magical idea—the idea that utterance of a word creates a physical reality. It's also a deeply religious idea, contained in the ancient Hebrew blessing: "Blessed is He who spoke, and the world was."[19]

There is a lot of sense behind this explanation of the phrase, but it doesn't answer one question: why on earth the nine-row inverted pyramid in Sammonicus's treatise? To answer why the number nine would be significant, there is one other possibility—that *abracadabra* isn't Aramaic at all but Hebrew.

Both Aramaic and Hebrew are written and read right to left and not (as English is) from left to right. Read that way, the first line of the pyramid reads not "abracadabra" but "arbadacarba." To anyone who knows Hebrew, a word jumps out immediately: *arba*.

Arba means "four," and thus at the beginning and the end of the incantation we have the word *four*—*arba-dac-arba*. Four and four might make sense, if the pyramid were eight rows instead of nine. So, what of that odd cluster of letters in the middle? Well, ancient amulets and formulae for warding off evil forces often misspelled or misarranged words—the theory being, perhaps, that the devil was easily confused (or just not that great a speller). Often a small but crucial word would have an inverted letter, simply to throw evil off the track. In this case, if the letters are arranged not as D-A-C but as A-C-D, the letters of the Hebrew word for *one* (*echad*) are represented. So the incantation would actually read four + one + four: *arba-echad-arba*.

Why would a magical formula Sammonicus picked up in the Middle East invoke the number nine? Because in Kabbalah, the ancient Jewish mystical tradition, the number nine is associated with the forces of darkness and evil. According to Kabbalah, there are ten *sefirot*, or divine attributes loosed in the world. Diminish that by one, teaches the Kabbalistic text *Sefer Yetzirah*, and you have nine, the ultimate number of imperfection and thus of evil. And why would the formula not simply use the Hebrew word for nine? Because *tesha*, Hebrew for "nine," has only four letters (in Hebrew), and nine letters are needed here. It is a basic principle of magic that the physical act must mirror the intention, something that Hogwarts students learn with their first "swish and flick." Thus, if the wearer of Sammonicus's amulet wants to repel the forces of nine (darkness), the number nine must be physically invoked.

As the final proof that the number nine is significant in his incantation, Sammonicus prescribed that the amulet with this inscription be worn for nine days, at which point the affliction would have been driven off and the sufferer would be free of evil influence. Perhaps Sammonicus had left his lucky amulets at home when the Emperor Caracalla invited him to dinner, but on the other hand, maybe he can be forgiven for not knowing exactly where he stood with the emperor: for Emperor Caracalla's family name, like that of his brother and his slippery father before him, was Severus. And thus, naturally, Sammonicus could not read the emperor's mind.

So the name Severus invokes not only violence—brother murdering brother, the halls of the imperial palace running with blood—but magic as well. Emperor Septimius Severus, the father of both Caracalla and Geta, was not himself of noble birth. He was a successful general who put down the unrest following the death of Emperor Commodus, and although he rose to the imperial purple, he must have been aware all of his life of his own status as a kind of "half-blood" among Rome's oldest and purest noble families.

Like another and later Severus, the legacy of the Severan dynasty is a mixed one: Caracalla might be famous for his brutality, but he is equally renowned for granting citizenship to all free residents of the empire—a pen stroke that changed forever Western notions of belonging and of nationhood. In the end, therefore, one could argue that Caracalla was working for the forces of light, like his wizarding namesake.

Perhaps Rowling simply intended to evoke the meaning of the Latin adjective *severus*—"harsh, merciless, severe." Certainly, the Harry Potter books are full of such name references, where the root of the word for someone's name reflects the traits that the character later displays: Albus for "white," Rubeus for "ruddy," Argus for the all-seeing guard dog of the gods, Minerva for the goddess of war and wisdom. Yet it's hard to avoid the idea that this particular name—Severus—with its baggage of blood and magic, might mean a little bit more.

As for why Rowling, in her quotation at the start of this section, translates *abracadabra* as "let the thing be destroyed," the probable answer is that she understands *dabra* to be an Aramaic form of the Hebrew word *deber*, which means "illness or pestilence." *Abra* could conceivably be a corruption of the Hebrew word for "blessing," *ha-berachah*. Thus, it could mean something like "a blessing on this pestilence!" and be used to ward off disease or death. It's not as convoluted an explanation as some of the others—and not nearly as much fun—but is as likely as any other.

In truth, there are probably hundreds of competing explanations for this enigmatic phrase, and a case can be made for each of them. Because Rowling has given this ancient phrase a new lease on life in contemporary consciousness, she can probably be allowed to think whatever she wants about it. After all, she is the one who spoke—and Harry Potter was.

Notes

1. All book quotes are taken from the American editions by J. K. Rowling as follows: *Goblet of Fire*, New York: A.A. Levine Books, 2000; *Order of the Phoenix*, New York: A.A. Levine Books, 2003; *Half-Blood Prince*, New York: A.A. Levine Books, 2005.

2. The scouring spell, meaning literally "I wipe clean." A favorite of Hermione Granger's, used in *Half-Blood Prince* to wipe ink from Ron's essay and blood off Harry's face, it also makes several appearances in *Deathly Hallows*.

3. The digging spell, meaning literally "I dig out." This one appears only in *Deathly Hallows*, when Harry, Ron Weasley, and Hermione use it to extricate themselves from the Gringotts Tunnels.

4. This spell that causes confusion means literally "I confuse" and is both used and referred to many times in the books, beginning with *Prisoner of Azkaban*, when Snape claims that Harry, Ron, and Hermione must have been confunded to believe Sirius Black. Hermione is guilty of using this spell against the hapless Cormac McLaggen, who goes up against Ron in *Half-Blood Prince*'s Quidditch tryouts.

5. This common Latin verb means literally "I go down" and is used twice in *Deathly Hallows* to make objects lower—the wall in the Room of Requirement, the stairs to the attic in Ron's room.

6. *Dens* (meaning "tooth") and *augeo* (meaning "I enlarge, increase"). It is famously deflected onto Hermione in *Goblet of Fire*, after Draco attempts to use it on Harry and causes Hermione's teeth to grow to the size of a beaver's.

7. *Libera* (the command meaning "free") and *corpus* (meaning "body.") This is another of Snape's creations and is used twice in *Deathly Hallows*, both times by Harry: once to free Ron from the *levicorpus* he accidentally cast on him, and once to free Griphook from the avalanche of red-hot treasure in the Lestranges' vault at Gringotts.

8. Just off from *hominum revelo*, which means "I unveil a person." Hermione uses this spell in *Deathly Hallows*, after the Tottenham Court Road attack, to reveal any lurking Death Eaters on their arrival at Grimmauld Place.

9. An apparent hodgepodge of the Greek *meteorologia* (meteorology), English *jinx*, and Latin *recanto* ("I revoke"). Arthur Weasley suggests this in Deathly Hallows as a way to clear up the rain in Yaxley's office—suggests it, in fact, to his own son, because Ron is at the time Polyjuiced into Reginald Cattermole from Magical Maintenance.

10. In the movie version of *Half-Blood Prince*, Luna Lovegood performs this spell. Harry, always a quick study, then uses it later in the same book on Gryffindor Chaser Demelza Robins to fix her mouth, after Ron has punched her accidentally during Quidditch practice.

11. It was the Greeks who first systematized the study of medicine and theorized as early as the first century B.C. that disease was caused by microbial organisms—deducing the existence of germs just as Greek physicists deduced the existence of atoms. It was Asclepiades and his pupils who insisted that disease itself, not merely extensive details of a patient's personal history, should be a physician's proper course of study and thus gave to the world diagnostic medicine.

12. Barry Strauss, *The Spartacus War* (New York: Simon & Shuster, 2009).

13. Daniel Garrison, *The Student's Catullus* (Norman: University of Oklahoma Press, 2004). Translation mine.

14. Interview at Edinburgh Book Festival, April 15, 2004.

15. Edward Champlin, "Serenus Sammonicus," *Harvard Studies in Classical Philology* 85 (1981): 189–212.

16. Quintus Serenus Sammonicus, *De Medicina Praecepta Salvberrima*, ed. Johann Gottlieb Ackermann (Leipzig: I.G. Müller, 1786), 150. See also, *Liber Medicinalis (texte etabli, traduit, et commenté)* (Paris: Presses universitaires de France, 1950).

17. Gospel of Mark 5:41.

18. Modern readers will note that there is a distinction in modern Hebrew between *bet* and *vet*; the difference is indicated by full punctuation marking—specifically, with the dagesh (or dot) marking in the center of the *bet/vet* letter. The presence of the dagesh makes it *bet* (with dagesh) or *vet* (no dagesh). In traditionally noted Hebrew and Aramaic (e.g., the Hebrew of the third century C.E.), however, no dagesh was written and thus no distinction was maintained between the two.

19. Alternatively, the Aramaic phrase could be understood as "I will create as I speak," thus uniting the idea of creation with speech itself. This idea is found in the first few lines of the Hebrew bible, when God says, "Let there be light," and light appears. Throughout the biblical creation narrative, speech is the essential factor, indeed the foundation of creation itself.

Beastly Books and Quick-Quills

Harry Potter and the Making of Medieval Manuscripts

Alexandra Gillespie

In the middle of the 1400s, a man named Robert Taylor decided that he needed a book.[1] Robert lived in a town called Boxford in East Anglia in England, about fifty miles from the medieval university of Cambridge. In 1450, Cambridge was thronged with students who came from as far away as Italy and France to take courses in grammar, logic, arithmetic, and astronomy. Among those students was a young man named Simon Wysbech. Having already passed his foundational courses, Wysbech was working toward a degree in canon law. He was qualified to teach other students for money, but he was undoubtedly short of cash: studying and teaching never made anyone rich. So in his spare hours, he took on jobs using the most saleable skill he had—that of bookmaking. He worked as a scribe.[2]

It's not clear how Taylor knew Wysbech, but we do know that the student made Taylor's book, because that book still survives. It is now in the collection of the Huntington Library in San Marino, California, manuscript number 1336 (MS 1336). On its last leaf is Wysbech's colophon or scribal signature. It reads, "Here ends the book of good governance . . . which book belongs to Robert Taylor of Boxford . . . so says Simon Wysbech, student of Cambridge."[3] The word *governance* suggests that what Taylor was after was a sort of medieval "self-help" book, full of tips on how to live a well-organized and healthy life.

Having looked through the contents of Taylor's "book of good governance," we might give the manuscript a slightly different name. His book contains recipes for medical potions of "roots" and "galingale" to take "until you be whole." An "herbal" lists some plants that make living creatures seem dead. There is a "charm" to stop merchants from cheating you in the marketplace. One recipe provides the secret of invisibility, so its user can make a man appear headless; another teaches the reader how to turn black crows white. Astrological calculations predict "great winds" in January, followed by a "battle." The book that Wysbech made for Taylor is, by any other name, a book of magic.

More than 550 years later, we have means of making and obtaining textual information that Wysbech and Taylor could only have dreamed about. They perhaps knew about printing. The printing press was invented by Johannes Gutenberg in about 1450, and its products were reaching England's shores by the late 1460s.[4] Yet our libraries are not merely collections of printed books. We have electronic archives, digital search engines, and digital copies of books. We can read using iPods, Kindles, and mobile phones. So various, so ubiquitous, and so powerful are our new methods of producing and disseminating texts that some critics believe that the twenty-first century marks the beginning of "the end of the book."[5] For Taylor and Wysbech, books—or at least, pages of some kind, including single leaves, folded pamphlets, and parchment rolls—were the only way of preserving and retrieving ideas in recorded form. Now the physical page is just one way of doing so and not necessarily the most convenient one.

So it is an especially significant moment when, in this late age of the book, a boy receives a letter, "addressed so plainly that there could be no mistake" to:

Mr. H. Potter
The Cupboard under the Stairs
4 Privet Drive
Little Whinging
Surrey

It is striking that Harry's entry into magical life comes in the form of a letter, not an e-mail or a phone call. It is not even a very modern-looking letter. It is not on thin modern paper, with its hot, dry smell of bleach and wood pulp. "The envelope was thick and heavy, made of yellowish parchment." Harry's letter has been made just as Wysbech made Taylor's book: from "parchment," animal skin treated to form a writing surface. The letter has been "written in emerald-green ink," rather than typed on a keyboard. The envelope has been sealed: "Turning the envelope over, his hand trembling Harry saw a purple wax seal bearing a coat of arms." (PS, 30)[6] All of this would have made sense to Taylor and Wysbech, who lived at a time when important documents, including the many letters that messengers carried around England, were usually sealed.[7] Near to where Taylor's magic manuscript preserves a recipe for different colored inks (folio 3) are instructions for making sealing wax in green or red (on folio 12).

The letter Harry receives is, of course, the one inviting him to take his place at Hogwarts School of Witchcraft and Wizardry. Hogwarts sends a penned, parchment letter with a wax seal because, as Hermione Granger explains to Ron Weasley and Harry—having, as usual, memorized the relevant section of Hogwarts, A History—computers and other electronic devices do not work within the walls of Hogwarts. Anyway, what use would a computer or similar technologies be to someone magical? The electrical plugs, the toasters, and even the cars that Mr. Weasley collects are occasionally handy things for witches or wizards to bewitch, but mostly they are merely intriguing evidence of how Muggle culture works. Vacuum cleaners are not necessary when you know how to "scourgify" a dirty surface.[8] Cars and even airplanes are pointless if Floo Powder, Portkeys, Thestrals, brooms, and flying horse-drawn carriages are available to help you avoid the traffic.

Yet whereas most Muggle technologies are merely substitutes for things that magic has always done better, the technology of the book and other forms of writing is one that the Muggle and the wizarding worlds share. There are magical ways of communicating in Harry Potter's world, of course: witness the surprising appearance of Amos Diggory's head in the fireplace of the Burrow in *Goblet of Fire*. But mostly, witches and wizards use very human ways of getting word to one another or taking note of what they think. They write on scrolls and keep inkpots; they use quills and send sealed letters. What is striking about these activities is not that the methods are magical but that they are antique. Muggles once did much the same as wizards: they sealed their letters with wax and had local scribes such as Simon Wysbech copy magic spells into their recipe books using quills. Yet they did so in a medieval, rather than a modern, age.

J. K. Rowling thus does something very interesting when she fills Harry Potter's world with "real" medieval books and documents. She transforms the book (and writing itself) back into something magical, just at the moment when, so we've been told, its days are numbered. We are reminded that unlike a car or a vacuum cleaner, a book *is* magic. It doesn't need a magical substitute. It has an almost supernatural power: to bear words that contain and then stimulate the extraordinary force of the human imagination. Rowling demonstrated this magic when, at the start of a new age of digital media, she wrote a series of books that by 2009 had sold more than 400 million copies worldwide.[9] She made the point in another way when she selected the book, out of all Muggle technologies, for a starring role in the wizarding world. The old books, quills, and scraps of medieval writing depicted in the Harry Potter novels have much to teach us—about the magic that is hidden in books that were made in an era when it was perfectly normal to mix up a potion to remedy an ill and about the magic *of* the book and its long and fascinating history.

From the Slaughterhouse into the Goblet of Fire: Making and Using Parchment

Perhaps the first thing that would be striking to any modern reader of Taylor's manuscript is the parchment from which it is made. Parchment, from medieval Latin *pergamenum*, was animal skin, treated to make a smooth surface suitable for writing.[10] Paper was not unknown in the medieval period: in the year 100 or so, methods of making paper from plant fibers were invented in China and then introduced to Europe via the Islamic world during the 1100s. By Taylor's time, paper was commonly used in England for the production of documents and records. Yet although it was more expensive, parchment remained the more durable and desirable material for scribal work up until the advent of printing.[11] The situation is much the same in the wizarding world. At the Ministry of Magic in *Deathly Hallows*, Harry comes across a dozen officials who are magicking pamphlets out of "squares of colored paper" (*DH*, 205). But like his first letter from Hogwarts, most of the magical writing that Harry encounters is written on parchment.

At the slaughterhouse, a medieval parchment maker in search of skins from sheep, goats, or calves needed to be choosy. The hides could not be too blotchy, nor could the animals be infected with many ticks or parasitic flies, because insect larvae leave holes in the skin. Once selected, skins were washed in running water, soaked in a solution of lime in great wooden tubs for ten days or so, and rinsed. This process loosened the hairs and the remaining flesh from the skin. Each skin was then attached to a wooden frame called a *circulus*; as it was stretched, the parchment maker took a large curved knife called a *lunellum* and scraped vigorously at the skin. Hair and residual flesh were removed and the surface of the skin smoothed and refined. When the skin was taken from the frame, the skin's rough outer edges were cut away, its surface buffed with chalk, and the resulting yellowish-white rectangular sheet was ready for use.

The rough off-cut edges of the parchment sheet also had uses. In Harry's world, during the Triwizard Tournament, hopeful competitors from Hogwarts, Durmstrang, or Beauxbatons must write their names on a "slip of parchment" and submit it to the goblet's magical judgment (GOF, 225). Medieval people also appear to have kept scraps of parchment handy for note taking. In Corpus Christi College, Cambridge, there is a book, MS 311, in which a tiny scrap of parchment has been loosely stitched. On it is note about the death of a "Mister Watts" from a "tertiary fever" and a "medicine not known" administered by a suspicious local apothecary.[12]

The treatment of parchment stripped away much of what was animal about the basic component part of a medieval manuscript: the folded pieces of skin that formed it. Yet this process was never wholly complete. If a manuscript became at all damp, the parchment would begin to spring back to its three-dimensional, beastly shape. This is why most medieval manuscripts have clasps, ties, or straps and pins on their bindings to keep them restrained. The trouble that wizarding students and bookstore managers alike have with copies of The Monster Book of Monsters in Prisoner of Azkaban is a suitable metaphor for the not-quite-tamed creature that lurks in every parchment book.[13]

Under the Eye of Madam Pince: Medieval Libraries and Their Books

Technologies such as parchment making and bookbinding were reintroduced to England after the departure of its Roman rulers around A.D. 400. Between that time and the seventh century, the Christian church's pilgrims and missionaries brought the word of God to the British Isles in book form. St. Augustine is said to have carried a copy of the gospels with him when he came to Kent from Rome to convert the Anglo-Saxons in 597. The precious manuscript was kept for centuries at the abbey in Canterbury that was founded in St. Augustine's name. The book went missing when the monastery was officially "dissolved" during the English Reformation in the 1530s, but Elizabeth I's archbishop of Canterbury found it in the 1560s, and it still survives in the library he bequeathed to Cambridge, Corpus Christi College, as MS 286.[14]

The library at Hogwarts is very much like one at a medieval monastery or a medieval university college. Special rooms for books were first set aside in English monasteries in the fourteenth century, but the books were stored in chests. During the sixteenth century, a system arose for storing books on shelves. These were arranged in the sort of "narrow rows" through which Harry must make his way by lamplight during his first illicit nighttime visit to Hogwarts Library (PS, 145).

Medieval libraries contained books for loan, sometimes in duplicate copies. The "Founders Statutes" of New College, Oxford, 1379, state that each fellow of the college can borrow two textbooks per year.[15] Hogwarts students can also borrow certain books. For instance, the library has lots of copies of Hogwarts, A History, although Hermione is distressed to find "all the copies" out on loan soon after the Chamber of Secrets is opened (COS, 112). Other books in medieval collections were like St. Augustine's copy of the gospels. They were centuries old, unique, and for use only in the library itself. Hermione must get special permission to borrow an ancient "damp-spotted" book of Moste Potente Potions, and usually she, Harry, and Ron must search through Hogwarts' "thousands of books" under the suspicious eye of the Hogwarts librarian, Madam Pince, whether they are looking for the elusive Nicolas Flamel in Philosopher's Stone or for a spell to help Harry breathe under water during the second task of the Triwizard Tournament (COS, 124 and PS, 145).

Scrivenshaft's and Flourish and Blotts: Shopping for Medieval Books

During the first few centuries after St. Augustine's arrival in England, books and also the art of bookmaking were largely confined to the country's monasteries and abbeys. There were no universities to produce student scribes like Simon Wysbech, and men such as Robert Taylor conducted their day-to-day business without much reference to written documents.

Around 1200, all of this began to change. A variety of circumstances converged: the rise of bureaucratic record keeping; the foundation of medieval universities such as Oxford and Cambridge; and the establishment of new schools for children. There was increased demand for books and so for writing materials and bookmaking skills.[16] Book crafts such as parchment making and bookbinding became commercial: they were a means by which an ordinary man or woman could earn at least part of a living. Records from English towns around about 1300 show that people were renting premises as "parchmeners," binders, "limners" (professional illustrators of books), and "scriveners" (copyists of legal writs and deeds).[17] By the time Wysbech was in need of parchment, whether for his own studies of law or for his part-time work as a scribe, he and others like him could readily obtain sheets from a local parchmener's "shop."

A scribe such as Wysbech did not have to get all of his supplies wholesale, however. There were also stationers' shops in medieval England, and Wysbech may have visited one in Cambridge during the 1450s. On his very first visit to Diagon Alley, Harry has to do the same. Rubeus Hagrid takes him "to buy parchment and quills"; "Harry cheered up a bit when he found a bottle of ink that changed color as you wrote." (PS, 61) The shop he visits on his first expedition into the magical realm is not named, but the shop in Hogsmeade where Hogwarts students can stock up on writing materials during the school year is called Scrivenshaft's Quill Shop. Of course, it is Hermione who directs attention away from Honeydukes to this more scholarly establishment, when she pauses to examine "a handsome display of pheasant feather quills in the window." (OOTP, 310–311)

Medieval stationers did not, oddly enough, start out by selling "stationery," whether parchment or "feather quills." Instead, stationers were traders, lenders, and appraisers of secondhand books. In the late 1200s and the 1300s, they set up stations—and so acquired their name—around medieval universities in Paris, Bologna, and Oxford and in great cities such as London.[18] Their shops looked less like Scrivenshaft's and more like the bookshop at Diagon Alley, Flourish and Blotts: its "shelves . . . stacked to the ceiling with books as large as paving stones [and] the size of postage stamps." (PS, 62) Some of Flourish and Blotts's books are secondhand, as were the books in medieval stationers' shops. That is how Ginny Weasley comes to have "a very old, very battered" Transfiguration book in her shopping cauldron into which Lucius Malfoy can then slip another used book, Tom Riddle's diary (COS, 51).

Not only a few books for the thrifty (Weasley) buyer, however, but *all* of the stock of a medieval book shop was secondhand. This is because it was such a slow and complicated business to get a new book made in the Middle Ages. Every new book had to be copied out by hand by a scribe such as Simon Wysbech. All copying was thus "bespoke," which means that books were "spoken for," made to order, as Wysbech's was for Taylor.

Yet medieval stationers did get involved in this bespoke trade. Like the manager of Flourish and Blotts who takes advance orders for Rita Skeeter's scurrilous *The Life and Lies of Albus Dumbledore*, stationers saw the advantage of responding directly to customer demand. If they did not have the book requested in stock, they could either borrow a copy and make a new manuscript themselves or subcontract one or more scribes to assist them. So Wysbech may well have supplemented his income by working for Cambridge stationers, as well as for patrons such as Taylor.

Readers of the Harry Potter series are never told exactly how the books in Flourish and Blotts are made, but Rowling does leave clues. Ordinarily, writing in Harry's world is done just as Wysbech did it—slowly and by hand. Think of the detention in *Chamber of Secrets* in which Harry must help Gilderoy Lockhart address his fan mail. He "moved his aching hand over what felt like the thousandth envelope . . . miserably." (COS, 92) In *Deathly Hallows*, he encounters more efficient writing techniques. At the Ministry of Magic, Harry passes "a frowning wizard who was murmuring instructions to a quill that floated in front of him, scribbling on a trail of parchment." (DH, 204–205) This probably comes as no surprise to Harry, who has spent so many memorable moments with

Rita Skeeter and her poisonous Quick-Quotes Quill. Yet neither Harry, Ron, nor Hermione has ever before seen a magical device like the one on which *The Quibbler* is being printed when they go to the Lovegoods' house. It is an "old-fashioned printing press," nothing like the modern machine that this essay was printed on. It looks "like the bizarre offspring of a workbench and a set of shelves," which is a very good description of the sort of wooden presses that were invented during Wysbech's lifetime (*DH*, 325).[19] Presumably, it's with books made on such machines—or by a small army of Quick-Quotes Quills—that Flourish and Blotts stocks its shelves.

Written in Blood: Putting Quill and Ink to Parchment

Perhaps because they were sometimes in the business of making books or at least ordering them from scribes, medieval stationers did sell stuff that we think of as "stationery." A French-English phrasebook of the mid-fifteenth century contains a description of the contents of a stationer's shop. It is full of secondhand books:

> George the book seller
> Hath more books.
> Than all they of the town.
> He buys them all:
> Such as they be
> Be they stolen or imprinted
> Or otherwise purchased

"George"—like Scrivenshaft's—also has writing equipment:

> Ink and parchment
> Pens of swans
> Pens of geese.[20]

We are not accustomed to think of a "pen" as something made from the feather of a goose or a swan. But in Middle English, the word *pen*, just like the word *quill*, always meant both "feather" and "writing instrument." For medieval people, the two things were inseparable.[21]

Medieval quills or pens were presumably sometimes prepared at home by scribes. Medieval households kept geese for their down (to stuff mattresses and pillows), fat, and meat, as well as for the long wing feathers that made such nice pens. Goose feathers or more luxurious pens from the white swans that sailed England's waterways could also be found at a local stationer's shop. In a medieval copy of the English poem *Piers Plowman*, written around 1425, the word *pen* (meaning "feather" *or* "pen") is followed by the line "for his painted feathers the peacock is honoured."[22] So it may be that the "enormous peacock quill" that Lockhart uses for book signing has medieval ancestry (COS, 123).

The feathers used for quills needed to be stiffened for use. They were either soaked in water and then heated or left for months in a warm, dry place. It took a "pen-knife" to finish them for use. A scribe would scrape away any skin or pith from the feather's shaft, pare each side of the tip to a sharp point for writing, and cut a slit up the center of that point to form a nib that would hold a bit of ink.

Medieval quills thus did not come with ink loaded into them, as do modern pens. This is why something seems curious to Harry when he sits down to write his lines in Dolores Umbridge's office in *Order of the Phoenix*. He cannot see an ink bottle, which are as ubiquitous in the wizarding world as they were in the workshops of medieval scribes, when scribes wore "inkhorns" around their necks or kept pots of ink on their desks.[23]

Ink is, of course, vital to the scene in Umbridge's office: the punch line of her sadistic joke is that the message that Harry "must not tell lies" will "sink in" as the pen draws blood from the back of Harry's hand (OOTP, 239–241). For very different reasons, there was a strong medieval connection between ink and blood. The gospels describe Christ as "the Word made flesh" (John 1:1), and the metaphor is drawn out in medieval texts such as the *Fasciculus Morum*, which describes the crucified Christ's skin as parchment and his blood as ink.[24]

Obviously, medieval scribes needed real, as well as metaphori-
cal, ink, and, as noted previously, Robert Taylor's manuscript contains recipes for making it. Among these is a semimagical recipe for
invisible ink; it advocates the use of egg white (folio 27). Invisible
ink turns up in the wizarding world, too. Hermione thinks that Tom
Riddle's diary might be written in it. In *Prisoner of Azkaban*, Severus
Snape assumes that there is invisible writing on the parchment
scrap he finds in Harry's pocket late one night. (The blank page
is actually the Marauder's Map, its "mischief managed.") Other
recipes in Taylor's book explain how to make the two sorts of ink
that medieval scribes ordinarily had in their pots. Some medieval
ink was made from a mixture of charcoal and gum. A much more
complicated recipe—one worthy even of the Half-Blood Prince—
requires ferrous sulfate, known as "copperas," and tannic acids that
were obtained by crushing dried "oak galls," which were growths
made by parasites on oak trees.[25]

A Twelve-Inch Essay for Potions:
Books versus Scrolls

Up to this point, we have seen that the bookish world of Simon
Wysbech and Robert Taylor was strikingly similar to the one Harry
Potter enters on his eleventh birthday. Yet there is one notable
difference between Wysbech's book, Huntington MS 1336, and
many of the textual objects we read about in the wizarding world.
Wysbech's book is a "codex." That means it is an object made up of
leaves of parchment folded together to form gatherings or "quires":
bundles of pages, stitched together, which themselves have been
stitched into covers. Most of us have worked with paper-based
"codices" from the moment we started writing exercises in books at
school.[26] Hogwarts students, by contrast, write their homework on
parchment scrolls.

The scroll was already associated with the past during the
Middle Ages. It had been developed in ancient Egypt thousands
of years earlier as a way to store text copied onto papyrus, a papery
substance made from reeds. By around the year 400, parchment

leaves had largely supplanted papyrus ones, and folding had for the most part replaced the practice of rolling pages into scrolls.[27]

The Harry Potter books thus teach us an important lesson about the history of any technology. The coming of the new does not necessarily signal the end of the old. The Middle Ages, the age of the book, still prized the roll format. First, scrolls were an excellent mechanism for the storage of short texts meant for display. Whereas books hide their text away so that it is visible only one opening at a time, when a scroll is fully opened the whole of its text is revealed. Umbridge's decrees probably started out as scrolls. They are opened up and pinned or nailed onto boards and walls around Hogwarts; each has its own "highly official-looking seal at the bottom." (OOTP, 313) In the Middle Ages, papal decrees, pardons, and royal injunctions were sent out in the form of rolls with papal or royal wax seals suspended from them by silk or parchment ties.[28]

Second, the medieval association between scrolls and antiquity gave them special cultural significance. They were used to preserve important historical texts, whether the records of the Court of the Common Pleas or genealogies such as that in Huntington Library MS 264, which rolls up the story of England's whole past from Adam and Eve to King Edward IV.[29] Magical secrets were sometimes kept in roll form for much the same reason. The scribe who copied alchemical symbols and rituals into Huntington MS 30313, a roll from the 1550s, also wrote that his information came from the time of the ancient philosophers. They have bequeathed the secrets of their magical alchemical "philosopher's stone." Because the ancients used rolls, it made sense for medieval scribes of these old texts to do the same.

Finally, the roll format remained a convenient way to store a single leaf of parchment, and it served for scribal exercises of various kinds. Queen's College, Oxford, MS 304 contains a picture of a young scribe in 1416 learning to write on a long roll of parchment. Hovering behind him is his supervisor, ready to scrape off any errors with his pen-knife. He looks like a medieval version of Hermione, hovering over her friends' homework, correcting Ron's "misspelled words with a tap of her wand" when his Spell-Check

Quill malfunctions during an essay on dementors (it spells the word "Dugbogs") (*HBP*, 449–450). Percy Weasley demonstrates another practical use for medieval scrolls when he scratches away on one during Harry's trial at the Ministry of Magic. Court reporters in the Middle Ages also made notes on short rolls of parchment. There is an image of such a reporter sitting near the feet of Henry V in British Library, MS Cotton Julius E.iv (drawn 1483–1493).[30]

A Magical Curriculum

Some time after the events described in *Deathly Hallows*, Minerva McGonagall gives permission for the publication of a set of notes by Albus Dumbledore to *The Tales of Beedle the Bard*, alongside a new translation of the tales by Hermione Granger. The runic letters that Hermione translates refer back to technologies of writing that can be easily overlooked in a broad history of the medieval book such as that presented here. Even before their conversion to Christianity, the Anglo-Saxon people of England had a written record. They had runes, which is what the original *Beedle the Bard* was written in: a whole alphabet of letter forms that Christian missionaries replaced with the Roman alphabet.

Ironically, most of what we know about runes comes not from the bone, horn, stone, and wooden surfaces on which the early Anglo-Saxons recorded writing but from the books that supplanted these traditional textual surfaces. Such books include the tenth-century manuscript, London, British Library, MS Cotton Otho B.x, that preserves an Old English "Rune Poem," which lists each runic letter and adds a stanza in Roman alphabet that explains the letter's meaning.[31] Such books also include the one that Dumbledore bequeaths to Hermione, "its binding . . . stained and peeling in places." (*DH*, 106)

Hermione's book is interesting not only as a reminder of ancient techniques of textual record that survive only in fragments, but also for what Dumbledore's notes suggest about the history of magic in England. According to the Hogwarts Headmaster, Beedle was a magician in the fifteenth century, the last century that permitted the open practice of magic in England. "The persecution of witches and wizards was gathering apace all over England in the early fifteenth century," he wrote, and the popular wizarding sentiment soon became "Let the Muggles manage without us!" (*TOBTB*, 13)

Aspects of the real histories of magic in England that lie behind this statement are discussed at more length elsewhere in this book.[32] Yet it is worth noting here that the book that Wysbech made for Taylor in the middle of the fifteenth century bears Dumbledore's statement out. Huntington MS 1336 mingles magical and non-magical materials in such a way as to suggest that magic was just an ordinary part of social existence in medieval England, during Beedle the Bard's lifetime. It was made at a time when it was not at all strange to ask a law student from Cambridge to help you make a magic book.

Notably, old magic manuscripts such as Taylor's—of which a great many survive from medieval England alone—contain a course of reading for which the curriculum of Hogwarts School would be excellent preparation.[33] To understand Taylor's manuscript, you would need Herbology, because there is an "herbal" between folios 1 and 2. You would need classes in Charms to make sense of the spell against deceit in the marketplace (folio 13). Transfiguration classes might help with the invisibility spell (folio 27); Potions would prepare you for all of those complicated recipes; and Divination would help with the astrological calendar on folio 35. There is nothing on Care of Magical Creatures, but readers of medieval manuscript "bestiaries" would find those classes useful for understanding sections on unicorns, sphinxes, and griffins.[34] There is nothing on the Defence against the Dark Arts in Huntington MS 1336, but the Dark Arts make their mark in surviving medieval English manuscripts, too. A manuscript such as Cambridge University Library, MS Dd.11.45, would presumably be kept in the Restricted Section of Hogwarts Library, under the closest supervision of Madam Pince, because it teaches its readers how to "conjure" fallen angels to wreak revenge on their enemies.[35]

One more thing is missing from Taylor's manuscript that is present in other English medieval manuscripts and that is a vital part

of the world into which Harry Potter is invited, by a signed and
sealed parchment letter, on his eleventh birthday: tricks and pranks.
Trinity College, Cambridge, MS 1081, is a mid-fifteenth-century
manuscript that belonged to a gentry family called Haldenby from
Northamptonshire. Like Taylor's manuscript, this book is a practical miscellany for day-to-day living, and it is full of magical material, including charms to catch thieves (folio 95) and accounts of
the magical properties of azure (folio 45). But between folios 93
and 97 are a series of spells that belong not so much in a Hogwarts
classroom as in one of the school's common rooms, especially one
occupied by Fred and George Weasley. On these folios of the manuscript are a series of magic tricks, and they are designed simply
to delight and amuse. One spell will make it seem as if the house
is full of water (folio 96). Another will, just briefly, set a mirror
ablaze—to the surprise of any especially vain onlooker (folio 97).[36]

When Harry gives Fred and George the gold they need to establish their trade in Weasley's Wizard Wheezes, he does so because
in the midst of all of the difficulties he sees ahead, he thinks people
will need "a few laughs." (GOF, 365) The Harry Potter novels allow
us to think in new ways about the rich history of our own society,
including its books. Their magic is that they make that learning process so much fun.[37]

Notes

1. For this book and others from this library described further on, see Consuela
Dutschke, *Guide to Medieval and Renaissance Manuscripts in the Huntington Library*,
2 vols. (San Marino, CA: Huntington Library, 1989).

2. Elisabeth Leedham-Green, *A Concise History of the University of Cambridge*
(Cambridge, UK: Cambridge University Press, 1996), 1–28.

3. This is the text on folio 36 recto of the manuscript, translated from Wysbech's Latin
and Middle English. All subsequent references to texts in languages other than English are
also in my translation unless otherwise stated.

4. Henry R. Plomer, "The Importation of Books into England in the Fifteenth and
Sixteenth. Centuries," *Library* 4 (1923–1924): 146–150.

5. See discussions in Geoffrey Nunberg, ed., *The Future of the Book* (Los Angeles:
University of California Press, 1996).

6. All book quotes are taken from the British editions by J. K. Rowling as follows:
Philosopher's Stone, London: Bloomsbury, 1997; *Chamber of Secrets*, London: Bloomsbury,
1998; *Prisoner of Azkaban*, London: Bloomsbury, 1999; *Goblet of Fire*, London:
Bloomsbury, 2000; *Order of the Phoenix*, London: Bloomsbury, 2003; *Half-Blood Prince*,

London: Bloomsbury, 2005; *Deathly Hallows*, London: Bloomsbury, 2007; *Tales of Beedle the Bard*, London: Bloomsbury, 2007.

7. On medieval English letters, see Richard Beadle, "Private Letters," in A. S. G. Edwards, ed., *A Companion to Middle English Prose* (Cambridge, UK: Brewer, 2004), 289–306.

8. First seen used by Tonks on Hedwig's cage in *Order of the Phoenix*, chap. 3.

9. The Bible has sold 2.5 billion copies, but it has had since record keeping began in 1815 to do so, according to the *Guinness Book of World Records*. In a decade, the Potter series has sold more than 400 million copies ("The Harry Potter Economy," *Economist* (December 17, 2009), www.economist.com/node/15108711?story_id=15108711.

10. *The Middle English Dictionary*, Middle English Compendium, University of Michigan Digital Library Production Service, December 2001, http://quod.lib.umich.edu/m/med/, s.v. "parchemin." Henceforth cited as *MED*.

11. Christopher de Hamel, *Scribes and Illuminators* (London: British Library, 1992), 8–16.

12. Folio iii, written in the late 1500s.

13. See Alexandra Gillespie, "Binding," in "Book Production outside of Commercial Contexts," in Alexandra Gillespie and Daniel Wakelin, eds., *Book Production in England, 1350–c.1500* (Cambridge, UK: Cambridge University Press, 2011); for trouble with the *Monster* book, see, e.g., *POA*, 45.

14. See R. Emms, "St. Augustine's Abbey, Canterbury, and the 'First Books of the Whole English Church,'" in R. N. Swanson, ed., *The Church and the Book* (Woodbridge, UK: Boydell and Brewer, 2004), 32–46.

15. B. H. Streeter, *The Chained Library: A Survey of Four Centuries in the Evolution of the English Library* (London: Macmillan, 1931), 7.

16. Michael Clanchy, *From Memory to Written Record: England 1066–1307*, 2nd ed. (London: Blackwell, 1993).

17. A. I. Doyle, "The English Provincial Book-Trade before Printing," in P. C. G. Isaac, ed., *Six Centuries of the Provincial Book-Trade in Britain* (Winchester: St. Paul's Bibliographies, 1990), 13–29.

18. *Oxford English Dictionary Online*, Oxford Online, 2009, www.oed.com/, s.v. "stationer." Henceforth *OED*; M. A. Michael, "Urban Production of Manuscript Books and the Role of the University Towns," in Nigel J. Morgan and Rodney M. Thomson, eds., *The Cambridge History of the Book in Britain: Volume II 1100–1400* (Cambridge, UK: Cambridge University Press, 2008), 168–194.

19. S. H. Steinberg, *Five Hundred Years of Printing* (London: British Library, 1996).

20. L. C. Harmer and J. C. T. Oates, eds., *Vocabulary in French and English: A Facsimile of Caxton's Edition, c. 1480* (Cambridge, UK: Cambridge University Press, 1964), 36 (my translation).

21. *OED*, s.v. *penne*.

22. *The Vision of Piers Plowman*, C-version; San Marino, Huntington Library, MS 137, Passus XV, 108.

23. See, for example, *Goblet of Fire*, pp. 142, 256. On quills and inkpots, see De Hamel, *Scribes and Illuminators*, 27–29, 32.

24. Siegfried Wenzel, ed., *Fasciculus Morum* (Philadelphia: Penn State University Press, 1989), 212.

25. Orietta da Rold, "Materials," in Gillespie and Wakelin, eds., *Book Production in England, 1350–c.1500*.

26. *OED*, s.v. "codex."

27. For more on this topic, see Colin Roberts and T. C. Skeat, *The Birth of the Codex* (London: Oxford University Press, 1983).

28. See, for example, Clanchy, *From Memory to Written Record*, Plates IX–XII.

29. The Plea Rolls are still stored in this format in the Public Record Office in Kew Gardens, London.

30. Kathleen L. Scott, "Representations of Scribal Activity in English Manuscripts c. 1400–c. 1490," in Michael Gullick, ed., *Pen in Hand: Medieval Scribal Portraits, Colophons and Tools* (Walkern, UK: Red Gull Press, 2006), 115–149.

31. R. I. Page, *An Introduction to English Runes* (Woodbridge, UK: Boydell Press, 1999).

32. See also Owen Davies, *Cunning-Folk: Popular Magic in English History* (New York and London: Hambledon, 2003).

33. Frank Klaassen, "English Manuscripts of Magic, 1300–1500," in Claire Fanger, ed., *Conjuring Spirits: Texts and Traditions of Medieval Ritual Magic* (Philadelphia: Penn State University Press, 1998), 3–31.

34. Debra Hassig, *Medieval Bestiaries: Text, Image, Ideology* (Cambridge, UK: Cambridge University Press, 1995).

35. Juris Lidaka, "The Book of Angels . . . Attributed to Osborn Bokenham," in Fanger, ed., *Conjuring Spirit*, 58–59.

36. This manuscript is the subject of a forthcoming study by Laura Mitchell. I am grateful to her for assistance.

37. Thanks to William and Isobel Binnie for advice and support.

Nicolas Flamel

The Alchemist Who Lived

Don Keck DuPree

ALBUS DUMBLEDORE
Currently Headmaster of Hogwarts.
    Considered by many the greatest wizard of modern times, Dumbledore is particularly famous for his defeat of the dark wizard Grindelwald in 1945, for the discovery of the twelve uses of dragon's blood, and his work on alchemy with his partner, Nicolas Flamel.
    Professor Dumbledore enjoys chamber music and tenpin bowling.

    —Chocolate frog card, *Sorcerer's Stone*[1]

No bureau of vital statistics records a cause of death or a date of death for Nicolas Flamel, the alchemist whose Philosopher's Stone frustrates Lord Voldemort and creates both mystery and adventure in the first book of the Harry Potter series. The real, historical Nicolas Flamel's dates (he lived roughly between 1330

and 1418) end with a question mark and an empty grave. His legend involves meeting a Spanish *converso* (a member of the group
discussed in chapter 10) around 1380, obtaining a copy of the
Book of Abraham the Jew, and allegedly solving the riddle of
the Philosopher's Stone in time to bring his wife, Perenelle, back
from the dead and gain immortality for himself. Flamel's "legend"
is grounded in medieval hagiography (biographies that idealized
their subjects), as much as it relies on murky history colored by
rumor and passed-down stories. Yet the real Nicolas Flamel was a
man of piety, generosity, and faith.

The faith underlying Flamel's life and work was the allegorical faith of the Middle Ages; he profoundly participated in a world
of seen and unseen realities, coexisting, mixing, and influencing
one another. A medieval theologian, for instance, might explain
the idea of an allegory like this: for everything in the physical
(seen) world, there is a corresponding thing in the spiritual (unseen)
world, so it makes sense to use allegories to explain truths from the
spiritual world, which we cannot see in the physical world. Indeed,
the medieval science of transformation that we know as alchemy
derives from this allegorical faith. Alchemy was a medieval science
that fused chemistry, philosophy, and magic in attempts to trans-
form (transfigure) base metals into gold and also in pursuit of what
alchemists called an "elixir of longevity." Allegories were crucial to
the science of alchemy.

Unlike chemistry in our own day, medieval alchemy wed physical knowledge to spiritual perceptions, book learning, and word-of-
mouth teaching. Armed, then, with the mysterious *Book of Abraham
the Jew*, the love of his wife, Perenelle, and an unshakeable reliance
on the communion of all creation, Flamel undertook the "work"
of magic in Paris during the fourteenth century in order to pursue
immortality and to create gold for him to do good works. These
saintly works and thoughts of the Flamels, husband and wife, rank
them among those Albus Dumbledore describes when he speaks of
love to Harry: "Your mother died to save you. If there is one thing
Voldemort cannot understand, it is love. He didn't realize that love
as powerful as your mother's for you leaves its own mark." (SS, 299)

Among other things, the real, historical Flamels funded the restoration of the Église (church) of Sainte-Geneviève-des-Ardents and left endowments to support the Hôpital (hospital) des Quinze-Vingts, both located in Paris. They began married life as impoverished scriveners (paid letter writers and document copyists), eking out livings among the craftsfolk and the artisans of Paris. They "ended" life with wealth, which they used to rebuild the church and endow a hospital. Achievement of the Philosopher's Stone and Flamel's fame as an alchemist brought them this.

Yet unlike Voldemort, whose lust turned to a craving for the crudely physical aspects of the Stone, the Flamels cherished the spiritual illumination represented by the Stone at the same time that they enjoyed its physical rewards: wealth and (according to Dumbledore) immortality. As Dumbledore reveals to Harry, the Flamels used the Stone to create the elixir that prolonged

A portrait of Nicolas Flamel and his wife, Perenelle (both kneeling), from a French engraving done in the late fifteenth century.

life indefinitely. The Flamels were apparently part of the wizarding world; after achieving success in Paris, they presumably left the Muggle world at some point (because they disappear from Muggle historical records) to take up residence in the wizarding community, where Flamel meets Dumbledore five centuries later.

The Flamel house exists to this day at 51 rue de Montmorency, Paris, France, satisfying any skeptical need to prove that there is real history behind their legend. Although Flamel's own writings remain a matter of scholarly dispute, what he learned from *The Book of Abraham the Jew* comes down to us in several authenticated manuscripts. The *Book* provides detailed instruction to readers for making the Philosopher's Stone:

When the 14 days and nights are over, . . . take a great cask, and make in such of straw and wood a grate; and lay such below in the cask, and thereon a quantity of [distillation sediment]; pour thereon dew, or Rain-water, taken from a thunder shower is very good, leave it 24 hours so standing, then make below on the cask a hole and fit a bung therein. And through it let the Water trickle down, till it all falls down. . . . In the same manner proceed also with the remaining [distillation sediment]; and then pour such clean Water into a copper kettle, till it be quite full, and lay on such three parts and seethe down; pour the kettle, seethe it down again, till on the third part, and thus continue 10 or 12 times, when now at last all is seethed down, and the third part is yet in the kettle, so pour in another clean kettle, set it into cold sand some days so will a Salt crystallize. . . . On this Salt pour clean dew, in order that it will dissolve. Then filter it and coagulate it so often, till it is pure and crystallized and prepared, so have you the right Salt [distillation sediment], which in the Sea of the World hovers and is concealed, without which nothing can be engendered and born, and also have you the fruit bringing Salt and the *prima Materialis Universal* prepared and *primam materiam* of the old Wine.[2]

Thus, making the Philosopher's Stone meant more than following a recipe of directions that could have come straight from a Potions textbook; it meant interpreting images correctly and conforming correctly to those images. Hogwarts undertakes to teach that interpretation and "conformation" in both Potions and Transformations classes.

Croton Capitatus, a Plant to Inspire

Sometime after the fall of Constantinople to the Turks in 1453, Cosimo de Medici (the ruler of Florence, Italy, and the patron of Fra Angelico and Donatello) commissioned Marsilio Ficino to translate the so-called *Corpus Hermeticum* — a collection of legendary and mysterious writings ascribed to one Hermes Trismegistus — as a way to understand Plato's vision of "*to agathon* (the good), the divinity of the human soul, the power of the word."[3] Like the fictional names in J. K. Rowling's work, Hermes is a manufactured name that was used to weave an aura about writings that contained magical instructions. Ficino must have found the neo-Platonism very much to his liking in Hermes's writings, which were a compendium of esoteric works, some as old as 300 B.C. (B.C.E.) and some dating from as late as around A.D. 300 (C.E.). This collection of alchemy, white magic, and exuberant philosophy exerted such an influence that rumors about it persisted all through the Middle Ages, even when no text existed anywhere in Western Europe. (Scholars often cite the mosaic depiction of Hermes on the floor of the cathedral in Sienna, Italy, to affirm the mysterious pull of this hermetic material.)

Scholars fleeing the wreckage of the Byzantine Empire after its fall to the Turks brought to Western Europe their ability to teach Greek, as well as Greek manuscripts, including some by Plato, Hermes, Homer, and others. Before this, Transfiguration and Potions (which alchemy is one branch of) at Hogwarts must have rested largely on popular hearsay and meager materials that could be brought from Sephardic/Islamic Spain. Yet with the renaissance of Greek texts and teaching in Western Europe during the fifteenth century, the scholars of Hogwarts would have come to know the most ancient alchemical treatises, combining Persian, Egyptian, Greek, and other sources. They would have been able to embark on wizardry much wider in scope and complexity than anything Flamel knew or could have known, despite his success with the Philosopher's Stone.

A bit of medieval literature can serve to illustrate the meager and narrow scope of alchemical understanding before Greek texts began to be taught in Western Europe after 1453. As Geoffrey Chaucer (1342–1400) described her in the famous *Canterbury Tales*, the Wife of Bath understands the folk science of transfiguration: "Of remedies of love she knew per chaunce,/For she koude of that art the olde daunce."[4] She's an herbalist and a conjurer, trained in the wood's lore of ancient Britain, the same as taught by the founders of Hogwarts: Godric Gryffindor, Helga Hufflepuff, Rowena Ravenclaw, and Salazar Slytherin. Her interest is love and pleasure. Chaucer's story has its own Voldemort figure, the Doctor of Physick. "For gold in phisik is a cordial,/Therefore he lovede gold in special."[5] His interest is profit and luxury, with no particular interest in curing his patients. Yet although magical practitioners in Chaucer's time knew about herbs, charms, and some potions, magic would be lifted to much higher levels once it was fertilized by the ancient texts that refugees from Byzantium brought with them to Western Europe.

Oddly, the Florentine translator Marsilio Ficino (1433–1499) remained as interested in what we might call the Wife of Bath's folk wisdom as he did in the "new" world of neo-Platonic astrology/astronomy. He knew that *Croton capitatus* (the herb called "hogwort" in common speech) is a powerful laxative. Purging the body, the Renaissance adepts taught, had to be done before a practitioner could master the higher levels of alchemy. The self-effacement that Flamel learned through poverty Dumbledore teaches by word and example. Hogwarts School derives its name from the plant that represents this first step—purging, self-knowledge, humility—on the ladder of alchemical science and practices. That ladder climbs toward the summit of human potential and power.

"Of course it is happening in your head, Harry, but why on earth should that mean that it is not real?" (*DH*, 723)

"We are all facing dark and difficult times . . . the time [might] come when you have to make a choice between what is right, and what is easy." (*GOF*, 724)

"Fascinating creatures, phoenixes. They can carry immensely heavy loads, their tears have healing powers." (*COS*, 207)

Anticipating Dumbledore's wisdom, Ficino's contemporary, Renaissance philosopher Pico della Mirandola, saw that summit of human perfection and described it in words he lifted directly from Ficino's translation of Hermes. Pico's work *Oration on the Dignity of Man* (1492) put it this way:

We have made you neither of heavenly nor of earthly stuff, neither mortal nor immortal, so that with free choice and dignity, you may fashion yourself into whatever form you choose. To you is granted the power of degrading yourself into the lower forms of life, the beasts, and to you is granted the power, contained in your intellect and judgement, to be reborn into the higher forms, the divine.[6]

Dumbledore's ideal of wizardry as the servant of moral wisdom and choice was thus descended directly from the philosophical teachings of the Renaissance adepts.

Sealing the parchment carefully, [Harry] climbed through the portrait hole and headed off for the Owlery.

"I would not go that way if I were you," said Nearly Headless Nick, drifting disconcertingly through a wall just ahead of Harry as he walked down the passage. "Peeves is planning an amusing joke on the next person to pass the bust of Paracelsus halfway down the corridor."

"Does it involve Paracelsus falling on top of the person's head?" asked Harry.

"Funnily enough, it does," said Nearly Headless Nick in a
bored voice. "Subtlety has never been Peeves's strong point."
(*OOTP*, 281)

The most famous of these Renaissance alchemists (featured
on Harry's and Ron Weasley's chocolate frog cards) were Agrippa
and Paracelsus. Alchemists were also philosophers, and along with
alchemy, Paracelsus (1493–1541) taught the worthiness and beauty of
human beings, the manifold dimensionality of creation, and the near-
divine possibility of human power. When we hear Paracelsus rhapso-
dizing about human power, we detect echoes of those alchemists from
Wittenburg, Hamlet and his friend Horatio, or that friend of English
humanists Giodorno Bruno (1548–1600), whose musing on other
worlds anticipated *Star Trek* and also got him burned at the stake.

Essentially, Paracelsus reminded his Renaissance world that
the concrete and the physical are not the sum of all there is: the
actual world does not exhaust all that is real, and human operation
is not confined or defined by physical boundaries. In the *Alchemical
Catechism*, Paracelsus dismissed as "vulgar" the attempt to reduce
all of reality down to the merely physical world. Dumbledore, of
course, agrees and would also label Voldemort's schemes disastrously
vulgar. The Dumbledore who saves Tom Riddle from the orphanage hopes to lead him on the way to the "white magic" of the Right
and the Good taught by thinkers such as Pico, Paracelsus, Agrippa, and
Bruno. Not surprisingly, Dumbledore sees Nicolas Flamel as one
in this line of wise wizards. This is, of course, the Platonic Good,
which Cosimo de Medici and the Renaissance desired to understand more fully: Plato's vision of *"to agathon* (the good), the divinity
of the human soul, the power of the word."[7]

Not all Renaissance alchemists shared the noble ideals of
Paracelsus and della Mirandola, however. Some used their alleged
abilities to create a Philosopher's Stone to commit fraud. The
sixteenth-century Italian alchemist Marco Bragadino, for example,
can only be seen as an Early Modern con artist. Originally from
Florence, he first deceived a Medici duchess into believing that he
could use a "magical powder" made from the Philosopher's Stone

to cure her infertility; he duped her into giving him enormous sums before he was forced to flee to Rome when no pregnancy resulted. Bragadino traveled across almost all of Western Europe, always taking great pains to move on to the next stop before his victims realized that he was a fraud; in the course of his journeys, he achieved a reputation for being a skilled gold maker, again by his supposed use of the Philosopher's Stone.

His machinations were eventually uncovered, however, after Bragadino was invited to the Bavarian court of Duke William V in 1590. Bragadino wheedled huge sums of money from the duke, enough to fund his own palace, where he started selling not only potions and ointments but also an elixir that he claimed was useful for making gold and curing all ills. William V was completely charmed by Bragadino and apparently very fond of him but eventually had to realize that there was no gold to be had. In March 1591, Bragadino was arrested and forced to confess that his magic was actually based on delusion and sleight of hand. Although Bragadino was accused of fraudulent sorcery—which would have meant death at the stake—the Bavarian duke and Bragadino's friends among the local Jesuits saw to it that the charges were reduced to mere fraud, which meant death by beheading (generally seen as preferable to being burned). Bragadino was executed on April 26, 1591.[8] Clearly, approaching alchemy and the Philosopher's Stone with cynical or self-seeking motives could rebound on the alchemist. At the same time, Bragadino's story shows how seriously Europeans took both the physical and the unseen worlds, because belief in the Philosopher's Stone was obviously widely shared.

Welsh Gingers at Hogwarts

Just a little imagination places the seventeenth-century Welsh literary twins Henry and Thomas Vaughan at Hogwarts, like their ginger-headed successors, Fred and George Weasley. (In an interview, Rowling admitted to a Welsh connection for the Weasleys.)[9] It's easy to imagine that the Vaughans were at Hogwarts around 1636. Seventeenth-century scientist-alchemists Samuel Hartlib,

Sir Cheney Culpeper, Benjamin Worsley, and the many years "retired" John Dee probably taught at or influenced the Hogwarts of the Vaughans' schooldays. Intellectuals throughout Europe referred to these men and their colleagues as being part of an "invisible college"; the scientist Robert Boyle referred to this college, for example, in letters written during the English Civil War, 1642–1651. It seems likely that the invisible college these men were referring to was indeed Hogwarts, because we know that the school is literally invisible to Muggle eyes.

Cheney Culpeper (1601–1663) was an avid herbologist who could easily have been one of Pomona Sprout's predecessors. Culpepper, along with his wife, produced alchemical "receipts" of medicinal, as well as culinary, benefit. Benjamin Worsley (1618–1673) was a practicing cryptographer and alchemist; his major published work was *De nitro theses quaedam*. Because Worsley was one of those said to be part of the invisible college by seventeenth-century Muggle scholars, he possibly taught or shaped the study of Transfiguration and Potions at Hogwarts and could have taught Runes or Arithmancy, as well. Worsley's pastime was map making; he may have produced an early version of the Marauder's Map.

Finally, alchemist Samuel Hartlib (1600–1662) would have made a Headmaster in the mold of Albus Dumbledore, if he had led the Hogwarts the Vaughans would have attended. His contemporaries called him an "intelligencer" because of his work to spread and promote knowledge itself, rather than focusing only on his own research. Like Dumbledore, he had little use for cryptic utterances and secret circles. Hartlib taught student and friend alike that knowledge was meant to be a universal human possession. He defined the universalist goal later echoed by the founders of Wikipedia, saying that he wanted "to record all human knowledge and to make it universally available for the education of all mankind."[10] Dumbledore, who supported the teaching of magic to all witches and wizards, whether Muggle-born or not, would have agreed.

Alchemists such as Hartlib and his colleagues and the Vaughans faced a century beset by the Dark Arts, much the way that Harry, Hermione Granger, Ron, and the rest of the wizarding world faced the effects of years of Dark Art magic during the lifetime of Voldemort. Sectarianism, political strife, and intellectual fear dominated the seventeenth century. Galileo suffered house arrest for gazing at the heavens, Bruno was burned at the stake, and tens of millions died in that century's wars of religion. The Vaughan twins had both been supporters of the deposed and executed British monarch Charles I. One of them withdrew during the English Civil War to the obscurity of Wales, while his brother sought the privacy of metropolitan London.

Like the political upheavals of England's Civil War, from which the Vaughan twins retreated, the Scientific Revolution of the seventeenth century sent alchemists and wizards and magicians into hiding across Europe. Empiricism, the approach promoted by the Scientific Revolution, assumes that something we call reality can be quantified, measured, catalogued, and predicted: it thus meant a real break with previous ways of creating knowledge. Medieval alchemists, however, had assumed that reality always and ever will escape quantification. The new approach to science denied magic and evidence from beyond our senses. Indeed, most European Muggle authorities no longer even accepted accusations of witchcraft by the late seventeenth century, because they no longer believed in magic.

Hogwarts and similar schools would have proved the last refuge for European wizards, witches, and magicians—and alchemists. When Harry Potter leaves the cupboard under the stairs, he discovers a magical world that even in the twentieth century still refuses precise empirical description. The triumph of science in the Muggle world has meant that all modes of thought outside the empirical can find a place only in the Diagon Alleys at the fringes of our world.

Thomas Vaughan retreated to find refuge in Wakefield, London, corresponded with Hartlib, and continued alchemical experimentation in collaboration with his wife, Rebecca. His alchemical work *Anthroposophia Theomagica* gained a measure of fame, and his translation of the *Fama Fraternitatis Rosae Crucis* ignited genuine interest in a multinational community of learning and charitable medical endeavors. The *Fama* made public the ideals of an invisible college and is seen as one of the most important documents produced by the Rosicrucians, a secret society of

mystics. Henry, the other twin, retired to Wales, practiced medicine, and wrote poems. His most famous poem, "I Saw Eternity the
Other Night . . ." testifies to an allegorical (alchemical) faith in seen
and unseen worlds mingling and influencing one another.

More than one critic has said that Vaughan's poem reads like
one of Flamel's enigmatic notebooks. In some ways, the poem
appears to describe an alchemical operation:

> I saw Eternity the other night,
> Like a great ring of pure and endless light,
> All calm, as it was bright;
> And round beneath it, Time in hours, days, years,
> Driv'n by the spheres
> Like a vast shadow mov'd; in which the world
> And all her train were hurl'd.[11]

Or this could just as easily be a page from that work of Abraham
the Jew that set Flamel to seek the Philosopher's Stone. At any rate,
there is no empirical science here; this is the visionary work of
poets, wordsmiths, and wizards.

Muggles and Mugwumps

Men such as Cheney Culpeper and Thomas Vaughan were marginalized and excluded when the Royal Society of London for the
Improvement of Natural Knowledge received the royal patent that
allowed it to open its doors on July 15, 1662. Yes, monarchy regained
its place in England after the Civil War Interregnum, but Roundhead
(Puritan) assumptions of the world pushed aside earlier adepts of the
invisible college and their allegorizing, magico-alchemical ways.
Understandings put forth by political philosophers such as Thomas
Hobbes and John Locke triumphed, and Natural Knowledge came
to mean empirical scientific knowledge to the exclusion of knowledge about unseen worlds, which might or might not exist.

In point of fact, the Puritans pushed magic out of England in
1642 when they closed the theaters and ripped down Shakespeare's

Globe Theatre several years later. Theater, particularly Shakespearean theater, requires imagination and magic. Theater time, alchemical time, runs neither forward nor backward per se; theater time folds in on itself, thick and ungiving at points, at others diaphanous as tiffany, jumping over months or years between scenes, strong as silk thread. Thomas Hobbes (1588–1679), the Machiavellian pragmatic political philosopher, whose *Leviathan* characterizes human life as "brutish," denied theater time and helped invent the busy Grunnings world of Uncle Vernon Dursley. As Hobbes put it, "The present only has a being in nature. Things past have a being in memory, only, but things to come have no being at all, the future being but a fiction of the mind, applying the sequels of actions past to the actions that are present."[12]

With the reduction of time to "time present," Hobbes struck an antialchemical blow in the cascading empirical Scientific Revolution of the seventeenth century. John Locke (1632–1704), the other great political thinker of the day and an influence on the founders of the American republic, called the mind a tabula rasa — a blank slate — thereby reducing the world to sensory data and quantifiable experience. Locke saw the world as "Bulk, Figure, Texture, and Motion." In other words, Locke confined "reality" to those things we might know empirically and record by the senses on that blank slate, the mind.

For many historians of philosophy and science, Locke proposes and Newton disposes. Sir Isaac Newton (1643–1727), the genius who is one of the founders of modern physics and mathematics, so the claim goes, codified Locke's rational, empirical insight, thereby "discovering" the eternal, immutable laws of the physical universe, such as momentum and inertia. Yet the other, lesser-known side of Newton, who also had allegorical-alchemical interests, wrote page after page not only investigating Locke's world of bulk, figure, texture, and motion but also exploring the world of alchemists such as Pierre Jean Fabré, whose *Panchymici seu anatomiae totius universa* sought to clarify the cohabitation of the seen and the unseen. Fabré (1590–1650) proposed a universal chemistry and an exploration of the whole universe, visible and invisible.

Although Newton's laws appear to reduce the universe to the surface of its parts, his alchemy probed the kaleidoscopic majesty and drama he discerned beyond the simplicity of the physical laws. His library contained works by Nicolas Flamel, Paracelsus, Agrippa, Thomas Vaughan, and all of the major seventeenth-century alchemical adepts. He owned, among his vast collection, this remarkable treatise: *Nicholas Flammel, His Exposition of the Hieroglyphicall Figures which he caused to be painted upon an Arch in St Innocents Church-yard in Paris. Together with The secret Booke of Artephius, And the Epistle of Iohn Pontanus: Containing both the Theoricke and the Practicke of the Philosophers Stone.*

Newton's fascination with the Philosopher's Stone suffuses the stunning body of his alchemical work; much of it still survives in manuscript form. Among his manuscripts, he left a translation of the *Emerald Tablet* (from the *Corpus Hermeticum*) and a commentary on that work. The *Tablet* asserts the same enthusiasm for human potential that Pico had crafted into a Renaissance credo in his *Oration.* Newton translated the passage "you shall have the glory of the whole world and thereby all obscurity shall fly from you." In his commentary on this, Newton observed, "[The Stone] . . . is the philosophical method of meliorating nature in nature, consanguinity in consanguinity."[13] Instead of a simple material empiricism, Newton perceived the allegorical potential of alchemy to gain access to both the seen and the unseen. Taken rather literally, the Philosopher's Stone makes each of us and everything in the universe *blood siblings.* The Stone metaphorically "meliorates" or mediates between the seen and the unseen in much the same way that a stage meliorates between an actor and an audience.

This explains Dumbledore's great friendship and collaboration with Nicolas Flamel: both are trying to mediate between things that seem very dissimilar. When Voldemort dismisses Dumbledore as "[T]hat champion of commoners, of Mudbloods and Muggles," he is not simply sneering because Dumbledore is a nice (inclusive) guy (*GOF*, 648). Voldemort rejects any rapprochement or mingling between the human and the wizard worlds because he is a proto-fascist beguiled by visions of "purity." Dumbledore and Flamel understand those visions of purity as disasters, whether they appear as programs of racial purity, scientific purity, or political purity.

It's a Longbottom, Short-Sell Kinda Day

When economist John Maynard Keynes (1883–1946) purchased the Newton alchemical archive in 1936 (about the time that Tom Riddle entered Hogwarts), he dismissed Newton's collection of manuscripts as an embarrassment, "unfit to publish." In a later article, Keynes wrote that Newton "was not the first of the age of reason. He was the last of the magicians."[14] Keynes, who hoped to bring scientific purity to economic study, could not abide the mushy science of Newton's monumental alchemical works. His reaction was not unusual: as the Muggle world regretted and derided earlier centuries' alchemical study, the wizarding world continued to expand and perfect that study. During the 1930s, alchemy was still alive and well at Hogwarts as a vital portion of the curriculum, as it was during Harry's years there.

Left unchecked by a social structure that could contain it, with its most scholarly practitioners withdrawn to Hogwarts and other places outside our world, magic in the Muggle world devolved into the parlor trick shows of people like Gilderoy Lockhart and the rather fuzzy sentimentalism of Sibyll Trelawney. Table tapping, séances, Ouija boards, and palmistry reflect this sentimental attachment to magic in the off-road world of mummery in our own day. Arthur Waite, a mystical scholar, and his contemporary Madame Sosostris brought tarot cards and clairvoyance to the respectable world of middle-class Americans during the early twentieth century. Astrologer Jeanne Dixon, who did forecasts for Nancy and Ronald Reagan, and L. Ron Hubbard, the founder of Dianetics, take their places as the Lockharts and the Trelawneys of the modern Muggle world, as sleights of hand and mirrors beget the television show *Wizards of Waverly Place.* Even Muggles still want to believe that there is magic in their world, long after they have driven it past the walls of Diagon Alley.

Fiction and history meet where allegory and empiricism collide. Rowling's Harry Potter saga itself collides with history at a time when readers and viewers have enough science and personal experience at hand to suspect that space and time as we experience them with our physical senses do not exhaust the sum of reality. Volumes and volumes of alchemical writing from the sixteenth and seventeenth centuries parallel the explosion of Harry Potter fan fiction in the twenty-first century. As Bernard Madoff goes to jail, we witness the downfall of a financial "wizard" who also tried to make something out of nothing; as we watch Voldemort's demise, we watch the logical unraveling of death eating death. Bald empiricism leads only to Privet Drive.

In other words, thousands of individuals in our own century recognize that the parameters of empirical science are not large enough to contain the sum of human experience. There is, indeed, an unseen world to be probed and explored. Both Dumbledore and Flamel know this, which is why in discussing Flamel's impending death at the end of the first book, Dumbledore notes simply that "to the well-organized mind, death is but the next great adventure." (SS, 297)

Voldemort understands this situation fully and speaks it in a moment of candor in a graveyard:

> "You know of course, that they have called this boy my downfall?" Voldemort said softly, his red eyes upon Harry, whose scar began to burn so fiercely that he almost screamed in agony. "You all know that on the night I lost my powers and my body, I tried to kill him. His mother died in the attempt to save him—and unwittingly provided him with a protection I admit I had not foreseen . . . I could not touch the boy." Voldemort raised one of his long white fingers and put it very close to Harry's cheek. "His mother left upon him the traces of her sacrifice . . . This is old magic, I should have remembered it, I was foolish to overlook it . . . but no matter, I can touch him now." (GOF, 652)

Harry discovers the "old magic" when he leaves the cupboard under the stairs. The old magic is "delight," which burns past the empirical scientific surface of things to the unseen grandeur;

"delight" can look back from this unseen majesty to perceive the empirical as anything but bare and bald. Voldemort remains unbodied in both worlds because he cannot see beyond desire and power in *this* world.

Flamel's Philosopher's Stone, talisman of brave delight, ignites actor and action. It transforms a homely railway platform into a theater of old magic far stronger than the Puritans, the Madoffs, or the Voldemorts, which are all that the empirical world can conjure.

Notes

1. All book quotes are taken from the American editions by J. K. Rowling as follows: *Sorcerer's Stone*, A.A. Levine Books, 1998; *Chamber of Secrets*, New York: Scholastic, 2000; *Prisoner of Azkaban*, New York: A.A. Levine Books, 1999; *Goblet of Fire*, New York: A.A. Levine Books, 2000; *Order of the Phoenix*, New York: A.A. Levine Books, 2003; *Deathly Hallows*, New York: A.A. Levine Books, 2007.

2. Taken from a 1774 edition of *The Book of Abraham the Jew*, reprinted by the British Museum in 1982 and available online at www.rexresearch.com/abrelzar/abrelzar.htm.

3. Michael J. B. Allen, Valery Rees, and Martin Davies, *Marsilio Ficino: His Theology, His Philosophy, His Legacy* (Boston: Brill, 2002), 116.

4. From the prologue, lines 475–476, in Geoffrey Chaucer and Larry Dean Benson, *The Riverside Chaucer* (New York: Oxford University Press U.S., 2008), 31.

5. Ibid., lines 443–444, in Chaucer and Benson, *The Riverside Chaucer*, 30.

6. Taken from Richard Hooker's 1994 translation of *Oration on the Dignity of Man*, available online at www.wsu.edu:8080/~dee/REN/ORATION.HTM.

7. Allen, Rees, and Davies, *Marsilio Ficino*, 116.

8. See Oswald Bauer, *Pasquelle in den Fuggerzeitungen. Spott- und Schmähgedichte zwischen Polemitk und Kritik*, Quelleneditionen des Instituts für Österreichische Geschichtsforschung, vol. 1 (Vienna and Munich: Böhlau and Oldenbourg, 2008), 100–117. I would like to thank Birgit Wiedl for sharing this anecdote and source with me.

9. For this interview, see "Rowling Reveals Debt to Welsh Friend Who Was Inspiration for Ron Weasley," *Western Mail* (Cardiff, Wales), June 2, 2004.

10. From Hartlib's papers, published by the Humanities Research Institute online at www.sheffield.ac.uk/hri/projects/projectpages/hartlib.html.

11. Jay Parini, *The Wadsworth Anthology of Poetry* (Boston: Wadsworth, 2005), 1251.

12. Thomas Hobbes, *The Leviathan* (London: Routledge, 1886), 21.

13. Stanton J. Linden, *The Alchemy Reader: From Hermes Trismegistus to Isaac Newton* (Cambridge, UK: Cambridge University Press, 2003), 245.

14. Quoted in Michael White, *Isaac Newton: The Last Sorcerer* (Cambridge, MA: Da Capo Press, 1999), 3.

Why the Statute of Secrecy?

Real Historical Oppression
of Witches and Wizards

Birgit Wiedl

The witch or wizard [being burned at the stake by Muggles]
would perform a basic Flame Freezing Charm and then pretend
to shriek with pain while enjoying a gentle, tickling sensation.
Indeed, Wendelin the Weird enjoyed being burned so much that
she allowed herself to be caught no less than forty-seven times in
various disguises.

— *Prisoner of Azkaban*, 2[1]

Innocent I came into prison, innocent I was tortured, innocent
must I die. [. . .] For they never leave off with the torture till
one confesses something; however pious he may be, he must be
a witch. [. . .] You may well presume that I am no witch but a
martyr, and die herewith, prepared. A thousand good nights, for
your father [. . .] will never see you more.

— From a letter of Johannes Junius, smuggled out of prison on
July 24, 1628, to his daughter Veronica[2]

Johannes Junius, the mayor of the German town of Bamberg, was put to death on August 6, 1628, after an extensive interrogation during which, aided by excruciating torture, he "remembered" the names of several other citizens who had conducted horrendous magical rituals with him. As a result, the leading politician of the territory and the wealthiest citizen of Bamberg were burned at the stake together with Junius, along with clerics, councilors, and members of the regional government: altogether six hundred witches, sorcerers, and black magicians had gotten their just deserts, or so claimed a pamphlet that circulated from 1629 onward.[3] Neither a Flame Freezing Charm nor a Statute of Secrecy had come to their aid, nor had their political reputation, their wealth, or their clerical status protected them from being confronted with one of the deadliest accusations a person in seventeenth-century Europe could face: the practice of witchcraft.

The Persecution of Witches: A Phenomenon through the Ages?

Thou shalt not suffer a witch to live.

—Exodus 22:18

Babbity fled from the bush, and the Brigade of Witch-Hunters set off in pursuit, unleashing their hounds, who bayed for Babbity's blood.

—"Babbitty Rabbitty and Her Cackling Stump," in *Tales of Beedle the Bard*, 72–73

According to the enthusiastic letter that Ron sent to Harry during the Weasleys' vacation in Egypt after Harry's second year, all that the wizards of ancient Egypt had to worry about were spells to punish the Muggles who had broken into their tombs.[4] Ron may have been downplaying (or misunderstanding) the situation in ancient Egypt, however. There was, and is, a firm belief in and fear of witchcraft to be found in most cultures and religions around the world. The belief in witchcraft and sorcery—and the subsequent persecution of those practicing it—was never limited to a particular time and place. Each time and region has had its own ideas about the ways magic constituted either a help or a threat (or both) to a society and how it was integrated into the society.[5]

Yet the image of threatening witches and their *maleficia* (malicious acts), as well as methods to counteract their evil deeds, appears in many cultures. In ancient Babylon, a person suspected of harmful witchcraft was put through the ordeal of being thrown into a river. Ancient Romans were as much afraid of harmful magic,

The execution by burning of Anna Vögtli, who had been accused of witchcraft and of stealing the wafers used in the Mass, held outside the city walls of Willisau (Switzerland) in 1447.

particularly *veneficium* (secret murder by means of magic), as any of their northern European contemporaries were.[6] And even though a wizarding community clearly still exists in Egypt, as proved not only by Bill Weasley's work but by Elphias Doge's encounter with Egyptian alchemists, sorcerers in ancient Egypt lived risky lives just as their Babylonian colleagues did: if their magic was deemed harmful, Egyptian sorcerers, too, were subjected to an ordeal.

With the rise of Christianity, ideas about magic underwent fundamental changes. The church fathers of early Christianity, particularly St. Augustine of Hippo, were quite adamant on the subject of sorcery: any kind of magic, even as "harmless" as the wearing of an amulet or astrological observations, was deemed superstition and implied some sort of contract between the human (who was relying on the item to have the desired effect) and a demon who made it work through magic. Thus, although magical skills could be acquired by learning, from a Christian point of view all magic derived from demons or the devil and was for the most part deception, while many pagan cultures tended to regard Christian teachings and practices as superstitious and "magical" as well.

However strict the "official" line between Christian "proper rites" and pagan "superstition" was drawn, the early Church still co-opted quite a significant number of pagan practices in the course of its struggle for supremacy, including those not only from Roman pagan cults but also from Germanic and Celtic Europe, as Christianity expanded northward. Christian ideas about magic and sorcery intersected with early non-Christian thinking, most of which was also quite familiar with the crime of (harmful) sorcery.

Manifold early medieval legal codes shed light on how witches were perceived and treated in European pagan societies. Early Germanic laws—if they had not adapted Roman law—levied heavy fees on all kinds of misdeeds carried out by witches and sorcerers, yet only seldom demanded the magician's life. A Burgundian man was allowed to divorce his wife if she was suspected of witchcraft. In the Visigothic realms of present-day Spain and southern France, sorcerers and witches were feared because they could devastate vineyards, use charms to harm humans and animals, ruin the harvest, and cause impotence. The practice of divination was generally considered a crime in those regions, as it was in the Lombard law that forbade any consultation with magicians, diviners, and witches who could conjure storms or cause madness by invoking demons.[7]

The same law, however, allowed women unjustly accused of being witches to turn to the king for protection. Witchcraft was not an accusation to be bandied about lightly: accusing someone of being a sorcerer was considered an offense in itself, if the accusation could not be proved; for example, in the law of the Alamanni, the accuser was fined if he or she wasn't able to prove the other person's magical abilities—with a considerably higher fine if the accused person was a woman.[8]

The havoc that Voldemort's Death Eaters wreaked on the poor Muggles of Great Britain puts them in a league with the witches and the sorcerers of the late classical and early medieval times: the conjuring of storms, lightning, hail, or droughts was a common accusation against "magic" people, both in still mostly pagan and in already widely Christianized areas, and many sources from Ireland, Spain, and France report of witches and sorcerers being killed by enraged locals for those crimes.[9] With the expansion of Christianity—namely, during the expansion of the Carolingian empire toward the still-pagan regions in the northeast—forbidding both the belief in witchcraft and any form of punishment of (alleged) witches became a political tool, because now those who believed "after the manner of pagans that some man or woman is a witch" were to be punished, rather than those they had accused of practicing malevolent magic.[10]

The actual existence of magic and witchcraft was, however, not generally denied. Ninth-century clergymen Hrabanus Maurus, the abbot of Fulda, and Agobard, the bishop of Lyon, ranted against the superstition of their time, with the latter deploring the lynching of weather magicians.[11] Their contemporaries at the royal court of Louis the Pious, the king of the Franks (778–840), however, were so fervent in their belief in divination that the learned abbot of Corbie became worried about how reason and judgment were given up in favor of omens, auguries, and other obscure sources that now dominated the king's politics.[12] The idea of witchcraft as a real or potential threat was still around and was put to use as a political tool, even against people of the highest social standing, such as King Louis's second wife and her (alleged) lover and her lover's sister, who were said to use magical practices in order to exert their influence on the king.

The Dark Ages Weren't So Dark

Toward the end of the first millennium, as Professor Binns tells his students, "the four greatest witches and wizards of the age" began to be concerned about the safety of the wizarding world and decided to become the founders of Hogwarts: "They built this castle together, far from prying Muggle eyes, for it was an age when magic was feared by common people, and witches and wizards suffered much persecution." (COS, 149) A separation between magical and nonmagical folk was thus created that obviously had not existed before. Even so, this separation did not go far enough for one of the founders, Salazar Slytherin, who demanded a complete break with the Muggle environment, at least in the area of education.

Slytherin needn't have worried. Except for a few (documented) cases, the majority of which can be attributed to political machinations, the early and High Middle Ages weren't a period when Muggles were very worked up over witchcraft. The helping hand that many wizards still seemed willing to give their neighbors, shown in the character of the deceased father in Beedle the Bard's tale "The Wizard and the Hopping Pot," would not have aroused much suspicion. The *Canon Episcopi*, a ninth-century compilation originally intended as an aid for bishops in their pastoral work, encouraged local authorities to search out sorcerers and witches within their scope of responsibility and exile them, but also discussed the questions of whether witches, magicians, and diviners truly existed; whether herbs could be used to magically heal humans and animals; and whether love or hate could be induced by use of magic.

The most extensively discussed question in the *Canon Episcopi* was, interestingly, something that witches and wizards in Harry

Potter's world debated as well: whether it was possible for humans to fly. Witches and wizards who experimented with the broomstick—a device that was easy to hide and that was to become the means of so much more than just transportation—during the tenth century would have been more concerned about the possibility of having "splinter-filled buttocks," as the twelfth-century Scottish wizard Guthrie Lochrin noted in *Quidditch through the Ages*, and less worried about what their Muggle neighbors might see (*QTTA*, 2).

Flight, which was to become a key feature of witchcraft in the minds of the Early Modern Europeans, was deemed impossible by high medieval scholars. Women who claimed to traverse great distances during the night, led by the Roman goddess Diana, were not practicing magic but were seen as merely delusional, betrayed by the devil who caused these hallucinations.[13] Belief in the existence of witches and their deeds, as well as in the power of demons to work transformations were all declared to be superstition. At least, here medieval Muggle scholars and wizards agreed: both thought that it was impossible for humans to fly unaided (*QTTA*, 1).

Yet in both circles, the question was still debated. Just as the witches and the wizards aimed to find a fitting object to fly on and—after finally settling on the broomstick—subsequently sought to adapt its shape to meet their requirements, so, too, did many medieval scholars theorize about whether humans could fly, coming up with quite different and often rather detailed solutions. The thirteenth-century Dominican inquisitor Étienne de Bourbon, for example, stated that "good women" ride on brooms (through the air), while evil ones ride on the backs of wolves.[14]

Wizards soon discovered how entertaining flying on broomsticks could be and how to incorporate it into sports: the tenth-century broomstick race in Sweden; the first games played in Germany, England, Ireland, and Scotland; and the tentative beginnings of what was to become Quidditch in the eleventh century, with the first teams founded some decades later (such as Puddlemere United, established in 1163). Yet at no time were the wizards overly concerned about Muggles detecting them at play in the air: the main precaution against Muggles spotting the Golden Snitch's predecessor, poor Golden Snidget, was its inherent ability to hide and its very great speed, resulting in "more Muggle broomstick sightings than any other pursuit." The first anti-Muggle precautions were not introduced until 1398, when Zacharias Mumps—in his first encompassing description of Quidditch, which had by then become the most popular wizarding game—noted that deserted moors should be chosen for game venues and Muggle-repelling Charms applied beforehand, precautions that are still taken today (*QTTA*, 15).

Yet were Slytherin's concerns completely unfounded? There are no hints in the medieval Muggle literature that Muggles ever suspected that a wizards' school existed up north in Scotland. Beauxbatons and Durmstrang, however, seem to have underestimated the prying eyes of the Muggles or might have cared less: rumors about schools of sorcery somewhere in the Auvergne (France) and in Turku (Finland) were already circulating in the sixteenth century. Neither of these two schools, however, nor any of the other alleged magical schools in Cracow, Padova, and Venice (to name but a few), managed to outshine the university that gained a reputation as *the* school of magical arts par excellence among medieval scholars starting around the time that Hogwarts itself was founded, a little before the year 1000: the University of Toledo, in Spain.

Legend has it that necromancy—communicating with the spirits of the dead in order to predict the future—was invented in Toledo. Books of such great power were kept there that they had to be chained to the shelves (in fact, a quite common practice in medieval libraries), and magical arts of all kinds, particularly divination and summoning the devil, were said to be taught there; these rumors did not subside after Arab rule in Spain had been replaced by Christian rule in 1085. Despite these allegations, however, scholars who had been educated at Toledo and other, partially still Arabic universities such as Salamanca, Seville, or Cordoba were much sought after. Some even rose to the highest honors, such as the Seville-schooled astronomer and mathematician Gerbert de Aurillac, who became Pope Sylvester from 999 to 1003, although later legends claimed that he was a shady devil worshipper and the founder of a school of sorcery in Rome.[15] However much fantasy was involved in stories about magician scholars trained at these universities, they reflect the high medieval approach to magic: it was discussed at universities and was, as the *artes magicae*, even integrated in the liberal arts.[16]

Scholastics such as the philosopher and theologian Thomas Aquinas theorized about the nature of the devil, demons, and magical arts, constructing an elaborate and highly complex system of the devil and his minions, who strove only to corrupt humankind. Yet ideas of "real" witchcraft that became central in later centuries, like the notion of a formal pact with the devil or the Witches' Sabbath (a wild orgy presided over by the devil), do not appear in medieval discussions of witchcraft, nor was there a single, unified opinion about magic, sorcery, and witchcraft.[17] The main concern of church authorities during the High Middle Ages was heresy—ideas that contradicted orthodox Christian teachings—particularly since the church itself was caught up in a permanent struggle for its identity. With the rise of heretical sects, ideas such as the sacrifice of children, sexual promiscuity, and the worship of the devil were associated with heresy, and malevolent magic was one aspect of heresy.[18]

None of these developments seemed to have bothered the wizarding world. On the contrary, the thirteenth century was obviously an important one in the development of wizarding culture: the International Warlock Convention was held in 1289, and about five years later, what became a centuries-long tradition was kicked off with the first celebration of the Triwizard Tournament. Quidditch was becoming increasingly popular during the same period, as can be seen in the foundation of new teams such as the Holyhead Harpies (1203), the Kenmare Kestrals (1291), and the Pride of Portree (1292). Perhaps the wizarding world was aware of (and relieved by) Pope Alexander IV's decree of 1260, which forbade any active persecution of witches: the decree stated that authorities should take action against a witch only if the matter was brought to their attention, but also emphasized that they should heavily punish the accuser if his allegations were proved wrong.

Two for the Stake: Wendelin the Weird and Petronilla of Meath

Students at Hogwarts—and possibly at Durmstrang, Beauxbatons, and other schools—learn from Bathilda Bagshot's A *History of Magic* that in the early fourteenth century, Muggles were very afraid and suspicious of magic and sorcery, yet lacked the abilities to recognize it properly. As a result of Muggle ignorance, Wendelin the Weird could enjoy the tickling sensation of being burned forty-seven times. This means, as the title of the essay Harry is obliged to write for his summer homework before his third year suggests, that "witch burning in the fourteenth century [was] completely pointless." (POA, 1) The more pressing question, however, is how many Muggles—who couldn't perform a Flame Freezing Charm, like Wendelin—suffered a more tragic fate, due to having been wrongly accused of witchcraft, but Professor Binns apparently doesn't consider this problem important enough to cover in his assignment.

If the wizarding world had spared a thought for the ill-fated Muggles, it would perhaps have been surprised at finding fewer victims to mourn than it would have anticipated. Despite Bathilda Bagshot's findings, accusations of sorcery and witchcraft were still rare in fourteenth-century Europe, although they were sometimes added to the more serious charge of heresy during investigations and trials. The connection with heresy was firm, and ideas about the two "crimes" were still closely intertwined, even inseparable. Like heresy, sorcery was seen as a threat to Christendom by both secular and ecclesiastical rulers, and, using papal authority, inquisitors would seek to track down heretics and sorcerers to remove them from the Christian community.[19]

In the fourteenth century, sorcery served as a "popular" political tool to denounce, denigrate, and, in the best of cases, oust your political enemy. People such as the English treasurer and chamberlain of Edward I or the bishop of Troyes, who had acquired many enemies during their rise to power and wealth, were classic targets of witchcraft accusations. In the ongoing rivalries between papal and secular powers, neither popes nor kings and emperors shied away from spreading rumors and even openly accusing one another of worshipping the devil: Pope Boniface VIII was even said to employ a private demon as his servant.[20] Yet despite the sometimes drastic accusations, none of these alleged celebrity sorcerers was actually executed: from death in prison to returning to their former positions (or even rising higher), anything might happen after an accusation was laid.

Petronilla of Meath, however, had no such luck. This Irish maidservant was neither capable of saving herself with a Flame Freezing Charm (least of all enjoying it) nor of sufficient importance that anyone came to her aid: she was burned at the stake on November 3, 1324. The accusations against her had been made during a much more wide-ranging trial that was centered on Petronilla's mistress, Alice Kyteler, a wealthy widow of Kilkenny. Several of her stepchildren accused her before the bishop of Ossory of having killed some of their fathers after having forced them to make wills leaving all of their property to her, and the bishop, Richard Ledrede, went quickly into action.

At the ensuing formal enquiry, however, charges were raised that went far beyond the accusations of homicide and fraud. Kyteler was said to preside over an organized heretical group that indulged in devil worship and sexual debauchery and summoned demons. At their nightly meetings, they allegedly concocted powders, ointments, and draughts and used to either kill others or induce love or hatred in them; they also burned candles made of human fat and sacrificed animals. Kyteler even had—just as Pope Boniface did—a personal demon. Under torture, Petronilla confessed to having seen the demon that had appeared on several occasions in a number of shapes—as a cat, a dog, or a black man (*Æthiops*)—and Kyteler had mated with him. In return, the demon taught her magic arts, and she had passed on the knowledge to her followers, including Petronilla.

While Kyteler, who had in turn accused Bishop Richard of defamation, managed to escape to England, most of her followers were given a variety of punishments. A few suffered Petronilla's fate at the stake, some were whipped, others excommunicated and exiled, some imprisoned for a time. Although certain elements mentioned in the accusations reappeared in later witch trials, the case against Kyteler was not a typical witch hunt of the Early Modern sort, which would occur in greater numbers a few hundred years later.

As in other cases, the supernatural aspects of the indictment against Kyteler had been brought not by some illiterate, still half-pagan peasants (which Kyteler and her followers weren't, anyway) of modern "Wiccan" fantasies but by the upper-class, scholarly bishop; many of the details of the accusation reflected the ideas of the literate elite about ritual magic and demon worshipping.[21] These additions had turned what had started off as a quite ordinary conflict among wealthy villagers into a trial that would have been more at home at the French or papal court—where, in fact, Bishop Richard had spent the time before his consecration. Neither the local secular nor the local and regional ecclesiastical authorities were happy with Richard's downright fanatical prosecution of the case, which resulted in his being summoned before the archbishop of Dublin and subsequently exiled for several years.[22]

Yet on an intellectual level, the fourteenth century prepared the grounds for the more numerous witch hunts of the Early Modern period. Along with fundamental changes in judicial procedures, such as the use of torture as a legal instrument, the definitions of and punishments for heresy became sharper, while new offenses were introduced.[23] As a "century of perpetual crisis" that saw famine, natural disasters, the Black Plague, permanent warfare, economic collapses, and the Great Schism of the papacy, the fourteenth century also witnessed an increasing fear of the coming of the Antichrist and of assaults of the devil that resulted in a new intensity of religious devotion that could easily swing the other way—of which the witch hunts were only one among many examples.[24]

Perhaps the Wizards' Council had employed the services of a fourteenth-century Sibyll Trelawney when they twice banned all Quidditch matches within fifty and a hundred miles of a Muggle settlement in 1362 and 1368, respectively (QTTA, 15–16). It remains open to speculation whether Muggles had ever listened to

Malécrit's play *Hélas, Je me suis Transfiguré Les Pieds*, with its reference to a Keeper, or to the verses of the Norwegian Ingolfr the Iambric, who waxed poetic on pursuing the Snitch (*QTTA*, 39), yet given the fantasy worlds that Muggle writers of that time unleashed on their audiences, they might merely have filed Keepers and Snitches away under yet another poet suffering from exuberant fantasy. During this period, however, the Wizards' Council was more concerned with defining the characteristics of a beast, rather than with implementing any kind of official precautions against being detected by Muggles, although it was evident from Muggle art and literature, and particularly Muggle bestiaries, that nonmagical Europeans also noticed magical creatures.[25] Their imperfect understanding, however, as Newt Scamander noted, eventually led to the fear and persecution of wizards.

Desiring with Supreme Ardor: Sir (Nearly Headless) Nicholas de Mimsy-Porpington, Lisette de Lapin, and Margery Jourdemayne

What was perhaps the most significant date in the history of European witch persecution — the publication of the *Hammer of Witches* in 1486, discussed further on — went by almost unnoticed by the wizarding population. There was an acute awareness that Muggles should not be given the opportunity to spy on witches and wizards when they used their powers. "Many in the magical community felt, and with good reason," Albus Dumbledore wrote in his commentary to "The Wizard and the Hopping Pot," "that offering to cast a spell on the Muggle-next-door's sickly pig was tantamount to volunteering to fetch the firewood for one's own funeral pyre." (*TOBTB*, 12) As early as the beginning of the fifteenth century, Dumbledore observes, the persecutions of witches and wizards had been gathering apace all over Europe, and wizards responded by withdrawing further and further from the Muggles.

Their greatest worry seems to have been about the most conspicuous of all wizarding activities: Quidditch. Attending to a concoction that was bubbling away in a cauldron might be explainable to a Muggle, because cauldrons were commonly used in kitchens across Europe, and a witch or a wizard could simply refuse to cure the neighbor's pig. But people buzzing through the air to and fro on broomsticks was something that could not be explained (unlike, perhaps, the occasionally ensuing brawl between the losers and the winners of a match). In fact, Kennilworthy Whisp observed that Quidditch was the "worst kept secret" of the wizarding world during this period (*QTTA*, 16). Quidditch had spread across Europe by the early 1400s (*QTTA*, 38–39), new teams were founded, and thus in 1419 the earlier regulations that had banned all Quidditch matches within a certain distance of a Muggle settlement had to be sharpened: under penalty of being "chained to a dungeon wall," no one was to play Quidditch at a place where he or she stood the chance of being seen by Muggles (*QTTA*, 16).

Nevertheless, it seems that the wizards still felt quite safe as long as they managed to stay among themselves—at least safe enough to hold Duelling Competitions, even the first All-England Duelling Competition in 1430, as we see from the Wizarding Card of the winner, Alberta Toothill. This attitude seems to have been common among wizards across Europe, because the first Quidditch world cup was held in 1473. Perhaps they should have been more cautious: only a decade later, in 1484, the papal bull that confirmed the existence of wizards was issued. Pope Innocent VIII responded to the request of the German Dominican priest Heinrich Kramer, who asked for papal support in his quest to persecute witches and heretics within the Holy Roman Empire (where he had found local authorities quite unwilling to cooperate) and in his bull *Summis desiderantes affectibus* (Desiring with supreme ardour), Innocent VIII gave full approval for Kramer to move against witches and use whatever means he deemed necessary (which did, however, still not result in the support of the local authorities).

Despite the fact that, as the wizarding editor of *Beedle the Bard* noted, "Genuine witches and wizards were reasonably adept at escaping the stake, block and noose," the fifteenth century was no longer the "safe" period that Bathilda Bagshot had described it as (*TOBTB*, 12, fn. 1). The term *witch* had been introduced into Muggle legal terminology by the beginning of the century, further easing the way for witches to be prosecuted by secular and ecclesiastical courts.[26] Tales of witches and their malicious deeds found their way into books that were also written for practical use by preachers, such as the highly influential *Formicarius* (The Anthill) of the German Dominican Johannes Nider, who included what he claimed were the true stories of a Swiss judge and his witch hunts.[27] Despite the fact that he became the most important authority on witchcraft of his time, providing one of the earliest descriptions of a Witches' Sabbath, Nider still didn't consider witchcraft a crime on its own but maintained the earlier close connection between witchcraft and heresy.[28]

Once the existence of witches and wizards was officially acknowledged, perhaps it became easier to identify and persecute them. Even real wizards could fall prey to Muggles during this period — for example, magical children who weren't able to control their magic and thus drew the attention of witch hunters. Sir Nicholas de Mimsy-Porpington, whom a Muggle executioner turned into Nearly Headless Nick, is one of the best-known examples of this upward tick in persecutions of wizards and witches. As Dumbledore's notes to "The Wizard and the Hopping Pot" reveal, the Muggles who incarcerated Sir Nicholas took his wand away, rendering him defenseless, a fact that — interestingly and tellingly — Sir Nicholas himself does not reveal to Harry when he tells him about his sad fate. On October 31, 1492, Harry learns, Sir Nicholas was "hit forty-five times in the neck with a blunt axe," yet he mentions neither his (alleged or actual) offense, nor the identity of his executor (*COS*, 123).[29]

It is again Dumbledore to whom we owe the knowledge of Sir Nicholas's social standing before he met his fate: he was "a wizard at the royal court." (*TOBTB*, 12) Given the year of his death, Sir Nicholas could have been at either the court of Henry VII, the king of England, or James IV, the king of Scotland, neither of whom was known for his witch-hunting proclivities.[30] Although the first major witch persecutions in Scotland — the North Berwick witch trials—affected many nobles of the Scottish court, they took place about a century later, between 1590 and 1592, at the court of James VI, an avid believer in witchcraft and the author of a handbook on demonology.[31]

Given the long life expectancy of wizards, it is possible that Sir Nicholas had witnessed a graphic warning against showing off his magic in public (or even trying to impress ladies he fancied). If he lived at the English court of King Henry VI, he would have been present during one of the "most sensational episodes of the mid-fifteenth century": the trial of Eleanor Cobham, the duchess of Gloucester.[32] Furthermore, if Dumbledore's account can be trusted, a genuine witch had been present at the court of Henry VI, as a trusted adviser and in the shape of a large white rabbit: Lisette de Lapin, who had so skilfully vanished from her prison in Paris in 1422 and had traveled across the English Channel in her Animagus form (TOBTB, 82).

Were Lisette and Sir Nicholas present at the English court in 1441, when (along with Eleanor) three clerics and a woman named Margery Jourdemayne were accused of having tried to kill the young king by means of witchcraft and necromancy? As the wife of Henry's uncle, the former lord protector (guardian and regent for the young king) and heir presumptive to the childless king, Eleanor had a rank as high as it came at that court, but neither high status nor widely respected scholarship saved the countess and her alleged accomplices. While Eleanor was sentenced to lifetime imprisonment, the two most "magical" characters of the plot—the Oxford scholar and astrologer Roger Bolingbroke, and Jourdemayne, the "witch of Eye next Westminster"—were punished with the full rigor of the law: Bolingbroke was hanged, drawn, and quartered, his head set on London Bridge, and his four body parts displayed in what were considered four centers of heresy as a warning to others.[33] Jourdemayne's fate, however, was sealed when the prosecutors found out that she had already been charged with witchcraft ten years earlier and released on condition that she abstain from the use of sorcery in the future. Not only had she relapsed, but she had added treason and heresy to her crimes, which led to her being burned at the stake on October 27, 1441.[34]

During the course of the fifteenth century, the concept of witchcraft had undergone profound changes that eventually resulted in the papal bull mentioned earlier and (even more important) in the publication of the *Malleus Maleficarum* (The Witches' Hammer, first published in 1486).[35] Although the book had not really developed any new witch stereotypes but rather only expressed them at greater length, and even though it was rejected by many, its impact was enormous: it was to become the most popular "handbook" of secular and ecclesiastical witch hunters in many parts of Europe. The author, the Dominican inquisitor Heinrich Kramer, not only confirmed that people who practiced malevolent magic indeed existed, but also described their ceremonies and rituals and listed methods of annihilating the witches' powers and evil actions through meticulous investigation and legal action.[36] Most important, the book included a "catalogue" of criteria that investigators should use to identify a witch. The list merged older medieval scholarly ideas about witchcraft with motifs from folk traditions, and it twisted (at points, even refuted) older notions in order to make the theory match the authors' imagination, such as Thomas Aquinas's concept of high magic requiring a pact with the devil, or the *Canon Episcopi*'s assertion of the impossibility of bodily flight.[37]

Like the French Dominican inquisitor Nicholas Jacquier, who published *A Scourge for Heretical Witches* in 1458, Heinrich Kramer came to the conclusion that the witches of his century had to be different from the delusional medieval women discussed in the *Canon*: they had to be real, in other words.[38] He backed up his theories by citing exemplary cases such as those provided by Johannes Nider and his tales about the Swiss sorcerer Staedlin. Following the publication of the *Malleus Maleficarum*, witch trials became more systematic and also rapidly increased in number. While in some countries the methods of investigating, prosecuting, and punishing the execution of witchcraft varied, the "witch craze" took off during the Early Modern period to become a pan-European phenomenon after 1500 that even crossed the Atlantic Ocean. A paradigm shift had taken place: witchcraft was now defined and prosecuted as a crime on its own, quite separate from heresy.[39]

Too Little, Too Late? The Wizarding International Statue of Secrecy and the Witch-Hunt Craze of the Sixteenth and Seventeenth Centuries

"Germany smokes everywhere with execution pyres," the Jesuit Friedrich Spee von Langenfeld wrote in his *Cautio Criminalis* (A Warning on Criminal Justice) in 1629–1631, a "cry of conscience from the very epicenter of witch-hunts," written in a decade that saw a particularly ferocious wave of witch hunts sweep through German-speaking Europe.[40] Spee's findings, however, would have been only slightly less true for the rest of Europe, at least north of the Alps.[41] It is difficult to give even an approximate estimate for the number of victims who fell prey to the witch hunts, particularly since not all trials ended in a death sentence, and not all of these sentences were actually carried out. Estimates range from 25,000 to 30,000 for the high point of the witch craze between 1530 and 1660 and may total 50,000 for the whole period from 1400 to 1800.[42]

"We were careless for too many centuries," Kennilworthy Whisp conceded in retrospect in his history of Quidditch (*QTTA*, 16). The object he was worried about, the broomstick, had now indeed become firmly associated with wizards in the Muggle mind, and this was but one of the problems that the wizarding world had to face in the Early Modern period. Nocturnal flight, by means of a broomstick or using some other method, had come to be one of the signature elements of a "true" witch in the explanations offered by Kramer and other Muggle witch hunters. Flight now had to be included in the confession drawn from suspected witches and wizards, a confession that the interrogators would use any means to extract.

What, then, made someone a witch in the eyes of Muggle prosecutors? In 1628, Johannes Junius confessed to having declared,

"I renounce God in Heaven and his host, and will henceforward recognize the Devil as my God," in the presence of the devil, who had first appeared to Junius in the shape of a woman but had then turned into a goat.[43] In the eyes of the authorities, Johannes had entered the pact with the devil willingly, an essential feature of the definition of witchcraft in Early Modern Europe, which marked a break with how their deceived and delusional medieval predecessors had been seen. After making this demonic agreement, Junius admitted that he had attended gatherings of witches frequently, to which a black dog had brought him. His confession thus included two more key features of the Early Modern understanding of witchcraft: first, that witches participated in the Witches' Sabbath, where they danced and met with other witches and the devil, whom they worshipped; and second, that they arrived at the Sabbath by means of flight, whether by straddling sticks, by riding on the backs of beasts or demons, or by using a flying ointment.

Yet witches were thought not only to worship the devil, in a perverted, topsy-turvy version of the rituals of the Christian faith.[44] They were also thought to have sexual intercourse with the devil, often as a part of the initiating ritual. The devil would also visit female witches, in the form of an *incubus*, a male demon, while in order to lie with wizards the devil took the shape of a *succubus*, a female demon, such as the "grass-maid" (*Grasmagd*) who had approached Junius first, and with whom he copulated frequently.[45] Muggle authorities thought that witches and wizards might also have sexual intercourse with the devil while he assumed the shape of a beast—usually a goat or a cat—or kiss the beast's anus as a token of their adoration.

As an integral part of the pact with the devil, during (and by) which the delinquent renounced the Christian religion, sexual intercourse with a demon also meant that the witch had crossed moral boundaries, thus disavowing a set of community or civic values. Most of this happened at the Witches' Sabbath, the place and the time where inversions of not only "proper" religious worship but also "normal" ways of social interaction took place.[46] The last (but not least) misdeed of a witch was the *maleficium* ("malicious deed"), whether it was accomplished through use of balms or potions, spells or hexes, or by touching or merely looking at the victim with the witch's evil eye. These constituted the evildoing, the actual actions that witches performed against individuals and/or the community as a whole.[47]

A witch or a wizard of the early fifteenth century would have been well-advised to be wary of curing the sickly pig of a Muggle neighbor with a spell, because doing so might indeed have triggered a witch hunt. Accusations against witches were often made by their immediate neighbors and could be the result of neighborhood tensions, threats uttered in anger or during a dispute, or when the accused had broken social norms.[48] Any of these could result first in rumors of witchcraft, then in suspicion, and finally in conviction for acts of witchcraft.[49]

By the mid-sixteenth century, the witch craze had taken hold of most of the territories in Europe, in both Protestant and Catholic territories. While Catholic inquisitors in Italy and Spain generally tried to curb the spread of witch hunts, keeping the number of both trials and executions in those areas comparatively low, mostly secular witch hunters were as busy in the Catholic regions of France and the Holy Roman Empire as they were in Protestant areas such as Scandinavia, Zwinglian Switzerland, Calvinist (Presbyterian) Scotland, and (to a lesser degree) Anglican England.[50] In most of Europe's legal systems, malicious witchcraft was now classified as a criminal offense, punishable by both ecclesiastical and secular authorities, such as in the *Constitutio Criminalis Carolina* (1532) for the Holy Roman Empire or the English Witchcraft Acts that were promulgated from 1542 onward.

Demonology was no longer a theological concept that only scholars brooded over but had become a daily reality in courts of law. Although there was a broad variety in both belief systems and patterns of prosecution, the witch craze nevertheless crossed borders of religion, culture, and mentality. The reasons proposed by historians to explain the craze are quite diverse: from conspiracy ideas that spread through all levels of society to the "little ice age" that began in Europe during the sixteenth century and its resulting crop failures, mass pauperization, economic changes, and demographic expansion, to witch crazes as a means of social discipline—all of these contributed to what was a pan-European phenomenon.[51]

Considering the fate that Muggles intended for magical folk such as Wendelin the Weird and Lisette de Lapin and the (actual) execution of Sir Nicholas, it is remarkably clear why witches and wizards of this period feared Muggle persecution. No distinctions were made between male and female in the wizarding world, something that Muggle prosecutors may have eventually guessed at, because recent research has confirmed that both male and female witches were accused and prosecuted.[52]

Although medieval misogynist traditions were reflected in the witch hunters' ideas and actions, and while it is undeniable that more women than men were tried for witchcraft in most regions, older arguments that the witch hunts were a "gynocide" and a means of driving midwives and other healing women out of an increasingly prestigious profession have been thoroughly debunked by modern research, and witchcraft today is seen by historians as a more sex-related than sex-specific crime.[53] At the end of the witch craze, suspicion shifted to focus on young itinerant men from the lower social strata, people who posed a threat to the emerging "law and order" states of the late seventeenth and eighteenth centuries.[54]

The danger of being persecuted by witch hunts did not pass unnoticed by the wizarding world, and some began to argue for more separation between the two worlds. Brutus Malfoy, the editor of *Warlock at War*, an anti-Muggle periodical of the late seventeenth century, ranted against wizards who showed fondness for Muggles and their society. His publication tried to convince his fellow wizards of the danger that came from associating with Muggles and sniped that "any wizard who shows fondness for the society of Muggles is of low intelligence, with magic so feeble and pitiful that he can only feel himself superior if surrounded by Muggle pig-men." (*TOBTB*, 15–16) Yet however successful his periodical might have been (and Dumbledore is careful not to tell us), Malfoy stood no chance against the sheer masses of leaflets and broadsheets that had literally been flooding Muggle Europe from the sixteenth century onward.

These broadsheets, both in plain text and with woodcut illustrations, did not so much disseminate general (and still quite complicated) ideas about witchcraft but showed either stereotyped figures—such as figures of a flying witch with a broomstick or witches kissing the devil's anus—or told the story of a specific case of witchcraft, thus translating a theoretical concept into everyday reality that was within the average reader's grasp. Even the first major persecution in Europe, in a tiny Lutheran lordship in southeast Germany in 1562, was made known to a wider public by a pamphlet titled the *True and Horrifying Deeds of 63 Witches*, which started to circulate while the ashes were still smoldering. Local incidents or accusations that a century earlier would have come to the attention of only those who lived nearby were now discussed hundreds of miles away, arousing fear and hatred in people from different religious faiths and regions.

The "dark days that preceded the wizards' retreat into hiding," and the "particularly bloody period of wizarding history": this is how Newt Scamander—rephrasing Bathilda Bagshot's *A History of Magic*—describes the period just before the passage of the International Statute of Wizarding Secrecy, and we can apply these words more generally to the whole of the seventeenth, if not parts of the sixteenth, century (*FB*, xv). Witch hunts had grown "even fiercer," compared to what the wizarding world had earlier suffered during the lifetimes (however long) of Lisette de Lapin and Sir Nicholas de Mimsy-Porpington (however cut short). And although the cry "Let the Muggles manage without us" had been heard as early as the fifteenth century, the centuries that followed saw the majority of the wizarding families leading double lives for fear of their safety, constantly casting concealment charms in order to protect themselves. The process that had begun in the era of de Lapin, as wizards separated themselves more and more from the Muggle world, gathered steam in the face of the imminent (and rapidly increasing) danger. Indeed, Dumbledore's commentary on "The Wizard and the Hopping Pot" notes that the changing climate led to mounting suspicion and even hatred against those wizards who, despite the smoldering evidence, still chose to fraternize with the enemy (*TOBTB*, 13, 15).

It may come as a surprise that we are given conflicting information about the year in which the Statute of Secrecy was enacted, considering that it is undoubtedly one of the, if not *the*, most important rules of the wizarding world. Yet while Dumbledore claims that "wizardkind voluntarily went underground" in 1689 (*TOBTB*, 13), Newt Scamander in his *Fantastic Beasts* gives the year 1692 as the date when the International Confederation of Wizards (including delegations of goblins, centaurs, and merpeople) met to enact the statute (*FB*, xv). Dumbledore's knowledge of all things magical notwithstanding, the later date seems more logical if we compare it with events happening in the Muggle world during that year.

The year 1692 witnessed one of the most (in)famous witch trials in Muggle history, which took place in a variety of towns in colonial Massachusetts, one of which gave the name to this particular witch hunt: Salem. Although the witch craze was already on the decline in Europe by this date, a "great intensity of anti-wizard feeling," as Kennilworthy Whisp recognizes, had been "exported from Europe" to North America. As a result, not only was Quidditch hindered from becoming as widespread and popular as it was in Europe at that time (which was Whisp's main concern), but the wizard settlers who "had hoped to find less prejudice" in the New World were forced to exercise great caution (*QTTA*, 43).

We do not know whether any "real" witches were affected by the Salem witch trials. Yet more than simply the name of the Salem Witches' Institute, which sent a delegation of middle-age witches to attend the Quidditch World Cup, reflects the American wizarding community's memory of New England's greatest (if not only) witchcraft persecution.[55] Despite Bathilda Bagshot's description of this time as a "particularly bloody period," there is no evidence of the wizarding culture having come to a standstill during the period of dire persecution in Europe. On the contrary, not only were the European Quidditch Cup and the British and Irish League established and books written on the wizards' most favorite sport, but we also know of magical research done during this period, such as the invention of a cure for the dragon pox and the discovery of the properties of Gillyweed. Cultural activities continued as before: music was being composed, societies founded, and social institutions such as St. Mungo's were established while the witch craze peaked in the Muggle world, as we see in the Famous Wizard Cards of Gunhilda of Gorsemoor, Elladora Ketteridge, Musidora Barkwith, Honoria Nutcombe, and Mungo Bonham.

"When Muggle persecution was at its heights," Kennilworthy Whisp tells his avid readers (albeit in a footnote), wizarding communities reacted to the danger not only by deciding to separate entirely from the Muggle world but also by outlawing any deliberate exposure of the wizarding community. Given such an obvious nudge from across the Atlantic, where their North American fellows had for the first time experienced the full blast of witch craze reality, magical folk from all over the world came together—where, we do not know—to discuss at full length the most pressing issues. The summit was presumably quite (over)crowded with witches, wizards, and other magical beings who were more often than not at variance with one another: the decision alone of how many and which species of magical creatures to hide from the Muggles' eyes took seven weeks to reach (FB, xv). As an eventual result, however, the Statute of Secrecy was enacted on an international level, declaring, as Harry learns during his second year at Hogwarts, that "any magical activity that risks notice by members of the non-magical community (Muggles) is a serious offense under section 13 of the International Confederation of Warlocks' Statute of Secrecy." (COS, 21) To be able to defend themselves (and to avoid suffering the fate of being Nearly Headless), wizards were now allowed to carry wands at all times, even during Quidditch matches (QTTA, 28).

Witch Hunts—Yesterday's News?

While the witches and the wizards in Colonial America were rightfully fearing for their safety and perhaps pushing for a solution to be found, European wizarding folk might have realized that the

Muggles were already becoming tired of the whole subject by the end of the seventeenth century. Although learned scholars from all disciplines, such as the fifteenth-century German humanist Johannes Trithemius or the sixteenth-century French political philosopher Jean Bodin, continued to argue about the various types and key features of witches and the means to counteract them, other voices became stronger by the seventeenth century: voices that challenged the belief in witchcraft and the endorsement of the persecution of witches.

Influential writers like the physician Johann Weyer sought to reform and soften both the law and the legal procedures concerning witches, while accusing the persecutors of massacring the innocents. Adapting older, medieval concepts of witchcraft, Weyer (himself a noted occultist) saw the accused witches as being delusional, betrayed by the devil or demons, or suffering from melancholy, and thus rather in need of medical aid.[56] Doubt of, and even resistance against, witch hunts began to spread through all social classes by the late seventeenth century, including from the influential Jesuit Friedrich Spee von Langenfeld to opposition from people who had personally witnessed witchcraft trials.[57]

Although the number and the intensity of persecutions decreased after 1590 in Protestant German-speaking regions, the rage went on in the Catholic areas of German Europe somewhat longer.[58] At the same time that one of the greatest hunts in the southern German regions was taking place in 1590, any critique of the five most important points of witchcraft (pact with the devil, sexual intercourse with the devil, flight, Sabbath, and maleficium) was declared heretical. Yet while Protestant Germans were turning away from the whole subject, the witch craze only then took off in other Protestant territories. England saw the last witch burn in 1682, at a time when witch hunts were still in full swing in Protestant Switzerland and in Calvinist (Presbyterian) Scotland, which had joined the legions of witch-hunting countries rather late in the game but was making up for this with a fierce intensity that put other countries to shame. Reaching their peak between 1660 and 1680, the Scottish witch hunts lasted—with varying intensity—until 1727, when the last execution was carried out.[59]

The wizarding community seemed aware that interest in witch hunts was beginning to die down, and perhaps its members were anxious not to provoke any revival of suspicion. Thus, in the course of the eighteenth century, wizarding regulations concerning contact with Muggles—or, rather, the avoidance of contact—were sharpened, particularly with regard to items and creatures that might accidentally reveal the wizarding world's existence to the Muggles. For example, in 1709 the Warlocks' Convention outlawed dragon breeding, in order to keep Muggles from noticing these very conspicuous beasts, and when the Statute of Secrecy was breached in 1749, the consequences were severe. Although we do not learn—thanks to Harry's inattention in History class—what the cause for that breach was (only that it involved vampires), clause 73 was added to the statute only one year later: as of that date, the governing bodies of the respective territories were "responsible for the concealment, care, and control of all magical beasts." (FB, xvi) It is quite likely more than a coincidence that in the same year, the Department of Magical Games and Sports was established, regulating the perhaps most pressing concern, the hiding of Quidditch (QTTA, 27).

By this time, European witch hunts had almost come to a halt: King Louis XIV had brought prosecution for witchcraft to an end in France by the late seventeenth century. In England and subsequently Scotland, a statute of 1735 officially determined that witchcraft was no longer a crime. In German-speaking Europe, the last witch trials were held in the mid-eighteenth century; the maidservant Anna Schweglin was the last witch to be sentenced to death in this region in 1775, although the execution was actually not carried out.[60] When the Swiss maidservant Anna Göldi was accused of having cursed her employer's daughter, her execution in 1782 caused a public outcry in Switzerland and Germany that prompted the officials to speak of her as a poisoner and *not* a witch in the verdict.[61]

The days of the Early Modern witch craze are now long gone. Witches and wizards of Kilkenny, Bamberg, North Berwick, and Salem have no reason to fear execution today, nor have those dwelling in a mansion in Wiltshire, in Ottery St. Catchpole, or at 12 Grimmauld Place. Stories of family members who fell prey to

Muggle witch hunters and only just escaped the stake or (in the best of all cases) outsmarted their persecutors are surely still being told in wizarding homes, however.

These tales no doubt encourage many to support the continuing enforcement of the Statue of Secrecy and to accuse those who advocate relaxing the regulations of risking not only the exposure but also the (ensuing) destruction of the wizarding world. Yet are their fears really that unfounded? The wizarding world, after all, is a global one, and on a global scale, the era that saw the most people killed for being suspected of witchcraft (to date) was the second half of the twentieth century.[62] In light of this, the Statute of Secrecy may still be, sadly, the wisest policy.

Notes

1. All book quotes are taken from the American editions by J. K. Rowling as follows: Chamber of Secrets, New York: Scholastic, 2000; *Prisoner of Azkaban*, New York: A.A. Levine Books, 1999; *Tales of Beedle the Bard*, New York: Children's High Level Group, in association with A.A. Levine Books, 2008; *Fantastic Beasts*, New York: A.A. Levine Books, 2001; *Quidditch through the Ages*, New York: A.A. Levine Books, 2001.

2. Lara Apps and Andrew Gow, *Male Witches in Early Modern Europe* (Manchester, UK: Manchester University Press, 2003), 159–166 (translation based on the abridged edition of 1883). The full original text can be found in Elvira Topalović and Iris Hille, *Perspektivierung von Wirklichkeit(en) im Hexenprozess*, at historicum.net (www.historicum.net/themen/hexenforschung/thementexte/unterrichtsmaterialien/hille/). Staatsbibliothek Bamberg, R.B. Msc. 148, Nr. 300, 1r–2v. Junius's daughter survived as a Dominican nun.

3. See Apps and Gow, *Male Witches in Early Modern Europe*, 76–86, Wolfgang Behringer, *Witches and Witch Hunts. A Global History* (Cambridge and Malden, MA: Polity Press, 2004), 112. The literature on witchcraft, witch hunts, magic, and so forth, fills up shelves as it is now, and the number of books, articles, and series dedicated to the topic is still growing rapidly. As basic works, the reader can consult the six-volume series *Witchcraft and Magic in Europe*, edited by Bengt Ankarloo and Stuart Clark (Philadelphia: University of Pennsylvania Press, 1999–2002), with the addendum volume *Witchcraft and Magic in Contemporary North America*, edited by Helen Berger (Philadelphia: University of Pennsylvania Press, 2005), in Europe published under the title *The Athlone History of Witchcraft and Magic in Europe* (London: Athlone Press). Anthologies of articles and book chapters on witchcraft have been put together in the six-volume series *New Perspectives on Witchcraft, Magic and Demonology*, edited by Brian P. Levack (London and New York: Routledge, 2001); *Witches of the Atlantic World: A Historical Reader & Primary Sourcebook*, edited by Elaine G. Brelsaw (New York and London: New York University Press, 2000); and *The Witchcraft Reader*, edited by Darren Oldridge (London and New York: Routledge, 2002). Also see the *Encyclopedia of Witchcraft: The Western Tradition*, 4 vols., edited by Richard M. Golden (Santa Barbara, CA: ABC-Clio, 2006); from 2006 onward, Michael David Bailey and Brian P. Copenhaver edited the journal *Magic, Ritual and Witchcraft*;

for a survey of witchcraft historiography, see *Palgrave Advances in Witchcraft Historiography*, edited by Jonathan Barry and Owen Davies (Basingstoke and New York: Palgrave Macmillan, 2007). In Germany, the centers for the research of the history of witchcraft at the universities of Trier (series *Trierer Hexenprozesse—Quellen und Darstellungen*, 8 vols. as of 2009) and Tübingen (series *Hexenforschung*, 12 vols. as of 2008); an interdisciplinary platform is being maintained by Gudrun Gersmann (University of Cologne) and Katrin Moeller (University of Halle-Wittenberg) at www.historicum.net/themen/hexenforschung/, with a lot of articles and the *Lexikon zur Geschichte der Hexenverfolgung* available online. Regarding the pamphlet circulating from 1629 onward, see the German text edited by Wolfgang Behringer, *Hexen und Hexenprozesse in Deutschland* (Munich: dtv, 1988; 2001), 261–264, no. 171.

4. The Harry Potter lexicon states in its timeline (www.hp-lexicon.org/timeline.html) that ancient Egypt and Greece were "an era of Muggle/Wizard cooperation; many political and religious leaders were witches and wizards," a statement that is not found in the Harry Potter books themselves, nor is this supported by historical research, but rather seems to be rooted in a romanticized concept of pre-Christian societies.

5. Michael David Bailey, "The Meanings of Magic," *Magic, Ritual, and Witchcraft* 1, no. 1 (2006): 1–23, discusses the important question of what contemporaries perceived as magic and the thin line between magic and religion.

6. Behringer, *Witches and Witch-Hunts*, 47–50; Michael David Bailey, *Magic and Superstition in Europe: A Concise History from Antiquity to the Present* (Plymouth UK: Rowman & Littlefield, 2007), 20–25; James B. Rives, "'Magic, Religion, and Law: The Case of the *Lex Cornelia de sicariis et veneficiis*'" in *Religion and Law in Classical and Christian Rome*, edited by Clifford Ando and Jörg Rüpke, Potsdamer Altertumswissenschaftliche Beiträge 15 (Stuttgart: Franz Steiner Verlag, 2006), 47–67, particularly 49–59.

7. See Karen Louise Jolly, Catharina Raudvere, and Edward Peters, *The Athlone History of Witchcraft and Magic in Europe*, vol. 3: *The Middle Ages* (London: Athlone Press, 2002), 188–191.

8. Karl August Eckart, ed., *Pactus Legis Alamannorum* 13. *Leges alamannorum*, Monumenta Germaniae Historica, Leges nationum germanicarum, vol. 1 (Hanover: Hahnsche Buchhandlung, 1966, 1993), 24; online at www.dmgh.de. See Jolly, Raudvere, and Peters, *The Athlone History of Witchcraft and Magic*, vol. 3, 188–189.

9. Jolly, Raudvere, and Peters, *The Athlone History of Witchcraft and Magic*, vol. 3, 194–196.

10. Charlemagne, Capitularies at Paderborn, 785, nos. 6 and 9, English translation in Patrick J. Geary, ed., *Readings in Medieval History*, 2nd ed. (Peterborough, ON: Broadview Press, 1989, 1998), 284.

11. Agobardus Lugdunensis, "Liber contra insulsam vulgi opinionem de grandine et tonitruis," *Patrologia Latina*, vol. 104, ed. Jacques Paul Migne (Paris: Garnier, 1864), c. 147–158.

12. Georg Heinrich Pertz, ed., *Ex Paschasii Radberti Vita Walae abbatis Corbeiensis*, Monumenta Germaniae Historica Scriptores 2 (Stuttgart: Hiersemann, 1976), 553–554; Valerie I. J. Flint, *The Rise of Magic in Early Medieval Europe* (Oxford: Clarendon Press, 1998), 63; and Dan Burton and David Grandy, *Magic, Mystery, and Science: The Occult in Western Civilization* (Bloomington: Indiana University Press, 2004), 155.

13. Werner Tschacher, "Der Flug durch die Luft zwischen Illusionstheorie und Realitätsbeweis. Studien zum sog. Kanon Episcopi und zum Hexenflug," *Zeitschrift der Savigny-Stiftung für Rechtsgeschichte* 116, Kan. Abt. 85 (1999): 225–276.

14. Christa Habinger-Tuczay, "Hexen," in *Dämonen, Monster, Fabelwesen*, edited by Ulrich Müller and Werner Wunderlich, Mittelalter Mythen, vol. 2 (St. Gallen: UVK Fachverlag für Wissenschaft und Studium, 1999), 320.

15. Christa Habinger-Tuczay, *Magie und Magier im Mittelalter* (Munich: dtv, 1992, 2003), 74–79 and 183–184; Bailey, *Magic and Superstition*, 91–93.

16. Habinger-Tuczay, *Magie und Magier*, 176.

17. Michael David Bailey, "Medieval Concepts of the Witches' Sabbath," *Exemplaria* 8, no. 2 (1996): 419–439, has quite convincingly identified the concept of the Sabbath that developed from the fifteenth century onward as one of the, if not the, most important differences from earlier notions of sorcery.

18. For the latter, see, with particular regard to the witchcraft/demonology aspect, Norman Cohn, *Europe's Inner Demons: The Demonization of Christians in Medieval Christiandom* (Chicago: University of Chicago Press, 2000), particularly 51–78, "The Demonization of Mediaeval Heretics," reprinted as an article within *The Witchcraft Reader*, 36–52.

19. On the role of "the inquisition" (and the problematic use of that term) in the persecution of heresy and sorcery, see Bailey, *Magic and Superstition*, 114–119.

20. Jolly, Raudvere, and Peters, *The Athlone History of Witchcraft and Magic*, vol. 3, 219–320.

21. For example, the trial against a Swiss farmer named Stedelen, where the essential elements of sorcery were supplied by the secular judge, Peter of Greyerz. See Cohn, *Europe's Inner Demons*, 204–205.

22. L. S. Davidson and J. O. Ward, eds., *The Sorcery Trial of Alice Kyteler: A Contemporary Account (1324)*, together with related documents in English translation, introduction and notes (Binghamton, NY: Medieval and Renaissance Texts and Studies, 1993); Cohn, *Europe's Inner Demons*, 197–205; Jolly, Raudvere, and Peters, *The Athlone History of Witchcraft and Magic*, vol. 3, 223–224; Russell, *Witchcraft in the Middle Ages*, 189–193. The incident was so remarkable that it was mentioned in the sixteenth-century *Annales Hiberniae* by James Grace of Kilkenny, proofread online version of the 1842 edition by Richard Butler, Irish Archaeological Society: http://celt.ucc.ie/publishd .html. Although Cohn, *Europe's Inner Demons*, 126–138, and Kiekhefer, *European Witch Trials*, have proved beyond doubt that "notorious" trials such as those of Catherine Delort and Anne-Marie de Georgel were in fact made up by Etienne de Lamothe-Langon in his *Histoire de l'inquisition en France*, 1829, their stories still figure high in Wiccan and "Holy Women" literature, such as Raven Grimassi, *The Wiccan Mysteries: Ancient Origins and Teachings* (St. Paul: Llewellyn Publications, 1997, 2003). Grimassi thrives on the—seemingly ineradicable—assumption of "paganism" as a uniform religion ("Stone Age cult") that somehow persisted in secrecy, defying both time and geography. See also, Kathrin Fischer, "Wicca—die Hexenreligion im deutschsprachigen Raum," in *Lexikon zur Geschichte der Hexenverfolgung*, ed. Gudrun Gersmann, Katrin Moeller, and Jürgen-Michael Schmidt, www.historicum.net/no_cache/persistent/artikel/7390/, with further literature.

23. Jolly, Raudvere, and Peters, *The Athlone History of Witchcraft and Magic*, vol. 3, 225–226.

24. Richard Kiekhefer, "Major Currents in Late Medieval Devotion," in *Christian Spirituality: High Middle Ages and Reformation*, edited by Jill Raitt, Bernhard McGinn, and John Meyendorff, World Spirituality series, vol. 17 (London: Routledge & Kegan Paul, 1987), 75–108.

25. Pamela Gravestock, "Did Imaginary Animals Exist?" in *The Mark of the Beast: The Medieval Bestiary in Art, Life, and Literature*, ed. Debra Hassig, Garland Medieval Casebooks, vol. 22 (London: Garland, 2000).

26. See, for early examples in today's Switzerland, Savoy, and Dauphiné, the works of Andreas Blauert, namely *Frühe Hexenverfolgungen. Ketzer-, Zauberei- und Hexenprozesse des 15. Jahrhunderts*, Sozialgeschichtliche Bibliothek bei Junius, vol. 5 (Hamburg: Junius Verlag, 1998); and (more generally) *Ketzer, Zauberer, Hexen: Die Anfänge der europäischen Hexenverfolgung*, ed. id. (Frankfurt a.M.: Edition Suhrkamp, 2000), particularly the contribution by Arno Borst, "Anfänge des Hexenwahns in den Alpen," 43–68, reprinted in an English translation as "The Origins of the Witch-Craze in the Alps," in *New Perspectives on Witchcraft, Magic and Demonology*, vol. 2: *Witchcraft in Continental Europe*, 299–320. See further *Hexen, Herren und Richter. Die Verfolgung von Hexern und Hexen auf dem Gebiet der heutigen Schweiz am Ende des Mittelalters. Les sorcières, les seigneurs et les juges. La persécution des sorciers et sorcières dans le territoire de la Suisse actuelle à la fin du Moyen Age*, ed. Georg Modestin and Kathrin Utz Tremp, *Schweizerische Zeitschrift für Geschichte* 52, no. 2 (2002), 103–162; Niklaus Schatzmann, *Verdorrende Bäume und Brote wie Kuhfladen. Hexenprozesse in der Leventina 1431–1459 und die Anfänge der Hexenverfolgung auf der Alpensüdseite* (Zurich: Chronos Verlag, 2003); and Laura Stokes, "Prelude: Early Witch-Hunting in Germany and Switzerland," in *Magic, Ritual and Witchcraft* 4, no. 1 (2009).

27. See, most recently, Catherine Chène, "Le *Formicarius* (1436–1438) de Jean Nider OP: Une source pour l'histoire de la chasse aux sorcières dans le diocèse de Lausanne?" *Hexen, Herren und Richter*, 122–126, who is working on a new edition of Nider's work; and Michel David Bailey, *Battling Demons: Witchcraft, Heresy, and Reform in the Late Middle Ages*, The Magic in History Series (University Park: Pennsylvania State University Press, 2003), particularly 91–117.

28. Bailey, "The Medieval Concept of the Witches' Sabbath," particularly 430–432.

29. In the first draft of *Chamber of Secrets*, a ballad sung by Sir Nicholas reveals what had happened: he had made "a mistake any wizard could make," insofar as he had met with a—supposedly Muggle—Lady for a stroll in the park. The Lady, Grieve by name, had been under the impression that Sir Nicholas could straighten her teeth—when he in fact only managed to have her sprout a tusk. Despite the fact that according to Dumbledore, wizards had already grown very wary of Muggle contacts at the beginning of the century, it seems that Sir Nicholas not only rubbed elbows with Muggles but let them know about his magical abilities (at least, the Muggles he wanted to impress). Maybe the refusal to let him participate in the Headless Hunt was actually due to that display of stupidity? See www .jkrowling.com/textonly/en/extrastuff_view.cfm?id=11.

30. Apart from the basic studies by Christina Jessy Larner, *Enemies of God: The Witch-Hunt in Scotland* (Baltimore: John Hopkins University Press, 1981), and *Witchcraft and Religion: The Politics of Popular Belief* (Oxford: Blackwell, 1984), Brian P. Levack has edited two anthologies in his series *Articles on Witchcraft, Magic and Demonology*, vol. 6: *Witchcraft in England*, and vol. 7: *Witchcraft in Scotland* (New York and London: Garland Publishing, 1992), as well as *New Perspectives on Witchcraft, Magic, and Demonology*, vol. 3: *Witchcraft in the British Isles and New England* (London: Routledge, 2001), and is the author of *Witch-Hunting in Scotland: Law, Politics and Religion* (London: Routledge, 2008), here on James VI and the North Berwick Trial, 34–54; further see *Witchcraft and Belief in Early Modern Scotland*, edited by Julian Goodare, Lauren Martin, and Joyce Miller, Palgrave Historical Studies in Witchcraft and Magic (New York: Palgrave Macmillan, 2007).

31. Levack, *Witch-Hunting in Scotland*, 81–97.

32. Jessica Freeman, "Sorcery at Court and Manor: Margery Jourdemayne, the Witch of Eye Next Westminster," *Journal of Medieval History* 30 (2004): 343. Elanor Cobham is referred to in William Shakespeare's play *Henry VI*, part ii, act ii, scene 3.

33. Freeman, "Sorcery at Court and Manor," 352.

34. Ibid., 345, 351.

35. The newest edition and translation can be found in Henricus Institoris and Jacobus Sprenger, *Malleus Maleficarum*, vol. 1: *The Latin Text and Introduction*, vol. 2: *The English Translation*, ed. and trans. Christopher S. Mackay (Cambridge, UK: Cambridge University Press, 2006; the translation as a one-volume paperback 2009); see also Hans Peter Broedel, *The Malleus Maleficarum and the Construction of Witchcraft: Theology and Popular Belief*, Studies in Early Modern European History (New York: Manchester University Press, 2003).

36. Mackay, *Malleus Maleficarum*, 1, 4.

37. Stuart Clark, *Thinking with Demons: The Idea of Witchcraft in Early Modern Europe* (Oxford: Clarendon Press, 1997), 151–152; Scarre and Callow, *Witchcraft and Magic*, 17.

38. Alan Charles Kors and Edward Peters, eds., *Witchcraft in Europe, 400–1700: A Documentary History* (Philadelphia: University of Pennsylvania Press, 2001), 170–172. See also, Broedel, *The Malleus Maleficarum*, 113; and William E. Burns, *Witch Hunts in Europe and America: An Encyclopedia* (Westport, CT: Greenwood Press, 2003), 45–46, who refers to Jeffrey Burton Russell, *Witchcraft in the Middle Ages* (Ithaca, NY: Cornell University Press, 1972).

39. Behringer, *Witches and Witch-Hunts*, 83; see also Christina Larner, "The Crime of Witchcraft in Early Modern Europe," in *The Witchcraft Reader*, 205–212 (reprint of a chapter of Larner's 1984 book *Witchcraft and Religion*); for the changing intellectual understandings of magic and magical practice, see the highly instructive article by Michael David Bailey, "From Sorcery to Witchcraft: Clerical Conceptions of Magic in the Later Middle Ages," *Speculum: A Journal of Medieval Studies* 76, no. 4 (2001): 960–990.

40. The latest English translation can be found in Friedrich Spee von Langenfeld, *Cautio Criminalis, or A Book on Witch Trials*, trans. Marcus Hellyer, Studies in Early Modern German History (University of Virginia Press, 2003), vii, 16 (quote).

41. See the table of the largest witch hunts in Europe 1580–1680, in Behringer, *Witches and Witch-Hunts*, 130.

42. Bengt Ankarloo, Stuart Clark, and William Monter, *The Athlone History of Witchcraft and Magic in Europe*, vol. 4: *The Period of the Witch Trials* (London: Athlone Press, 2002), 13–16; Behringer, *Witches and Witch-Hunts*, 156–157. The enormous numbers still circulating in popular literature and magazines that go up to nine million victims go back to a very faulty eighteenth-century calculation that is based on one particular case study (Quedlinburg); see Wolfgang Behringer, "Neun Millionen Hexen: Entstehung, Tradition und Kritik eines populären Mythos," *Geschichte in Wissenschaft und Unterricht* 49 (1998): 664–685.

43. For a concise case study on Junius, see Apps and Gow, *Male Witches*, 76–89.

44. Stuart Clark has pointed out that inversion was not particular to witchcraft; see Clark, "Inversion, Misrule and the Meaning of Witchcraft," *Past and Present* 87 (1980): 98–127, reprinted in *The Witchcraft Reader*, 151.

45. Roper, *Witch Craze*, 82–103 (intercourse with female witches).

46. Bailey, "Medieval Concepts of the Witches' Sabbath"; Cohn, *Europe's Inner Demons*, 206–224. See, further, Carlo Ginzburg, *Ecstasies. Deciphering the Witches' Sabbath*, trans. from the Italian by Raymond Rosenthal (Chicago: University of Chicago Press, 1989); and—on the since then famous Benandanti—Carlo Ginzburg, *The Night*

Battles: Witchcraft and Agrarian Cults in the Sixteenth and Seventeenth Centuries, trans. from the Italian by John and Anna Tedeschi (Baltimore: Johns Hopkins University Press, 1992), who argues for traces of shamanistic cults; see also Wolfgang Behringer, *Chonrad Stoecklin und die Nachtschar. Eine Geschichte aus der frühen Neuzeit* (Munich and Zurich: Piper, 1994), published in English as *Shaman of Obersdorf: Chonrad Stoeckhlin and the Phantoms of the Night*, trans. H. C. Erik Midelfort, Studies in Early Modern German History (Charlottesville: University of Virginia Press, 2007), particularly 151–154 (referring to the German edition).

47. Robert Rowland, "'Fantasticall and Devilishe Persons': European Witch-Beliefs in Comparative Perspective," in *Early Modern European Witchcraft*, 165–167, argues convincingly for the pact with the devil, the Sabbath, and the *maleficium* as the three main features of early modern witchcraft, into which the other qualities such as flight and sexual intercourse are integrated. See also, Cohn, *Europe's Inner Demons*, 99–102.

48. Éva Pócs, *Between the Living and the Dead: A Perspective on Witches and Seers in the Early Modern Age* (Budapest: Central European University Press, 1999), 9–11.

49. Behringer, *Hexenverfolgung in Bayern*, 169–195, which has a wonderful case study on the moments and/or the events that triggered several large-scale witch hunts in 1590.

50. For inquisitors in Italy and Spain, see Ankarloo, Clark, and Monter, *The Athlone History of Witchcraft and Magic*, vol. 4, 44–49; on the role of the Roman Inquisition, see Rainer Decker, "Gerichtsorganisation und Hexenprozeßrecht der römischen Inquisition. Neue Quellenfunde zu Theorie und Praxis," in *Hexenprozesse und Gerichtspraxis*, eds. Herbert Eiden and Rita Voltmer, Trierer Hexenprozesse, Quellen und Darstellungen, 6 (Trier: Paulinus Verlag, 2002), 455–474. For other regions, see Ankarloo, Clark, and Monter, *The Athlone History of Witchcraft and Magic*, vol. 4, 22–23 (Germany).

51. For a concise survey of the witch persecution of the sixteenth and seventeenth centuries, see Scarre and Callow, *Witchcraft and Magic*, 21–28.

52. Rolf Schulte, *Man as Witch: Male Witches in Central Europe*, trans. from the German by Linda Froome-Döring, Palgrave Historical Studies in Witchcraft and Magic (Basingstoke and New York: Palgrave Macmillan, 2009); Apps and Gow, *Male Witches*; see also Clark, *Thinking with Demons*, 106–133; Clark, "The 'Gendering' of Witchcraft in French Demonology: Misogyny or Polarity?" *French History* 5 (1991): 426–437; Bailey, *Battling Demons*, 48–53. For a focus on female witches, see Lyndal Roper, *Witch Craze: Terror and Fantasy in Baroque Germany* (New Haven: Yale University Press, 2004), particularly 125–178; and Walter Stephens, *Demon Lovers: Witchcraft, Sex, and the Crisis of Belief* (Chicago: University of Chicago Press, 2002), particularly 32–57, who, however, bases his reasoning solely on the *Malleus Maleficarum*.

53. For Iceland, where the witch craze struck rather late and claimed up to 90 percent male victims, see Kirsten Hastrup, "Iceland: Sorcerers and Paganism," in *Early Modern European Witchcraft: Centres and Peripheries*, ed. Bengt Ankarloo and Gustav Henningsen (Oxford: Clarendon Press, 1998), 383–401, particularly 399; Ankarloo, Clark, and Monter, *The Athlone History of Witchcraft and Magic*, vol. 4, 84–85. See also the table of witchcraft persecutions by sex by Apps and Gow, *Male Witches*, 45. For research that debunks the older idea that witches were targeted because they were "wise women," see Bailey, *Battling Demons*, 49; David Harley, "Historians as Demonologists: The Myth of the Midwife Witch," in *New Perspectives on Witchcraft, Magic and Demonology 5: Witchcraft, Healing and Popular Diseases*, 49–74 (reprinted from 1990). See also, Christina Larner, "Was Witch-Hunting Woman-Hunting?" in *The Witchcraft Reader*, 273–275.

54. Behringer, *Hexenverfolgung in Bayern*, 341–355, 411.

55. While it is not explicitly stated that this institute is a school, J. K. Rowling has asserted in an interview in 2000 (www.accio-quote.org/articles/2000/0700-swns-alfie.htm) that there is a school for the American pupils, which would be mentioned in book 4. Because the Salem Institute is the only American organization that is mentioned in said book, it seems quite safe to assume that the school is housed there. The many scholarly and popular works on Salem include Mary Beth Norton, *In the Devil's Snare: The Salem Witchcraft Crisis of 1692* (New York: Vintage paperbacks, 2003); and the still essential studies by Bernard Rosenthal, *Salem Story: Reading the Witch Trials of 1692*, Cambridge Studies in American Literature and Culture (Cambridge, UK: Cambridge University Press, 1995); and Paul S. Boyer and Stephen Nissenbaum, *Salem Possessed: The Social Origins of Witchcraft* (Cambridge: Harvard University Press, 1974), who also edited the three-volume set of *The Salem Witchcraft Papers* (New York: Da Capo Press, 1977), available online at http://etext.virginia.edu/salem/witchcraft/texts/transcripts.html. The reader *Witches of the Atlantic World* has dedicated four chapters on Salem ("A Case Study of the Primary Documents," "Historians' Commentaries on the Salem Case," "Medical and Psychological Interpretations," and "The Salem Legacy"), 355–524. For other witchcraft accusations in New England, see, basically, Carol F. Karlsen, *The Devil in the Shape of a Woman: Witchcraft in Colonial New England* (New York: Norton, 1987); and Richard Godbeer, *The Devil's Dominion: Magic and Religion in Early New England* (Cambridge, UK: Cambridge University Press, 1992).

56. For a detailed study of a pro and con discussion, see Wolfgang Behringer, *Hexenverfolgung in Bayern. Volksmagie, Glaubenseifer und Staatsräson in der Frühen Neuzeit* (Munich: Oldenbourg, rev. ed. 1997), 405–410. An English translation was published by Cambridge University Press as *Witchcraft Persecutions in Bavaria: Popular Magic, Religious Zealotry, and Reason of State in Early Modern Europe*; all quotes here refer to the German edition.

57. Behringer, *Witches and Witch-Hunts*, 165–195.

58. Behringer, *Hexenverfolgung in Bayern*, 228.

59. Levack, *Witch-Hunting in Scotland*, 131.

60. Wolfgang Petz, *Die letzte Hexe. Das Schicksal der Anna Maria Schwägelin* (Frankfurt a.M.: Campus Verlag, 2007).

61. Historisches Lexikon der Schweiz, www.hls-dhs-dss.ch/texles/d/D43539.php.

62. Behringer, *Witches and Witch-Hunts*, 196–228.

PART TWO

After the Statute of Secrecy
Parallel Worlds

Upon the signature of the International Statute of Secrecy . . .
wizards went into hiding for good. It was natural, perhaps, that
they formed their own small communities within a community.

—Bathilda Bagshot, *A History of Magic,*
quoted in *Deathly Hallows,* 318–319

Was Voldemort a Nazi?

Death Eater Ideology and National Socialism

Nancy R. Reagin

Lizo Mzimba: "Voldemort's a half-blood too."
J. K. Rowling: "Like Hitler! See! I think it's the case that the biggest bully takes their own defects and they put them on someone else."

—Interview with BBC *Newsround* in fall 2000[1]

Was Lord Voldemort really like Adolf Hitler? Were the Death Eaters' ideas similar to those of the Nazis?[2] It seems clear that J. K. Rowling intended to suggest very strong parallels in the Harry Potter series between Tom Riddle and the man whose name is a byword for evil, and the followers of each. Rowling compared Hitler to Voldemort in more than one interview, and her readers had picked up on the similarities between the Death Eaters and the Nazis years before *Deathly Hallows*—which contains scenes that seem to be modeled on the history of Nazi

Germany—was published. Rowling herself sees the two groups as having very similar worldviews:

> The expressions "pure-blood," "half-blood" and "Muggle-born" have been coined by people to whom these distinctions matter, and express their originators' prejudices. As far as somebody like Lucius Malfoy is concerned, for instance, a Muggle-born is as "bad" as a Muggle. Therefore Harry would be considered only "half" wizard, because of his mother's grandparents.
>
> If you think this is far-fetched, look at some of the real charts the Nazis used to show what constituted "Aryan" or "Jewish" blood. I saw one in the Holocaust Museum in Washington when I had already devised the "pure-blood," "half-blood," and "Muggle-born" definitions and was chilled to see that the Nazis used precisely the same warped logic as the Death Eaters. A single Jewish grandparent "polluted" the blood, according to their propaganda.[3]

It seems likely that both Hitler and Voldemort would have rejected this comparison. We can be sure that Voldemort would have resented any comparison with a Muggle, while Hitler would have thought that anyone who staged a coup to gain control over a population of (probably) less than ten thousand—and then held on to power for less than a year—was a piker.

Moreover, Hitler was not a "half-blood," although Rowling was voicing a widely shared belief about his ancestry in her interview.[4] More important, Voldemort had none of Hitler's political charisma and power as a speaker: Hitler's speeches often threw his audiences into raptures, whereas Voldemort avoided any public appearances. Given how Voldemort looked, this was probably for the best. And while Hitler did have some of his followers arrested and shot, he never (as far as we know) had them eaten by a giant snake.

Yet although the resemblance between Voldemort and Hitler (at least, on a personal level) is not a striking one, there are certainly parallels between the ideology of Voldemort's followers and that of the National Socialists. The systems that both attempted to implement have marked similarities, although they are hardly comparable in scope or scale. But then again, Voldemort had less than a year to realize his ideas, and he seems to have spent most of those months looking for a better wand.

Hitler was, unfortunately, not unique in his atrocities. He had contemporaries who were equally vicious, such as Josef Stalin. Rowling probably chose to use symbols and language that would remind her audience of Hitler (instead of some other historical villain) because the Nazis are a sort of historical shorthand that all readers would understand; she thus invoked a fictional scenario with particular ideas about power and social hierarchies, good and evil, and political movements.[5] What is distinctive about Hitler and the Nazis among fascist movements—what made them such a useful comparison for Rowling—was their racial policies. Nazi Germany was what historians call "a racial state": very similar to what Dolores Umbridge and other pureblood extremists were trying to build in Deathly Hallows.[6]

Toujours Pur?

"Come on, Harry, haven't you seen enough of this house to tell what kind of wizards my family were?" said Sirius testily.

"Were—were your parents Death Eaters as well?"

"No, no, but believe me, they thought Voldemort had the right idea, they were all for the purification of the wizarding race, getting rid of Muggle-borns and having pure-bloods in charge. They weren't alone, either, there were quite a few people, before Voldemort showed his true colors, who thought he had the right idea about things."

—Order of the Phoenix, 112[7]

In creating a New Order in Deathly Hallows, Umbridge and her allies in the Ministry of Magic were expanding and reworking what seems to have been a long-established set of pureblood prejudices regarding magical ability. Wizarding society ought to be a hierarchy that included several categories of persons, by such pureblood reckoning: purebloods with magical ability; purebloods who were Squibs (Squibs are not quite Muggles, because they are able to see magical beings and Hogwarts itself); "half-bloods," a term that is apparently not very pejorative, because Severus Snape uses it to refer to himself in *Half-Blood Prince*; and Muggle-born magical folk at the very bottom ("Mudbloods" is the insulting term for such people).[8] Most wizards and witches, according to what Ron Weasley tells Harry and Hermione Granger, are of "mixed ancestry," because there are very few pureblood families left.

A consciousness of ancestry—and of categorizing people by the amount of magical ancestry they possess—must be very common in Harry's world, because almost all of the witches and the wizards we see use most of the terms listed previously quite unself-consciously, with the exception of the insulting "Mudblood." Yet although Harry hears these terms, there is evidence of a change in popular attitudes toward these categories in wizarding society in the century before Harry's time.

While some extremists in the magical community campaigned to persuade the Ministry to classify Muggles as beasts rather than human beings, Sirius Black's parents and other traditionalist pure-bloods considered wizards to be an entirely separate race from humans ("the wizarding race"). Yet there must have been a high rate of intermarriage between purebloods and Muggle-born or half-bloods for several generations before Harry's birth to produce the large number of people with mixed ancestry whom he meets; this argues that many purebloods had rejected the Black family's world-view. The stigma attached to producing a Squib seems to have less-ened, too, because Ron's aunt Muriel and Elphias Doge tell Harry (at Bill Weasley and Fleur Delacour's wedding reception) that during the nineteenth century, the existence of a Squib child used to be "hushed up" by pureblood families, who saw these children as a shameful family secret (*DH*, 155).

But Wait: Isn't Grindelwald the German Villain Here?

Gellert Grindelwald's ideas also seem to have been rooted in this older set of pureblood prejudices, and it can sometimes be difficult to sort out which wizard is supposed to be more similar to Hitler:

Voldemort or Grindelwald? In 1899, the attractive young Gellert met Albus Dumbledore (who had just taken his N.E.W.T.s), and the two entered into a brief but passionate relationship, agreeing that wizards should revoke (or overthrow?) the Statute of Secrecy in order to institute wizarding rule over Muggles "for the greater good." Dumbledore noted in the letter reprinted by Rita Skeeter that Grindelwald claimed, "Wizard dominance [was] FOR THE MUGGLES' OWN GOOD—this, I think is the crucial point. Yes, we have been given power and yes, that power gives up the right to rule, but it also gives us responsibilities over the ruled." (DH, 357)

This approach does constitute a charming departure from the later language of Voldemort and his supporters, which veered between brutal domination and (in the Ministry during Deathly Hallows) a chillingly flat and bureaucratic phrasing. Yet although it expresses an old-fashioned sense of wizarding noblesse oblige, the intent to establish a hierarchy based on "pure" ancestry still seems clear.[9]

In several other ways, Grindelwald seems designed to remind the reader of Hitler. Dumbledore defeated Grindelwald in the same year that Hitler was finally defeated by Britain (and her allies): in 1945. Both Grindelwald and Hitler mounted a scheme of sweeping conquests. Grindelwald also has a Germanic name (it is the name of a small village in Switzerland, in fact) and studied at Durmstrang.

The exact location of Durmstrang is never mentioned in the Harry Potter series. It seems to be a community that is home to a mélange of Slavic and German languages and cultural influences and is almost certainly located somewhere in Central or Central Eastern Europe. Because the wizarding community in this region would have separated from the Muggle world long before World War II, there is no reason for German-speaking wizards to ever have left or been expelled from the area (as happened with Muggle ethnic Germans after 1945). Durmstrang thus has pupils with German names and others who seem to be Slavic speakers, such as Viktor Krum. The wand maker patronized by most of its pupils, Gregorovitch, has a Slavic name, although members of his household speak German (DH, 232–233).[10]

Both Hitler and Grindelwald were from German-speaking Europe and were defeated in the watershed year of 1945 by British opponents (although the British had considerable help, in Hitler's case). The final parallel would seem to be in their foreign policy: both attempted to conquer populations outside their own communities, something that Voldemort did not seem to have any systematic plan for. Dumbledore tells Harry when the two meet at "King's Cross" in *Deathly Hallows* that Grindelwald sought the Resurrection Stone in order to raise "an army of Inferi," with the ultimate goal of "Muggles forced into subservience. We wizards triumphant. Grindelwald and I the glorious leaders of the revolution." (*DH*, 716) In scale, this comes closer to Hitler's attempts to conquer most of Europe than anything we see Voldemort attempting in *Deathly Hallows*, where almost all of the action is interior to the wizarding world.

Voldemort's New Order

Voldemort came to power using quite different means than did Hitler, and once in control, he seems to have been most concerned with safeguarding his own personal power and immortality. He spends a good deal of that year tracking down the Elder Wand and checking on the Horcruxes' safety, once he realizes that Harry is searching for them.

Although Voldemort seems to have focused primarily on the Elder Wand during *Deathly Hallows*, he was certainly willing to let his followers pursue their vision of pureblood superiority while he was abroad. He had made use of preexisting prejudices among those at the top of wizarding society (such as Sirius's parents) during his schooldays and thereafter to build a following, and then, starting in the 1950s, he inducted *their* children into the organization known later as the Death Eaters.

After Voldemort's supporters seized control of the Ministry, they went to town while their master was off trying to upgrade his wand, and it is in the New Order created by the likes of Yaxley and Dolores Umbridge—glimpsed by Harry during his Polyjuiced visits to the Ministry and Diagon Alley—that we see the most striking parallels with Nazi Germany during the mid- and late 1930s. Harry spends most of *Deathly Hallows* on the run—at 12 Grimmauld, in a tent, or at Shell Cottage—and we only get a good look at how the wizarding world is being restructured under Voldemort during the Trio's break-in at the Ministry and from occasional snippets thereafter. What we do see is very suggestive and offers a basis for extrapolation about what was happening to Muggle-borns and half-bloods in the broader wizarding world while Harry was in pursuit of the Horcruxes.

The Rule of Law? Edicts and Decrees in the Racial State

Lupin pointed at the *Daily Prophet*.

"Look at page two." [. . .]

"Muggle-born Register!" she read aloud. "'The Ministry of Magic is undertaking a survey of so-called 'Muggle-borns' the better to understand how they came to possess magical secrets.

"Recent research undertaken by the Department of Mysteries reveals that magic can only be passed from person to person when Wizards reproduce. Where no proven Wizarding ancestry exists, therefore, the so-called Muggle-born is likely to have obtained magical power by theft or force.

"'The Ministry is determined to root out such usurpers of magical power, and to this end has issued an invitation to every so-called Muggle-born to present themselves for interview by the newly appointed Muggle-born Registration Commission.'"

—*Deathly Hallows*, 209

As soon as the National Socialists came to power in Germany in the spring of 1933, they issued a slew of edicts, decrees, and new policies aimed at isolating and impoverishing Jewish Germans and other so-called undesirables. Some historians call this a "cold pogrom." The word *pogrom* was borrowed from the campaigns of mob violence against Jews in the Russian Empire that forced many Russian Jews to emigrate to the United States and elsewhere

between 1880 and 1920. The Nazis' persecution-through-decree
was a slower, relentless—and, on the surface, usually nonvio-
lent and hence "cold"—way to marginalize and drive out Jewish
citizens.

By 1939, a blizzard of new decrees affected almost every aspect
of German Jews' lives and the lives of others whom the Nazis considered undesirable. Health insurance funds would no longer reim-
burse Jewish physicians for their services. The civil service fired all
Jewish employees. Jewish tax consultants lost their licenses. The
government imposed a 1.5 percent quota on "non-Aryans'" university admissions and then banned Jewish students entirely a few
years later. Jewish attorneys were prohibited from serving as officers
of the court and then from the practice of law. There was a gradual
process of excluding Jews from every profession. Many Nazi decrees
also restricted women's opportunities regarding education and the
professions, because the Nazis were sexist as well as racist, an area
where the Death Eaters do not seem to be parallel.

At first, these decrees contained some loopholes, but those were
gradually closed, and the restrictions multiplied like noxious dox-
ies. By the late 1930s, German Jews could not go to beaches, parks,
sports stadiums, restaurants, theaters, and cinemas, nor could their
children attend public schools. "No Jews allowed" became a commonly posted sign, although many Jewish Germans (often afraid
of being refused service or humiliated) had begun to avoid restaurants and theaters even before they were legally prohibited from
setting foot in many public spaces. At the same time, Nazi authorities put enormous economic pressure on Jewish-owned businesses,
forcing them to pay fines or new taxes or to sell out to "Aryans" at
a fraction of their property's true value, a process referred to as the
"Aryanization" of a business or organization. As a result, by 1938
the number of Jewish-owned businesses in Nazi Germany had been
reduced by two-thirds.[11]

The Nazis' most famous racist laws were the Nuremberg
Decrees of 1935. The government issued the decrees to create a
legal definition of who was and was not Jewish, because this was
not always evident. Since the nineteenth century, there had been

many intermarriages between German Jews and Christians, and some Jews had converted to Christianity in order to escape anti-Semitism and to obtain better social and professional opportunities.[12] As a result, one historian estimates that although there were about half a million Jews in Germany in 1933, there were also hundreds of thousands of Germans in 1933 who had a Jewish parent or grandparent or who had parents, grandparents, or great-grandparents who had converted to Christianity (and whose families had been Christians for generations, but whom the Nazis saw as Jews, due to their ancestry).[13] The Nazi leadership wanted to label and identify all of these citizens, in order to use these categories as a foundation for persecution.

In *Deathly Hallows*, the Ministry issues a set of decrees that seeks a parallel goal: to identify those who have wizarding ancestry and those who don't. When Remus Lupin visits Harry at 12 Grimmauld, he explains that

> unless you can prove that you have at least one close Wizarding relative, you are now deemed to have obtained your magical power illegally and must suffer the punishment. [. . .] Attendance [at Hogwarts] is now compulsory for every young witch and wizard. That was announced yesterday. It's a change, because it was never obligatory before. [. . .] This way, Voldemort will have the whole Wizarding population under his eye from a young age. And it's also another way of weeding out Muggle-borns, because students must be given Blood Status—meaning that they have proven to the Ministry that they are of Wizard descent—before they are allowed to attend. (*DH*, 209–210)

The Muggle-borns were the first and primary targets of the Ministry, but there were other magical folk whom the purebloods sought to subordinate, as well. Both the National Socialists and the pureblood supremacists thought in terms of hierarchies that contained a number of categories (with themselves at the top of the pecking order). The golden Fountain of Magical Brethren that

Harry saw in the Ministry's Atrium in *Order of the Phoenix* reflected this magical hierarchy, with its "noble-looking" wizard and beautiful witch holding their wands aloft, who were gazed at adoringly by the (wandless) goblin, the centaur, and the house-elf.

Similarly, the National Socialists proposed an elaborate set of "racial" classifications that targeted more than only Jewish Germans. Their schemes of identifying, labeling, and discriminating against a long list of "undesirables" (both political and "hereditary") also included the Sinti and the Roma ("gypsies"), gays and lesbians, Germans with "hereditary illnesses" (for example, the mentally ill or those with alcoholism), Jehovah's Witnesses, communists, socialists, people with "asocial" tendencies, and others.[14]

Lupin, who falls into another category of the Ministry's "undesirables," offers an acute and dispassionate analysis of why Voldemort's "cold pogrom" is so effective. By operating within the bounds of what is apparently the "law," bureaucratic process, and the regular means of choosing a leader (because Voldemort allows the Imperius'ed Pius Thicknesse to operate as Minister), Lupin tells Harry that Voldemort has not "provoked open rebellion. Remaining masked has created confusion, uncertainty, and fear." Because the regime change seems to be operating legally, Lupin observes that the wizarding population is tolerating the fact that "Muggle-borns are being rounded up as we speak." (*DH*, 208–209)

Left-wing opponents of the Nazis understood this dynamic very well: many waited for a moment when the National Socialists were clearly staging an illegal overthrow of the Weimar government, so that they could protest and resist a Nazi coup. Yet although Hitler and the Nazis came to power using extraconstitutional means (because the "Enabling Act" they passed was akin to putting the previous German constitution under Imperius), they seemed to be operating under the rule of law as they went about establishing their New Order. As in the wizarding world, the moment for organized protest against a clear overthrow of the previous government never arrived, because each of these New Orders was being established under the rule of law and implemented by decrees.

The cold pogroms operated under a veneer of law and bureaucracy, but in both Nazi Germany and the fictional world of Voldemort, they were also accompanied by frequent and unpredictable acts of lawlessness. Those the regime despised had lost the ordinary protections of civil law and society, both large and small, and were therefore vulnerable to all kinds of exploitation. The postman could decide not to deliver a Jewish German family's mail, but instead leave it to be trampled on the apartment lobby floor or in the mud, knowing that the family risked being denounced to the government if they filed a complaint. Non-Jewish landlords or suppliers could refuse to honor contracts with Jewish tenants and businesspeople, because for a Jew to appeal to a civil court would be fruitless, even dangerous.[15] Lawlessness could easily escalate into violence: Jewish citizens were arrested and tortured on the flimsiest of pretexts. A Jewish woman who lived in Nuremberg during the 1930s remembered that "the most frightening fact at this moment was being deprived of the protection of law. Anybody could accuse you of anything — and you were lost."[16]

A similar sort of lawlessness lurks just beneath the surface in the wizarding world during *Deathly Hallows*. When Harry is shocked at the Death Eaters' use of brute force against Nymphadora Tonks's parents, Lupin tries to make him realize how rapidly the constraints of civil society have broken down: "What you've got to realize, Harry, is that the Death Eaters have got the full might of the Ministry on their side now. [...] They've got the power to perform brutal spells without fear of identification or arrest." (*DH*, 206–207) Fenrir Greyback can now terrorize parents by threatening their children without hindrance. Just as the Nazis took female relatives of political opponents hostage, to force politically active Jewish or socialist men to give themselves up, the Death Eaters also imprisoned Luna Lovegood in order to put pressure on her father. As Lee Jordan reported on the underground resistance radio broadcast *Potterwatch*, "Muggle slaughter is becoming little more than a recreational sport under the new regime." (*DH*, 439)

What's on *Your* Family Tapestry?
Blood Status and Denunciation

"This lot need to leave before you seal the exits," said Harry with
all the authority he could muster.

The group of wizards in front of him looked at one another.

"We've been told to seal all exits and not let anyone—"

"Are you contradicting me?" Harry blustered. "Would you
like me to have your family tree examined, like I had Dirk
Cresswell's?"

"Sorry!" gasped the balding wizard, backing away. "I didn't
mean nothing, Albert, but I thought . . . I thought they were in
for questioning and . . ."

"Their blood is pure," said Harry, and his deep voice echoed
impressively through the hall. "Purer than many of yours, I
daresay. Off you go," he boomed to the Muggle-borns, who
scurried forward into the fireplaces and began to vanish in pairs.

—*Deathly Hallows*, 265–266

Lawlessness and rule by decree soon produced fear and social frag-
mentation in both cultures, as people withdrew from acquaintances
and colleagues, anxious that a joke or an incautious comment—
saying Voldemort's name in a moment of anger, for example—
could have serious consequences. The National Socialists didn't
need to put a Taboo jinx on jokes about Hitler, because denunciation by someone who overheard you was often enough.

Soon after the Nazis came to power in 1933, for example,
Dr. Kuno Ruhmann went to a party in the small town of Northeim;
after having a few drinks, he did a good imitation of Hitler. His host-
ess reported him to local Nazi headquarters the next day, and soon
the townspeople realized that parties might not be safe amusements
under the new regime. "Social life was cut down enormously—you
couldn't trust anyone any more," said one person.[17]

Wizards and witches very quickly came to similar conclusions,
according to Remus Lupin:

"There has been such a dramatic change in Ministry policy
in the last few days, and many are whispering that Voldemort

must be behind it. However, that is the point: They whisper. They daren't confide in each other, not knowing whom to trust; they are scared to speak out, in case their suspicions are true and their families are targeted." (*DH*, 208)

Their fears were well founded, because the Death Eaters' push to determine the Blood Status of all magical folk (and punish Muggle-borns) went steadily forward. Those who tried to conceal Muggle ancestry were vulnerable to being found out and turned in, because in such a small population, those who had "unusual" (not traditional wizarding) names must have stuck out. Dirk Cresswell, one of Arthur Weasley's colleagues in the Ministry, apparently tried this and was denounced by Albert Runcorn, the Death Eater Harry impersonates in his visit to the Ministry in *Deathly Hallows*, much to Weasley's disgust: "'Don't pretend, Runcorn,' said Mr. Weasley fiercely. 'You tracked down the wizard who faked his family tree, didn't you? [. . .] [I]f he survives Azkaban, you'll have to answer to him.'" (*DH*, 255)

Faked pureblood family trees were nothing new, however: Muggle Germans had produced plenty of their own during the 1930s. The National Socialist regime made proof of "Aryan" ancestry a requirement for many government benefits and positions; those who wanted higher-ranking positions in the Party or the government (for example, SS officers) might even have to produce proof of "pure" ethnic German ancestry going back to 1750. At first, Christian clergy and staff were hired by the state to compile enormous card indexes listing the names of those who had converted from Judaism to Christianity (often several generations back) or who had mixed ancestry.

Ultimately, the task of investigating the ancestry of every person in Germany proved so large that the Nazi government established the Kinship Research Office to collect records and issue so-called Aryan Passes, which summarized a person's ancestry. Germans needed to show proof of "Aryan" ancestry so often that a huge demand was created for professional genealogical researchers, who could do the work of tracking down your great-grandparents' baptismal and marriage records (probably off in a small church office somewhere) for you.[18] In a sense, these researchers—who would research all of the records and compile a tidy "pureblood" family tree for you to show to an employer or the state—resembled a macabre sort of real estate title searcher.

To mandate such documentation is to invite falsification, of course, as those whose ancestry is not completely pure scrambled to cover their tracks. Ron saw the implications immediately, when Lupin laid out the new Muggle-born registration regulations to him, Harry, and Hermione during a visit to 12 Grimmauld Place:

> Ron glanced at Hermione, then said, "What if purebloods and half-bloods swear a Muggle-born's part of their family? I'll tell everyone Hermione's my cousin—"
>
> Hermione covered Ron's hand with hers and squeezed it.
>
> "Thank you, Ron, but I couldn't let you—"
>
> "You won't have a choice," said Ron fiercely, gripping her hand back. "I'll teach you my family tree so you can answer questions on it." (*DH*, 209–210)

Germans with "mixed" ancestry found other ways around the Aryan Pass requirement during the 1930s. One man employed at the Central Jewish Archive specialized in "finding" a (now-dead) Aryan man who might have had a real or (more likely) fictitious affair with a Jewish female ancestor. The "discovery" of such a "German-blooded" person in someone's family tree would thus render a current German citizen (someone who was either Jewish or with mixed ancestry) apparently "less" Jewish in Nazi eyes.[19] Had the Death Eater regime lasted somewhat longer, one can easily imagine Umbridge and her allies instituting a Wizarding Pass for their own community and the Weasley twins finding spells to create false passes.

But what if you couldn't produce a pass for love or money, like Mrs. Cattermole, who was called in for questioning by Umbridge's Muggle-Born Registration Commission? Her pureblood husband, Reg, was desperate to help her when the Trio ambushed him, and

Ron took his place. The pressure on "mixed" marriages became horrendous in both Nazi Germany and the wizarding world under Voldemort, as "pureblood" or Christian spouses were pushed to leave their "undesirable" partners or made to pay a penalty if they refused to abandon their husbands or wives.

In *Deathly Hallows*, Death Eater Yaxley mocks Cattermole because his wife is a Muggle-born, asking, "Already given her up as a bad job, have you? Be sure and marry a pureblood next time." (*DH*, 243) In Nazi Germany, "Aryan" Germans who were married to Jews also faced threats to their jobs and public derision. Nonetheless, like Reg Cattermole, many (but not all) "Aryan" Germans refused to abandon their spouses despite the pressure.[20]

Yaxley sneered at the "half-blood" offspring of such unions when Mrs. Cattermole mentioned her three young children during her interrogation by Umbridge, saying that "the brats of Mudbloods do not stir our sympathies." (*DH*, 259) Even so, the Death Eaters don't seem to have been particularly concerned with punishing those who had only one wizarding parent. Because their theory was that all magical ability had to be inherited from a wizarding parent, this meant that half-bloods were not suspected of "stealing" a wizard's or a witch's magic. They were therefore allowed to attend Hogwarts and hold Ministry positions.

Here, the parallel to Nazi Germany breaks down. "Half-bloods" in Nazi Germany were called *Mischlinge* (the term was applied to anyone with one or two Jewish grandparents) and were treated better than "full Jews" but were not remotely equal to "Aryans" in their civil rights and social position.[21] Their situations varied enormously and were often full of painful, sharp-edged contradictions.

Helmut Krüger's mother was Jewish; his father was not. His father lost his job after the Nazis came to power, and Helmut's brother was forced out of his scouting troop and later dropped out of school because of harassment from teachers. Krüger joined the military during World War II, hoping to protect his mother by compiling a good military record. He received the Iron Cross for distinguished service and later recalled, "How can I explain what a decoration meant for me at that time? I believed I had saved myself and my mother for good."[22] Children might react quite differently, however, and even blame their parents for the constant harassment at school. One boy was angry at his Jewish mother "for the fact that I am being discriminated against in school" and supported the Nazis because he felt so alienated from his "Jewish part."[23] Because the Death Eaters believe that magic is inherited through reproduction, half-bloods in Harry's world seem to be protected from such treatment, even at the peak of Voldemort's reign.

The "Wandless" and Social Death

Yet those who were married to "Aryans" or were of mixed ancestry were, in most cases, still much better off in Nazi Germany than so-called "full Jews," who faced what some scholars have described as "social death" years before they were actually deported to the camps. The term *social death* comes from the work of Orlando Patterson, who used it to describe the position of slaves in a civil society, but this term is also useful in analyzing the position of Jews and other "racial undesirables" in Germany during the 1930s.

Through relentless propaganda inculcated in educational institutions, in popular culture, in "scientific" discussions, and elsewhere during a period of several years, the National Socialists had constructed a racial community (a *Volksgemeinschaft*) of so-called "Aryan" Germans and persuaded much of the nation that *they* belonged to this fictional community, which consisted only of Christian Germans of ethnic German ancestry. Jews or members of other minority groups could not be "Germans," according to this definition. German citizens of Jewish ancestry were therefore cast out of this community, excommunicated from both the body politic and daily social life. Social death included the social isolation, the economic destruction, and the political disenfranchisement of "undesirables," because they now stood outside of the moral community of those to whom one owed consideration or any moral duties.[24]

By the end of *Deathly Hallows*, the Muggle-born seem to be in a similar position: now wandless, they have been excluded from the community of those who are owed any consideration at all by "real" wizards who have documented magical ancestry. When the (mostly Polyjuiced) Trio approach Gringotts to steal Hufflepuff's cup, they see a group of these now wandless witches and wizards in Diagon Alley:

> A number of ragged people sat huddled in doorways. He heard them moaning to the few passersby, pleading for gold, insisting that they were really wizards. One man had a bloody bandage over his eye. [. . .]
>
> Though the Death Eater looked offended, he also seemed less suspicious. He glanced down at the man Ron had just Stunned.
>
> "How did it offend you?"
>
> "It does not matter, it will not do so again," said Hermione coolly.
>
> "Some of these wandless can be troublesome," said Travers. "While they do nothing but beg I have no objection, but one of them actually asked me to plead her case in the Ministry last week. 'I'm a witch, sir, I'm a witch, let me prove it to you!'" he said in a squeaky impersonation. "As if I was going to give her my wand." (DH, 525, 527)

The Muggle-born have now lost even the right to be referred to as "he" or "she," but are now referred to as "it," a sure sign that they are now completely dishonored in the eyes of Voldemort's supporters and are socially dead. Lacking wands, they cannot support themselves in the wizarding world, and (because they are now beggars) one assumes that the regime has confiscated their property as well. Taking their wands paves the way for their economic destruction in the same way that Nazi policies of "Aryanization" had done for German Jews, and the lack of a wand seems to stigmatize them almost as effectively as wearing a Star of David had for Jews.

Some readers of *Deathly Hallows* have objected that the speed with which Muggle-born are excluded from the wizarding community seems implausible, because it takes Voldemort's supporters only a few months to completely change what can be said and done, at least in public. Yet selective terror, widespread propaganda, and the fear of denunciation worked almost as rapidly in Germany after 1933. Sirius, describing the years just before Harry's birth, when the Death Eaters weren't even yet in charge of the Ministry and couldn't control education and popular culture (as the National Socialists could, after March 1933), tries to explain to Harry why some witches and wizards cooperated with them: "Imagine that Voldemort's powerful now. You don't know who his supporters are, you don't know who's working for him and who isn't; you know he can control people so that they do terrible things without being able stop themselves. You're scared for yourself, and your family, and your friends. Every week, news comes of more deaths, more disappearances, more torturing." (GOF, 27)

Selective terror was supported, in each case, by broad programs of "reeducation." In Nazi Germany's schools, pupils had to take courses in "racial studies," and Departments of Racial Studies were established at German universities. We can assume that the Muggle Studies courses taught by Alecto Carrow at Hogwarts worked toward similar ends. In Deathly Hallows, during Harry's visit to the Ministry, he caught a glimpse of the sorts of readings being prepared for these courses and for wider public education:

> Harry crept closer [. . .] and he slid a completed pamphlet from the pile beside a young witch. He examined it beneath the Invisibility Cloak. Its pink cover was emblazoned with a golden title:

> ### MUDBLOODS
> *and the Dangers They Pose*
> *to a Peaceful Pure-Blood Society*

> Beneath the title was a picture of a red rose with a simpering face in the middle of its petals, being strangled by a green weed with fangs and a scowl. (DH, 249)

Even a brief visit to the Ministry makes it clear to Harry that the Muggle-born would be better off leaving the wizarding world. After he rescues Mrs. Cattermole from Umbridge, he tells her, "Go home, grab your children, and get out, get out of the country if you've got to. Disguise yourselves and run. You've seen how it is, you won't get anything like a fair hearing here." (*DH*, 263) He advises all of the Muggle-born waiting for questioning outside to go abroad, if they can.

This was easier said than done, of course. Muggle-born witches and wizards had the enormous advantage, compared to German Jews, of being able to dispense with exit permissions and visas in order to enter Muggle Britain. Having been born in the Muggle world, they could presumably turn up in London and reacquire identity papers. German Jews found it much harder both to get permission to leave Germany and to find a new country that would accept them.[25]

If the situation of the Muggle-born was anything like the historical reality for German Jews, then the costs of leaving would have been daunting. German Jews had to leave homes, businesses, jobs, and property, often with no way to get a fair price for them. Perhaps the Ministry of Magic held auctions to sell off hastily abandoned homes and personal properties, as Nazi authorities did. The (former) neighbors of Jews who had fled Germany or been deported called these the "Jew auctions," and many eagerly snapped up bargains on linens, china, jewelry, and silver.

Muggle-borns might have found that like German Jews in new countries, their credentials would not easily translate into a new setting. No matter how many N.E.W.T.s you'd earned at Hogwarts, this wouldn't be a help in the Muggle world. German Jews found that many of their professional licenses or degrees, work history, and other sorts of training couldn't be put to much use in New York City or London. If the risks were the same as in Nazi Germany, however, many families other than the Cattermoles must have concluded that their only choice was to leave the wizarding world after Voldemort came to power.

But Draco's Not Really a Member of the
Hitler Youth, You Know

Yet while the wizarding world under Voldemort maps on to the situation of German Jews during the 1930s fairly closely—and little wonder, because Rowling clearly had this historical precedent in mind when she was writing *Deathly Hallows*—in many important respects, the Death Eaters were *not* like the National Socialists. To begin with, Nazi policies regarding women, sexuality, and the family were quite different from what Umbridge and her allies seem to have had in mind.

The National Socialists pursued a vigorous set of policies designed to push women out of careers that weren't "traditional" women's work and to force up the birth rate among "German-blooded" women. They instituted a quota for women in university admissions and ruled out some areas of study for female students altogether. The regime also offered working women interest-free "marriage loans" if they would quit their jobs and stay home when they got married. The Nazi government even attempted to compel or persuade women with "desirable" ancestry to bear more children by outlawing birth control and abortion and through massive pronatal propaganda campaigns.[26] There is no hint of any parallel policies toward witches in *Deathly Hallows*.

In addition, the Nazis targeted and persecuted gay and lesbian Germans of all ethnic backgrounds, because they condemned homosexuality as a deviation from what they considered to be "healthy" (that is, heterosexual) activity. Gay and lesbian Germans went deep into the closet during the 1930s, hiding in order to survive. Those who were caught were often sent to concentration camps and made to wear a pink triangle, part of the Nazis' color coding system for "undesirables," just as Jews had to wear a yellow Star of David.[27]

Whether the Death Eaters would have treated gay and lesbian wizards similarly is open to question, although it seems doubtful, given the fact that we don't see any new and sexist decrees targeting witches introduced in *Deathly Hallows*. How the wizarding world felt about gay and lesbian magical people is just another one of those aspects of magical society that we don't see much from Harry's point of view, so it's open to speculation. The fact that Dumbledore (who was gay, according to Rowling) never hints at this fact in any discussion in the series, and Rita Skeeter's snide allusions to his "shocking" "great new friendship" with the handsome Gellert Grindelwald in her biography of Dumbledore could also support the inference that gay wizards faced some social stigma (DH, 358). Or perhaps it was simply that Dumbledore chose not to share details about his private life with a pupil (Harry) and that Skeeter was, as always, acid-tongued. We can't know for certain. As far as one can tell, the Death Eaters did not develop anything similar to the Nazis' persecution of gay and lesbian Germans.

Beyond these important differences in laws and official targets of persecution, the Death Eaters don't seem to have tried to reorganize civil society in a comprehensive fashion, as the Nazis did. The Nazis created "affiliate" organizations for every imaginable professional and demographic group: National Socialist teachers' organizations, lawyers' associations, and so on, along with groups for every age and both sexes, such as the Hitler Youth. The Nazi Party itself was for the most dedicated National Socialists (or the most ambitious). Tens of millions of Germans joined such Nazi affiliate groups or were compelled to do so.

We don't see any comparable takeover of the magical world's civil society in *Deathly Hallows*. In part, this is explained by the fact that the wizarding world doesn't seem to possess much of a civil society (the sphere of organized social activity that is outside the family but not under the state's control). As Susan Halls notes in another chapter in this book, the Ministry of Magic seems to regulate many parts of life (for example, organized sports) that would be under the control of a private organization in the Muggle world. Yet another reason might be that the Death Eaters themselves don't seem much interested in formal organizations: there is no actual Pureblood Party, nor does Voldemort create any affiliate organizations apart from his Death Eaters (who seem to be a fairly small, trusted group of early supporters). Of course, simply by taking over the Ministry of Magic, the Death Eaters achieved a much greater degree of control than winning an election in the Muggle world would bring to the victors.

The Nurmengard Trials?

After Dumbledore defeated Grindelwald in 1945 and took the Elder Wand from him, Grindelwald was imprisoned in the topmost cell of Nurmengard Prison, a looming, jet-black tower. Grindelwald originally built the prison to house his enemies, and he carved his motto, "For the Greater Good," over its entrance, much as the Nazis had notoriously carved one of *their* mottos, "Arbeit Macht Frei" (work will set you free), over the entrance to a concentration camp. The name *Nurmengard* resembles that of Nuremberg, the town where a series of famous trials of former Nazis and other war criminals was held after World War II.

If the prison's name is any guide to go by, however, no thorough accounting or punishment of the Death Eaters' crimes took place after Voldemort's death: the Nuremberg Trials got a great deal of publicity, but they brought only a small number of perpetrators to justice, and indeed the selection of those tried there by the victorious Allies was almost arbitrary. Some of the people who had helped organize the Holocaust or committed other atrocities were tried at Nuremberg or in other tribunals established by the Allies in the various jurisdictions they established in defeated and occupied Germany. Yet many of those who had participated in crimes against Jews and other "undesirables" were able to escape any reckoning or got off relatively lightly.

The epilogue to *Deathly Hallows* doesn't give us any information about what happened to Death Eaters such as Lucius and Draco Malfoy, Avery, Amycus and Alecto Carrow, Mulciber, Nott, the Lestrange brothers, Yaxley, and those who were simply Voldemort supporters. Many Death Eaters survived the Battle of Hogwarts, and we're not sure how comprehensive the trials that *should* have followed actually were. The turmoil in the Ministry following two rapid regime changes in less than a year probably made any thorough purges less likely, because (as the Allies found when they sought to replace large numbers of Nazis in the German government) it is difficult to find a sufficient workforce of new, trained civil servants on short notice. Rowling has said in an interview that the Malfoys were simply allowed to go home after the Battle of Hogwarts, because they "weaseled their way out of trouble (again)."[28] She noted that Umbridge was tried and imprisoned, however, so perhaps some of those responsible for persecuting the Muggle-born were indeed punished.

A post-Voldemort society in which certain people who harshly persecuted the Muggle-born were themselves punished, while others—equally guilty—were allowed to go free would complete the considerable set of parallels between the wizarding world under Voldemort and Germany during the 1930s. Even so, we should remember that the scale and the scope of the crimes committed by these two regimes are hardly comparable: Voldemort and his supporters ruled over a tiny population, and the number of Muggle-borns persecuted by the Death Eaters is miniscule when we think of how many people fell victim to the Nazis. Hitler and the National Socialists carried out staggering programs of conquest and genocide that claimed millions of victims. In that sense, there really can be no comparison, and indeed there are many other important differences between the Death Eaters and the Nazis.

Yet what we witness in *Deathly Hallows* is chilling and horrid enough, although we see only small snippets—limited by Harry's perspective—of what was happening. We can assume that much worse was going on than what Harry actually saw firsthand: neighbors denouncing one another, the random use of terror, and a daily feast for the dementors that were employed by the Ministry. When we survey all of these parallels and think of the anguish and humiliation suffered by the Muggle-born whom Harry does *not* see, we are glad, finally, that the reminder often thrown at deeply engaged fans (sometimes by exasperated family members) is indeed true: these characters didn't *really* exist. Unfortunately, however, the historical counterparts they're modeled on were all too true.

Notes

1. A transcript of this interview can be found at www.accio-quote.org/articles/2000/fall00-bbc-newsround.html.

2. The literature on Hitler and National Socialism is far too vast to be mastered by any single person. For this essay, I have chosen English-language sources that are either considered classics in their area or that would serve as good introductions for a reader who wanted to learn more on a given topic.

3. From the FAQ at J. K. Rowling's official Web site, www.jkrowling.com/textonly/en/faq_view.cfm?id=58.

4. Hitler's father, Alois Hitler, was born out of wedlock, although he was later legitimized after the man who was presumably Alois's father married Alois's mother. It is thus possible that one of Hitler's grandparents was Jewish (although there is no particular reason to think so). The accusation that Hitler had some Jewish ancestry was first proposed by his political opponents later in his life, and although—as one judge famously observed—maternity is a fact, while paternity is an opinion, historians have not generally taken this assertion very seriously. Certainly, Hitler did not see himself as a "half-blood." See Ian Kershaw, *Hitler: A Biography* (New York: W. W. Norton, 2010).

5. I would like to thank Jennifer Hock for this insight.

6. The classic study of the distinctive features of Nazi racial policies is Michael Burleigh and Wolfgang Wippermann, *The Racial State: Germany 1933–1945* (New York: Cambridge University Press, 1993). See also Robert Gellately, *The Gestapo and German Society: Enforcing Racial Policy, 1933–1945* (Oxford: Oxford University Press, 1990).

7. All book quotes are taken from the American editions by J. K. Rowling as follows: *Goblet of Fire*, New York: A.A. Levine Books, 2000; *Order of the Phoenix*, New York: A.A. Levine Books, 2003; *Deathly Hallows*, New York: A.A. Levine Books, 2007.

8. When Hermione is attempting to pass herself off as Penelope Clearwater (when she, Harry, and Ron are caught by Fenrir Greyback in *Deathly Hallows*), she also calls herself a "half-blood."

9. We must remember the source here, because the letter was contained in Rita Skeeter's salacious exposé of Dumbledore. Even so, I am inclined to accept this as having been written by Dumbledore for several reasons. First, Skeeter's book includes an image of the original letter. Taken as a whole, the letter also seems too eager to do right by the Muggles for it to have been penned or heavily edited by Skeeter, who would have heightened the anti-Muggle tone, in order to make it more damning. Finally, discussing the letter with Harry, Hermione (usually a very reliable guide) clearly accepts that Dumbledore is its author.

10. I agree here with the persuasive speculations on the history and the location of Durmstrang offered by Eric Oppen in his essay on the languages probably spoken at Durmstrang; see www.hplex.info/essays/essay-durmstrang_lang.html. Oppen doesn't mention the medieval and Early Modern communities of Baltic Germans (who were prominent in the governance and trading routes of this area for centuries), but it seems quite possible that they were among the founders of Durmstrang.

11. The U.S. Holocaust Memorial Museum has a succinct summary of this legislation at www.ushmm.org/wlc/en/article.php?ModuleId=10005681. This site overall is a good source of straightforward, accurate summaries of information on the history of Jews in Nazi Germany. Another excellent online source containing many images and documents is maintained by the German Historical Institute at www.germanhistorydocs.ghi-dc.org/section.cfm?section_id=13.

12. For an analysis of intermarriage between Jews and Christians, see Marion A. Kaplan, *Between Dignity and Despair: Jewish Life in Nazi Germany*, 2nd ed. (New York: Oxford University Press, USA, 1998), 247–249; for the conversion of Jewish Germans to Christianity in previous generations, see Deborah Hertz, *How Jews Became Germans: The History of Conversion and Assimilation in Berlin* (New Haven: Yale University Press, 2009). Some of these conversions were no doubt done out of sincere conviction, but many were done to avoid anti-Semitic prejudice.

13. Estimates varied of how many people there were in Germany with mixed ancestry, but the Nazis themselves thought that there might be as many as 750,000 (a figure that historians think was probably exaggerated). See Kaplan, *Between Dignity and Despair*, 10–12, 247–249.

14. Many of these categories of "undesirables" are discussed in Burleigh and Wippermann, *The Racial State*; see also Robert Gellately and Nathan Stoltzfus, *Social Outsiders in Nazi Germany* (Princeton, NJ: Princeton University Press, 2001); Götz Aly, Peter Chroust, and Christian Pross, MD, *Cleansing the Fatherland: Nazi Medicine and Racial Hygiene*, 1st ed. (Baltimore: Johns Hopkins University Press, 1994).

15. Martyn Housden, *Resistance and Conformity in the Third Reich* (New York: Routledge, 1997), 142–143, recounts the story of a Nazi Party member, Heinrich Gross, who owed a Jewish merchant some money in 1935. When he met the merchant one day on the train, Gross began to insult and shout at him, then beat the merchant after both got off at their station. Needless to say, the merchant never attempted to collect on the debt.

16. Quoted in Kaplan, *Between Dignity and Despair*, 20.

17. William Allen, *Nazi Seizure of Power: The Experience of a Single German Town 1922–1945*, rev. (Danbury, CT: Franklin Watts, 1984), 188–189.

18. Hertz, *How Jews Became Germans*, 3–7.

19. Ibid., 6–7. From a Jewish standpoint this made no difference, because Jewish tradition reckons descent through the mother alone. Yet a hypothetical "Aryan" grandfather, who had allegedly had an affair with a Jewish grandmother, could help improve someone's position in Nazi Germany.

20. For an account of the most famous (and successful) protest staged by "Aryan" spouses against the Nazis' imprisonment of their Jewish spouses, see Nathan Stoltzfus, *Resistance of the Heart: Intermarriage and the Rosenstrasse Protest in Nazi Germany* (New Brunswick: Rutgers University Press, 2001); see also Kaplan, *Between Dignity and Despair*, 148–150.

21. The legal situation of *Mischlinge* was complicated, and their treatment depended on whether their parents had had them baptized as Christians, whom they themselves chose to marry, the attitude of their Christian relatives, and other factors. Kaplan, *Between Dignity and Despair*, 83–87; see also Stoltzfus, *Resistance of the Heart*, 57 ff.

22. Kaplan, *Between Dignity and Despair*, 87.

23. Ibid.

24. Kaplan, *Between Dignity and Despair*, 5; For an eloquent and accessible account of how Jews and others were thrust outside of the German "moral community" during this period, which prepared many Germans for the atrocities that would follow, see Claudia Koonz, *The Nazi Conscience* (Cambridge, MA: Belknap Press of Harvard University Press, 2005).

25. For the difficulties that Jews faced in getting out of Germany and into somewhere else and the reasons many might have been reluctant to leave, see Kaplan, *Between Dignity and Despair*, 62–73.

26. For Nazi policies on women and the family, see Nancy R. Reagin, *Sweeping the German Nation: Domesticity and National Identity in Germany, 1870–1945*, 1st ed. (New York: Cambridge University Press, 2008), 110–180; see also Lisa Pine, *Nazi Family Policy, 1933–1945* (Oxford: Berg Publishers, 1997); Dagmar Reese, *Growing up Female in Nazi Germany* (Ann Arbor: University of Michigan Press, 2006); see also the interviews with women from all walks of life in Alison Owings, *Frauen: German Women Recall the Third Reich* (New Brunswick: Rutgers University Press, 1995).

27. For the treatment of gays and lesbians in Nazi Germany, see Günter Grau and Claudia Shoppmann, *The Hidden Holocaust?: Gay and Lesbian Persecution in Germany 1933–1945*, Ill. (New York: Routledge, 1995); see also Geoffrey Giles, "The Institutionalization of Homosexual Panic in the Third Reich," in Robert Gellately and Nathan Stoltzfus, *Social Outsiders in Nazi Germany* (Princeton, NJ: Princeton University Press, 2001), 233–254.

28. See the interview transcript at www.the-leaky-cauldron.org/2007/7/30/j-k-rowling-web-chat-transcript.

"Magic Is Might"

How the Wizarding Government Gained Its Power

Janice Liedl

"But for heaven's sake—you're *wizards*! You can do *magic*!
Surely you can sort out—well—*anything*!"

—An anonymous Muggle prime minister, *Half-Blood Prince*, 24[1]

The frazzled Muggle prime minister quoted above during the crisis-ridden summer of 1996 was unsettled to learn from his magical counterparts, the outgoing Minister for Magic, Cornelius Fudge, and Fudge's replacement, Rufus Scrimgeour, that the Brockdale Bridge collapse and other disasters of that year weren't natural events but collateral damage from the Second Wizarding War. The poor PM had already struggled to cope with the knowledge that a world of magic users existed in parallel to ordinary Britain, governed by a Minister for Magic who communicated via talking portraits and traveled by a fireplace network. Although the PM was wrong about the extent of magical power, looked at another way, he was right about wizarding power. The Minister for Magic ruled with more independence and authority than any Muggle prime minister, who was constrained by a constitutional tradition that emphasized the rights of parliament, relied on a cabinet of colleagues, and managed the state through a growing network of ministries.

Despite the striking differences between the Muggle and the magical worlds, the parallel traditions and structures of their governments enabled the PM and the Minister for Magic to find some common ground. Rather like modern-day Britain, Harry Potter's wizarding world is full of bureaucratic ministries that enforce laws and promote education, as well as work to keep magic secret from Muggles. Yet despite the many similarities between a prime minister and a Minister for Magic or the Wizards' Council and the Great Council, the wizarding world was already developing its own distinctive government and political traditions, probably as far back as the time of Hogwarts' founding. Those traditions emphasized the need for separation and secrecy to protect the wizarding world, which also helped increase the independence and authority of its leaders through the centuries, so that by Harry's time, they exercised far greater power over their population than any Muggle politician ever could hope to achieve in a democratically elected government.

Wise Men and Wizengamots

A little more than a thousand years ago, around the time that Hogwarts was established, kings of England formally and frequently met with important subjects to consider pressing business. They summoned churchmen, such as bishops and abbots, as well as noblemen, such as *ealdormen* (chief royal officials in a shire or a county) or *thegns* (royal retainers or lesser aristocrats), to these gatherings. These advisers were described as *witan*, from the Old English term signifying "wisdom," and their meetings were sometimes referred to as *Witenagemots* or *witans* for short. The English didn't admire kings who ruled without council: Aethelred, the king from 978 until 1016, demonstrated that in his cultural legacy. Whereas his given name meant "noble council," later writers derided his reign for the lack of council or unwise council that led to England's conquest by Canute and dubbed him "Unraed" or, as he is sometimes known today, Ethelred the Unready.[2]

There was no set membership of Anglo-Saxon Witenagemots: on some occasions where simple land transactions were witnessed, no churchmen attended. At other times, such as during the reign of Athelstan in the early tenth century, as many as a hundred men were in attendance at the Witenagemot, including Welsh kings and ordinary priests. If someone was summoned to a meeting of the Witenagemot, whether as member or subject, and failed to attend, he or she could be fined or outlawed. To resist the authority of the Witenagemot was to subvert the authority of the monarch at its most awe-inspiring, and punishments were in proportion to that offense.

Witenagemots were held wherever the king thought convenient and appropriate: Winchester and Westminster were common sites for meetings, and London held the pride of place for the most frequent summoning of advisers, but gatherings were called as far afield as York, Gloucester, Bath, and Exeter. A variety of business was conducted at these meetings, from trials and legislative activity to seeking advice on important policy matters; in Harry's time, the Wizengamot still does all of these things. The Witenagemot also authenticated royal wills and significant grants of land, but all of its powers depended on what the king wanted the session to consider.[3] Witenagemots were not independent government institutions with set memberships, officers, privileges, and powers but simply meetings of advisers summoned at the king's convenience.

Given their close similarity in names, the Wizengamot must have its roots in the same culture and customs as the Anglo-Saxon Witenagemot. Like the Muggle-world version, it would have originated as a royal advisory council, but of wizards rather than ordinary subjects. These meetings could even have been held alongside the nonmagical Witenagemot or integrated seamlessly into the more mundane events of royal governance. If so, the magical attendees made sure to leave no written record of their attendance or wizarding status in the records that survive today. Equally possible, the Wizengamot could have evolved as another, smaller group called separately to meet with the monarch during times of magical problems or threats and assuming its own institutional identity over the course of the Middle Ages. This second possibility appears the most likely, given that the Wizengamot has endured with its traditional name and sense of identity right down to Harry's day.

Although the medieval Witenagemot remained clearly an advisory council dependent on the king, the Wizengamot endured as a key part of the wizarding world's government. Harry found the Wizengamot a serious concern when it summoned him in all of its state, as a court of wizarding law, to answer charges regarding the unlawful use of magic as an underage wizard. The summons that brought Harry to trial was based entirely on the authority of the wizarding world's institutions. Unlike a Muggle court, no monarch was mentioned in the summons or the trial account, but Cornelius Fudge, as Minister for Magic, was the highest authority invoked (although Amelia Bones, the head of the Department of Magical Law Enforcement and a member of the Wizengamot, presided over the trial). Given what we know about the Anglo-Saxon background, how could this rapid transformation of an advisory council into an independent institution of wizarding government have come about?

To answer that, we should understand what became of the Muggle world's Witenagemot. The years after 1066 saw Norman and Angevin rulers summon Witenagemots to advise the monarch, although in the Norman French of the day, *parliament* became the word most commonly used to describe these events. Yet these gatherings were hardly the elected bodies of representatives we associate with the word today. Indeed, they were sometimes not even elected, because major landowners could appoint members in some cases (called "pocket boroughs") or simply "arrange" for votes in thinly populated electoral districts (called "rotten boroughs") right up until 1832, when British electoral laws were reformed.[4]

Powerful subjects, seeking to maintain their influence on the king and the law, helped make Parliament central to the political identity of medieval England. Parliament resisted absolute royal power by promoting the role of noblemen, church leaders, and prominent citizens as advisers to the monarchy. In the Magna Carta (Latin for "Great Charter") of 1215, barons and church leaders detailed their freedoms, which also limited the king's power. One of the most important rights that the Magna Carta reinforced was the right to a trial by one's peers, as the concept was understood at the time: people of similar station or situation. Magna Carta not only supported the role of a jury of peers (for many nobles, this would be the lords in Parliament), but also promised special judgment according to the laws of your own people: Welsh law was to be used to try Welsh subjects, and Scottish rules for the Scots.[5]

The philosophy of Magna Carta would have justified the creation of a more robust system of separate governance for the wizarding subjects of the English monarchs. If the Welsh had a right to be judged by their own laws, so, too, did the wizarding subjects. Even more than the protection implied by the Magna Carta's clauses, though, British wizards might have sought something more enduring to protect them from a society that feared and loathed magic users. The era of Magna Carta for Muggles might well have inspired a wizarding-world equivalent. Albus Dumbledore, when he testified on Harry's behalf in the trial before the Wizengamot, made reference to the Wizengamot Charter of Rights under which Harry as the "accused has the right to present witnesses for his or her case." (OOTP, 131) The wizarding Charter of Rights could well have been established shortly after the Magna Carta, leading to a gradual split between the governance of Britain's magical and Muggle populations. If so, this could have cemented the basic rights of wizards and witches that led to increasing self-government of the wizarding world, while Muggle Britons had to wait until 1689 for the establishment of a much more modest Bill of Rights.[6]

Medieval parliaments laid the foundation for British representative government. One example would be the "Model Parliament" of 1295, which set the standard for how representatives were allocated to counties and boroughs. In 1332, representatives of the shires, the cities, and the boroughs met apart from the nobles and the church leaders for their deliberations, dividing Parliament between the city folk and the modest landowners who made up the House of Commons and what became the House of Lords.[7] Parliamentary authority grew with a precedent established in 1334 that rulers could collect customary taxes (property taxes known as fifteenths and tenths) only if they got the agreement of the Commons, a concession Edward III made to finance his expensive campaigns of the Hundred Years' War.[8] By the end of the fourteenth century, English subjects recognized Parliament as the best venue to make their concerns known about taxation, whether it was the fifteenths and the tenths levied on lands and movable goods or specialized taxes of customs and exchange such as tonnage and poundage.[9]

Even if taxation never became an important part of the wizarding world, the later Middle Ages saw a parallel political development in the magical world. The Wizengamot clung to its name and became the integral wizarding government under the leadership of a Chief Warlock, who seems to have held power equivalent to the speaker of the Commons.[10] This position might have developed in the same way and around the same time as the first Muggle speaker of the Commons, Sir Peter de la Mare, an MP (member of Parliament) for Hereford, was chosen in 1376. For his outspoken criticism of the corrupt court power-brokers, de la Mare was celebrated in ballads as a champion of the people.[11] It wasn't always easy to be speaker, and the same can be said of the wizarding world's equivalent. When Dumbledore refused to be silent on the subject of Voldemort's return, he lost his position as Chief Warlock and was reinstated only the following summer.

Not all speakers were so independent-minded. Fifteenth-century kings assumed the right to both select and pay a salary to the speaker. It wasn't until 1679 that the Commons recovered the original right and tradition of selecting a speaker not nominated by the Crown.[12] In modern times, the speaker is elected from among all members of the House of Commons. Once in office, the speaker presides over all parliamentary debates and enforces the rules for all members to follow. Medieval Chief Warlocks or Witches of the Wizengamot, like all wizards and witches, probably lived and worked free from royal interference from a much earlier date in history.

Parliaments also functioned as courts, just as the Wizengamot did with Harry's case, although the last such trial of an English subject like Harry in Parliament was held in 1454.[13] After that, nobles accused of misdeeds were usually tried in private venues, before a limited audience, and Parliament was involved only after the fact.[14] Medieval rulers had good cause to bypass the sometimes difficult-to-control Parliament when it came to trying cases. This didn't seem to hold true outside of the Muggle world, though. While Parliaments focused on legislation and taxation, the Wizengamot retained a judicial role right up into the modern day.

Finally, the Wizengamot seemed to have a quality that Parliament couldn't secure until well into the seventeenth century: institutional security. Parliaments existed only on the say-so of the monarch, who summoned these meetings at will and could prorogue (sending members away until they were recalled) or dismiss Parliaments as he or she wished. A ruler such as Henry VIII had good reason to say that in the sixteenth century, "we at no time stand so highly in our estate royal as in time of Parliament, wherein we as head and you as members are conjoined and knit together into one body politic."[15] Yet he could also rule for years without summoning a Parliament. The Wizengamot might not enjoy such praise from a king, but its relative invisibility in the body politic allowed the wizarding government to grow unhindered.

King's Councils and the Wizards' Council

Even if the Wizengamot no longer concerned itself much with the Muggle monarch, British rulers might still have consulted with representatives of the wizarding world. To do so in a public or individual way would have been risky, however, as poor Henry VI discovered. The king, who was overthrown during the fifteenth-century Wars of the Roses, was widely thought to be suffering from insanity. But Professor Dumbledore suggested that the monarch's reputation for madness might have been augmented by his apparently taking counsel from a rabbit. In this case, it seems to have been an Animagus witch, Lisette de Lapin, who Dumbledore tells us sometimes acted as Henry's counselor (*TOBTB*, 81). Perhaps other monarchs took less outrageous counsel from their magical subjects? The name of the second great body in wizarding government, the Wizards' Council, suggests this could be true.

In the fifteenth and sixteenth centuries, monarchs regularly took advice from councils personal (or "privy") and public. A Wizards' Council might well have been one of these various sources of advice used by English kings and queens. Parliament could be considered a particularly special case of a council, but because it focused more on statutes and taxation, different royal councils provided policy advice, answered petitions from subjects, and acted as specialized royal courts. The three most important of these specialized councils were the Great Council, the Privy Council, and the Star Chamber.

The Great Council was first mentioned in the 1330s as a flexible alternative to Parliament, lacking a set membership or institutional authority.[16] When a child ruled, councils assumed the work of governance, as was the case when Henry VI became king. His great-uncles were accused of using the council for their own profit. When the sixteen-year-old Henry began to rule in his own name in 1437, he was undermined by the continuing power of some councilors who used their position to attack other political rivals.[17] Historians have been less positive about another council known as the Star Chamber, which was the king's council sitting as a law court from 1487 onward. The Star Chamber (so called because it customarily met in a room in Westminster where the ceiling was painted as a starry nighttime sky) was, at first, a useful alternative to common-law courts, hearing cases involving threats to public order, such as riots and rebellion, but by the reign of Charles I in 1625, the term had become synonymous with the abuse of royal authority.[18] The Privy Council was the only one of these groups to endure, beginning as a small group of prominent advisers and officers to the monarch and shifting, over time, to become integrated into the ministries of Muggle parliamentary government.

The Wizards' Council flourished during the same period that medieval and Renaissance monarchs were governing Muggle England through personal rule, Parliaments, and councils. One key difference was that with the history of the Wizards' Council, no mention occurs of monarchs or Muggle advisers. Instead, the Council was headed by a Chief of the Council who exercised a great deal of power. Take the case of wizard Barberus Bragge, who, in 1269, used his power as Chief of the Council to levy an immediate punishment against the witch Modesty Rabnott. She documented the Chief's authority in a letter outlining her own disruptive protest of his use of a Golden Snidget in a Quidditch match: "Chief Bragge was very angry and for a moment I thought I'd end up a horned toad, or worse, but luckily his advisors calmed him down and I was only fined ten Galleons for disrupting the game." Later in her letter, she noted, "Chief Bragge would have lost my vote if I'd had one." (QTTA, 13)

From this, we can deduce two things: first, that as Chief of the Wizard's Council, Bragge had the authority to preemptively punish or fine wizards and witches for their violations of wizarding custom or laws. Modesty Rabnott's complaint also shows us that the Chief of the Council was not elected by all adult wizards: whether Bragge was elected by only a section of the wizarding population (until the nineteenth century, only men who owned substantial property could ordinarily vote in Muggle elections) or chosen in some other fashion, clearly not every magical subject had a voice in his selection.

Both the Chief and the Council that he or she headed were an important force in governing the wizarding world. The Wizards' Council not only made policy judgments or issued decisions on difficult questions of the law but ruled over magical subjects, just as a royal council governed Muggle subjects when the monarch was underage or unavailable. Bragge's high-handed actions showed one extreme of the Wizards' Council's powers, but it was far from the only case where the Council assumed extraordinary authority. Take Chief Burdock Muldoon, who persuaded the Wizard's Council in the Middle Ages to issue a decree that any member of the magical community that walked on two legs would hence-forth by granted the status of "being," but all others would remain "beasts." When a wealth of two-legged creatures, from trolls to pix-ies, packed a summit called by the council to discuss new magical laws relating to their interests, Muldoon and others were outraged by what they saw as an impudent disruption of their meeting. Chief Muldoon, we are told, "forswore any further attempts to integrate non-wizard members of the magical community into the Wizards' Council." (FB, x–xi)

Yet the power of the Council could also be used for positive change, if the Chief so chose. Elfrida Clagg headed the Wizards' Council in the seventeenth century, and being "considerably more enlightened" than some of her predecessors, under her direction the Council made "the Golden Snidget a protected species, outlaw-ing both its killing and its use in Quidditch games." (QTTA, 14) In all of these cases, the Chief of the Council appears to have a great deal of personal authority over the Council and its activities. In no cases is the Muggle monarchy mentioned at all, which argues that the wizarding world had established a de facto independent system of self-government before the end of the seventeenth century.

The PM and "the *Other* Minister"

Although a monarch sits on the throne of the United Kingdom today, in reality, power rests with political parties and the prime min-ister. The prime minister's office slowly evolved out of the practical and personal politics of British government. Without the political freedom enjoyed by witches and wizards in governing their increas-ingly isolated community, ambitious and charismatic Muggles rose to power in medieval England mostly through royal favor.

Take, for instance, Piers Gaveston, a Gascon-born minor land-owner who rose to power and prominence in the service of King Edward II. Gaveston's rivals at the court denounced the favorite as low-born and evil, who used his influence to enrich himself at the expense of the monarch and the people.[19] When Edward appointed Gaveston as regent during the king's absence in 1307, discontent mounted. Many lords were further outraged by the newly created earl's public insults (Gaveston dubbed the heavy-set earl of Lincoln "Burst-Belly"). King Edward was forced to exile his favorite but recalled Gaveston time and again. In 1312, Gaveston's noble opponents got their revenge: they captured the favorite when he made an unauthorized return to England and convened a court of nobles, which ended with Gaveston's execution.[20]

Thomas Cromwell, a merchant's son, was a cannier politician than Gaveston. Even though he, too, came from a humble background, Cromwell trained as a lawyer and built up valuable skills in royal administration. Although he wasn't a close friend of Henry VIII, Cromwell served his king well and benefited handsomely up until his execution in 1540. It was Cromwell who engineered Henry VIII's divorce from Catherine of Aragon (and sparked the English Reformation) to permit the king to marry the supposed Squib, Anne Boleyn. Cromwell later helped Henry dissolve that second union so that Henry could marry Jane Seymour.[21] Individuals such as Gaveston and Cromwell rose to prominence only as long as they enjoyed the monarch's support and protection.

During the seventeenth century, British monarchs struggled to control the Muggle government with mixed success. King Charles I believed Parliament should have no input on his foreign policy or appointment of ministers and was executed on orders of the victorious parliamentary forces at the end of the English Civil War of 1642–1649.[22] In 1688, King James II fled England after falling out with many of his own subjects. His daughter, Mary, and her half-English husband, William of Orange, succeeded him in a bloodless coup, known as the Glorious Revolution. This was accompanied by the passing of a Bill of Rights, which limited royal interference in the law and further guaranteed parliamentary liberties. Bit by bit, the monarch's authority was being eroded in Muggle Britain.

Still, it wasn't until well into the eighteenth century that ministers and political parties dominated the government. Even then, monarchs could still invite an individual who wasn't the preferred choice of the parliamentary majority to create a new government. Within the wizarding world, however, the independence of the

Wizards' Council, combined with the magical world's increasing need for secrecy to protect wizards and magical beings, led to a more powerful governmental administration within Britain — headed by the Minister for Magic — as well as to the expansion of the International Confederation of Wizards (*FB*, xiv). This was probably already the case during the middle of the century, given that Mnemone Radford, who died in 1649, served as "First Ministry of Magic Obliviator" and could use her power to eliminate unfortunate memories from Muggle minds.[23]

The newly founded Ministry found purpose as wizards and witches moved to separate from the Muggle world. Although the Brigade of Witch-Hunters featured in the tale of "Babbitty Rabbity and Her Cackling Stump" seems fictitious, the Brigade's royally directed mission drove all real witches, even Babbitty at first, into hiding (*TOBTB*, 64), and a fear of witch hunts inspired witches and wizards, worldwide, to hide their powers from Muggle authorities. In 1692, the Confederation passed the International Code of Wizarding Secrecy, requiring witches and wizards to keep Muggles from learning about the wizarding world. The Minister for Magic and counterparts in every country pledged to uphold this code in order to protect magic users and magical creatures from persecution at the hands of witch-fearing Muggles. The critical need to enforce this code across the board meant that the Ministry of Magic quickly grew in authority, especially with regard to laws and enforcement, during the following centuries. The Minister's position concentrated so much power into the hands of one individual that Dumbledore turned down the position more than once, for fear of that power corrupting him.

Long after the wizarding world had accepted that its Minister for Magic would be the dominant force in its government, the Muggle world slowly witnessed the expansion of its prime minister's office. Yet the emergence of a powerful Muggle PM was more an evolution shaped by the two major political parties that emerged in the seventeenth century, the conservative Tories and the liberal Whigs, and the actions of one man, Robert Walpole, than an organized and deliberate reform. Walpole had been educated to work in the church but, after the deaths of his older brothers, fell heir to his father's estate and political tradition. First elected to Parliament in 1701, Walpole was welcomed into the aristocratic leadership of the Whig Party's political circle. He rose to prominence as secretary of war but was later charged with embezzlement and imprisoned. Ironically, this cemented his political reputation. Combined with his financial wizardry (sadly, entirely of the Muggle kind!), which restored the English economy after a disastrous investment scheme known as the South Seas Bubble collapsed in 1720, Walpole's political power was unstoppable. After 1722, he became the clear master of Parliament, as well as King George I's trusted minister.[24] Enjoying the confidence of both Parliament and ruler, Walpole can rightly be considered Britain's first prime minister, but, unlike modern PMs whose positions are drawn from their party leadership, his powers still relied on royal and parliamentary support, as well as the cooperation of his cabinet of fellow ministers who helped to run the government.

We know that the Minister for Magic also felt some pressure to conform to public opinion, especially as expressed through the Wizengamot, which had the power to appoint and fire the governmental leader.[25] In the summer before Harry's sixth year, Cornelius Fudge stepped down as Minister for Magic. He explained to the prime minister that "I was sacked three days ago. The whole wizarding community has been screaming for my resignation for a fortnight." (*HBP*, 20) Fudge's comment shows that a Minister for Magic could not remain in office if public opinion turned entirely against him or her. Just imagine being pelted with angry letters delivered by owl at any time day or night, containing a steady stream of Howlers. It would make the modern media barrage and paparazzi experienced by Muggle politicians seem pale in comparison! Similarly, the Chief Warlock or Witch of the Wizengamot could be forced out of office (presumably by the Minister for Magic), as Albus Dumbledore revealed that he had been asked to leave the Wizengamot.

Still, Ministers for Magic must have been able to withstand protests and bad publicity, at least to some extent. We know that when

Artemisia Lufkin became the first female Minister for Magic in 1798, she was met with some protests and resignations by members of the Wizengamot. Minister Lufkin nevertheless held office until 1811.[26] So the protests over Fudge must have been extraordinary indeed to force his resignation. Fudge might well have held on so long because he enjoyed the support of the *Daily Prophet*, the wizarding world's newspaper. Muggle political leaders such as Walpole well understood the need to cultivate a good relationship with the press: his government spent fifty thousand pounds during a ten-year period to pay for wildly positive press in newspapers such as the *London Journal* and the *Daily Gazetteer*. These papers produced a flurry of pseudonymous articles penned by reliable scribes such as Mathew Concanen and James Pitt, passionately defending the Whig government, its policies, and its ministers.[27] Given this history, Fudge's assiduous courting of media attention via the *Daily Prophet* seems entirely in character for politicians, whether Muggle or magical.

"Welcome to the Ministry of Magic"

When Arthur Weasley brought Harry to the Ministry of Magic offices, the Muggle-raised youth was rendered speechless by the magical sights of "a very long and splendid hall . . . [whose] peacock blue ceiling was inlaid with gleaming golden symbols that kept moving and changing like some enormous heavenly noticeboard." (*OOTP*, 117) The multilevel building was crowded with Ministry employees and crammed with departments. In contrast to the Ministry of Magic's centralized site, Muggle Britain lacks the elegance of a single governmental site and ministerial unity, even if individual buildings such as the Horse Guards and the Old Admiralty in Whitehall are impressive sights for tourists.

The lack of unity in British administration goes for its history, as well as its geography. Political scientist Gillian Peele noted that "The process whereby the British government acquired more functions over the nineteenth and twentieth centuries was not . . . a linear one."[28] Indeed, since the early nineteenth century, government offices were staffed and organized in a haphazard fashion. It wasn't until 1854 that standardized recruitment and administration were mandated. Even then, it took more than a century for the British government to standardize ranks and responsibilities in the civil service.[29] Instead of a centralized, rationalized model of administration, national agencies were created and expanded in response to parliamentary commissions or public outcries and were often regarded with suspicion.

Parliament's passage of the Education Act in 1870 didn't substantially enlarge any national government when it mandated education for all children ages 5 to 12. Instead, the act laid the responsibility on school boards, such as the School Board for London, which was charged with enforcing attendance. Between 1887 and 1903, more than a quarter of a million convictions were issued by London's courts of summary justice for parents who neglected to ensure that their children were educated in accordance with the law.[30] Matters changed substantially near the end of World War II, when the limits of local administration became clear as schools weren't evacuated during air raid sirens. A new Ministry of Education soon emerged after the Education Act of 1944.[31] In this case, the resistance of Hogwarts faculty and Dumbledore's Army to the mercurial decrees of "High Inquisitor" Dolores Umbridge could well mirror the reaction of some local boards, staff, and students to national oversight.

Charged with enforcing the International Code of Wizarding Secrecy, the Department of Magical Law Enforcement appears to be the largest department within the Ministry of Magic. It has a rough equivalent in the Muggle government department know as the Home Office, which is responsible for security, order, and immigration control.[32] It loomed large in Harry's life, beginning with the letter he received from Mafalda Hopkirk of the Improper Use of Magic Office, unfairly charging him with violating the "Decree for Reasonable Restriction of Under-Age Sorcery, 1875, Paragraph C" because of Dobby's use of the Hover Charm, all the way to his eventual service as Head of the Auror Department (COS, 21).[33] The Ministry also administers the one wizarding prison in Britain: Azkaban.

In Muggle law enforcement, it wasn't until 1877 that the Prison Act enabled the creation of a national Board of Commission of Prisons under the authority of the Home Office.[34] Muggle Britain's legal system has always been less centralized than the wizarding world's administration, although the creation of a centralized Crown Prosecution Service in 1985 increased national oversight of prosecutions. The Police and Magistrates Courts Act of 1994 gave the central government the authority to set national objectives for police forces but could not overcome strongly seated resistance to the idea of a national police force.[35]

"Magic Is Might"

The caption for the fountain that decorates the Ministry of Magic is a telling expression of the attitudes of many witches and wizards, especially those who hold power during the final stages of Harry's fight against Voldemort. While public opinion, the press, and opposition parties worked for centuries to steadily limit the independence of Muggle government, the Ministry of Magic, even as late as Harry's day, had little oversight or restraint on its authority. The fact that the Ministry was charged with enforcing the Statute of Secrecy had resulted in a growing divergence from Muggle notions of individual rights and government processes and the steady expansion of the Ministry's power over ordinary wizards.

From Hagrid's imprisonment without trial in *Chamber of Secrets* to the high-handed judgment that led to Buckbeak's fatal sentencing in *Prisoner of Azkaban*, Susan Hall, in the essay "Harry Potter and the Rule of Law: The Central Weakness of Legal Concepts in the Wizard World," shows how the Ministry enjoyed almost unlimited power over not only witches and wizards but also over most other beings, magical or Muggle, who came to its notice.[36] Harry and Hermione Granger, with their Muggle upbringings, were often at a loss to cope with the whimsical and autocratic tendencies of law and government as practiced by the Ministry and its personnel.

Legal scholar Benjamin H. Barton succinctly captures how Muggles would see the Ministry when he asks us to imagine:

What would you think of a government that engaged in this list of tyrannical activities: tortured children for lying; designed its prisons specifically to suck all life and hope out of the inmates; placed citizens in that prison without a hearing; ordered the death penalty without a trial; allowed the powerful, rich, or famous to control policy; selectively prosecuted crimes (the powerful go unpunished and the unpopular face trumped-up charges); conducted criminal trials without defense counsel; used truth serum to force confessions; maintained constant surveillance over all citizens; offered no elections and no democratic lawmaking process; and controlled the press?[37]

The actions he lists (which are all committed by the Ministry in the course of the Harry Potter books) hardly suggest an enlightened, modern, and humanitarian state, where the ideas of justice, freedom, and equality guide the government. Yet all of those activities are carried out by representatives of the wizarding world's government, demonstrating a fatal weakness in the development (or lack thereof!) of witches' and wizards' political philosophy. The old-fashioned and cozy world of witches and wizards appears, from this perspective, to be a reactionary and cruel culture.

Hall makes the case that the wizarding world lacks the concept of the rule of law and that without this principle in force, abuses naturally flourished. While Muggle governments became more democratic and accountable over the centuries, the Ministry showed little change from the whimsical policy-making and judgments of medieval times. Hall points out how the Muggle government of Britain continues to adapt its structures and processes even today, for example, with the 1998 integration of the European Convention of Human Rights into British law. This further protected the rights and freedoms of individuals and minorities. Hall notes that "the wizard world offers no equivalent."[38]

Indeed, the International Confederation of Wizards seems more interested in self-preservation than in principled ideas when it decides that secrecy will be its highest priority. Perhaps because the wizarding world bypassed the centuries-long struggles between

Muggle monarchs, nobles, and Parliaments, which led to a modern political system of checks and balances, it also failed to develop sophisticated principles of legal rights (and wrongs). Barton argues that the Ministry of Magic consequently became a "corrupt, self-perpetuating bureaucracy," where the self-interest of individuals such as Scrimgeour and Umbridge, rather than principles, determine ministry policy.[39] Despite the brave efforts of Sirius Black, Dumbledore, the Weasleys, and the rest of the Order of the Phoenix, the traditions of wizarding government allow Voldemort's supporters to take over the wizarding government relatively easily and quickly, by exploiting loopholes that Muggle politics had long ago closed.

Ironically, given the old-fashioned air of the wizarding world, the Ministry of Magic provides a much more centralized and authoritative, even abusive, government than Muggle Britain has known. Establishing agencies with strong central powers, first with the Wizengamot, then with the Wizards' Council, and finally through the development of the Ministry of Magic after the Statute of Secrecy was passed, the wizarding world's leaders faced few of the challenges to their independence and authority that their Muggle counterparts experienced. Royal interference in wizarding society seems to have been nonexistent, so much so that after the International Code of Wizarding Secrecy came into effect in 1692, the only checks on the wizarding world's government came from the court of public opinion and the few members of the Wizengamot. Where parallels existed, such as those between the Minister for Magic and the Muggle prime minister, it was always the wizarding government that enjoyed the greater degree of freedom and authority. And as Harry and his friends found, time and again, the Ministry's power was very often used for the worst possible ends.

Notes

1. All book quotes are taken from the British editions by J. K. Rowling as follows, with the exception of *Fantastic Beasts* (Vancouver: Raincoast Books, 2001): *Chamber of Secrets*, London: Bloomsbury, 1998; *Order of the Phoenix*, London: Bloomsbury, 2003; *Half-Blood Prince*, London: Bloomsbury, 2005; *Tales of Beedle the Bard*, London: Bloomsbury, 2007; *Quidditch through the Ages*, London; Bloomsbury, 2001.

2. Frank Barlow, *The Feudal Kingdom of England, 1042–1216*, 5th ed. (London: Longman, 1995), 34–35.

3. Henry Royston Loyn, *The Governance of Anglo-Saxon England, 500–1087* (Stanford, CA: Stanford University Press, 1984), 100–105.

4. G. I. T. Machin, *The Rise of Democracy in Britain, 1830–1918* (New York: Palgrave, Macmillan, 2001), 5.

5. Charles Petit-Dutaillis, *The Feudal Monarchy in France and England, from the Tenth to the Thirteenth Century* (London: Taylor & Francis, 1966), 333–335.

6. Roger Lockyer, *Tudor and Stuart Britain, 1485–1714*, 2nd ed. (London: Longman, 1985), 361.

7. Maurice F. Bond, *Guide to the Records of Parliament* (London: Her Majesty's Stationery Office, 1971), 20–21, 201–202.

8. G. L. Harriss, *King, Parliament, and Public Finance in Medieval England to 1369* (Oxford, UK: Oxford University Press, 1971), 362.

9. Roger Schofield, *Taxation under the Early Tudors, 1485–1547* (Oxford, UK: Blackwell, 2004) 27–28; and W. Mark Ormrod, "The Origins of Tunnage and Poundage: Parliament and the Estate of Merchants in the 14th Century," *Parliamentary History* 28, no. 2 (2009), 222–223.

10. For an interesting discussion of the Wizengamot, the Chief Warlock/Witch, and the Ministry, see "The Minister for Magic," www.redhen-publications.com/Minister.html, July 25, 2008. A brief survey is also available at the Harry Potter Lexicon: "The History of the Ministry," www.hplex.info/essays/essay-ministry-history.html, March 31, 2006.

11. John Smith Roskell, "Sir Peter de la Mare, Speaker for the Commons in Parliament in 1376 and 1377," in *Parliament and Politics in Late Medieval England*, vol. 2 (London: Hambledon Press, 1981), 1–7.

12. Conrad Russell, *The Crisis of Parliament: English History, 1509–1660* (Oxford, UK: Oxford University Press, 1971), 40–41.

13. Helen Miller, *Henry VIII and the English Nobility* (Oxford, UK: Blackwell, 1986), 40.

14. John Bellamy, *The Tudor Law of Treason: An Introduction* (London: Routledge, 1979), 211.

15. Henry VIII, quoted in John Hamilton Baker, *The Oxford History of the Laws of England, 1483–1558* (Oxford, UK, Oxford University Press, 2003), 55–56.

16. Henry G. Richardson and George O. Sayles, "Parliaments and Great Councils in Medieval England," in *The English Parliament in the Middle Ages* (London: Hambledon Press, 1981), xxvi, 16–20.

17. Ralph A. Griffiths, *The Reign of King Henry VI* (Berkeley: University of California Press, 1981), 275–282. Despite these failures, historians Henry Richardson and George Sayles argue that "great councils became a less elaborate and less cumbersome device for dispatching business which might otherwise have come before the council in parliament." See Richardson and Sayles, "Parliaments and Great Councils in Medieval England," xxvi, 20–21.

18. G. R. Elton, *The Tudor Constitution: Documents and Commentary* (Cambridge, UK: Cambridge University Press, 1960), 158–163.

19. Maurice H. Keen, *England in the Later Middle Ages: A Political History*, 2nd ed. (London: Routledge, 2003), 11–12.

20. J. S. Hamilton, "Gaveston, Piers, Earl of Cornwall (d. 1312)," *Oxford Dictionary of National Biography*, Oxford University Press, September 2004, online edition, January 2008, www.oxforddnb.com/view/article/10463.

21. Howard Leithead, "Cromwell, Thomas, Earl of Essex (b. in or before 1485, d. 1540)," *Oxford Dictionary of National Biography*, Oxford University Press, September 2004, online edition, May 2009, www.oxforddnb.com/view/article/6769.

22. Ann Hughes, *The Causes of the English Civil War*, 2nd ed. (London: Palgrave Macmillian, 1998), 149–152.

23. J. K. Rowling, "Wizard of the Month Archive," www.jkrowling.com/textonly/en/wotm.cfm.

24. Stephen Taylor, "Walpole, Robert, First Earl of Orford (1676–1745)," *Oxford Dictionary of National Biography*, Oxford University Press, September 2004, online edition, January 2008, www.oxforddnb.com/view/article/28601.

25. Proof for the practice of appointing Ministers comes from J. K. Rowling's "Wizard of the Month Archive," www.jkrowling.com/textonly/en/wotm.cfm, where Grogan Stump is mentioned as having been appointed as Minister for Magic in 1811.

26. J. K. Rowling, "Wizard of the Month Archive," www.jkrowling.com/textonly/en/wotm.cfm. For the Wizengamot protest, see "The W.O.M.B.A.T. Grade 3," www.hp-lexicon.org/wizworld/wombat/wombat3comments.html.

27. Simon Targett, "A Pro-Government Newspaper during the Whig Ascendancy: Walpole's *London Journal* 1722–1738," *Journal of History and Politics* 7 (1989): 3, 24.

28. Gillian Peele, *Governing the U.K.*, 3rd ed. (Oxford: Blackwell, 1995), 52.

29. John Greenaway, Steve Smith, and John Street, *Deciding Factors in British Politics: A Case-Studies Approach* (London: Routledge, 1992), 140.

30. Sascha Auerbach, "'Some Punishment Should Be Devised': Parents, Children, and the State in Victorian London," *Historian* 71, no. 4 (Winter 2009): 758.

31. Richard Aldrich, *Lessons from the History of Education: The Selected Works of Richard Aldrich* (London: Routledge, 2005), 66–67.

32. Peele, *Governing the U.K.*, 73.

33. J. K. Rowling, "Wizard of the Month Archive," www.jkrowling.com/textonly/en/wotm.cfm.

34. Alyson Brown, *English Society and the Prison: Time, Culture, and Politics in the Development of the Modern Prison, 1850–1920* (London: Boydell Press, 2003), 107.

35. Peele, *Governing the U.K.*, 437–444.

36. Susan Hall, "Harry Potter and the Rule of Law: The Central Weakness of Legal Concepts in the Wizard World," in *Reading Harry Potter: Critical Essays*, ed. Giselle Liza Anatol (Westport, CT: Prager, 2003), 156–157.

37. Benjamin H. Barton, "Harry Potter and the Half-Crazed Bureaucracy," *Michigan Law Review* 104 (May 2006): 1523.

38. Hall, "Harry Potter and the Rule of Law," 158–159.

39. Barton, "Harry Potter and the Half-Crazed Bureaucracy," 1531.

Were the Malfoys Aristocrats?

The Decline and Fall of the Pure-Blooded

Laura Loiacono and Grace Loiacono

"Some wizarding families are much better than others, Potter."
— Draco Malfoy, *Sorcerer's Stone*, 108

In the Harry Potter series, it soon becomes clear that Lucius, Narcissa, and Draco Malfoy fill an important role. Although Lord Voldemort doesn't speak to Harry for the first time until the final chapter of the first book, the Malfoys—specifically, Draco and Lucius—are conduits through which Voldemort's ideas are articulated from the very beginning, when Harry encounters Draco at Madam Malkin's. Voldemort's beliefs are not revolutionary or unprecedented. They are grounded in the simple politics of elitism that rich purebloods such as the Malfoys might well find attractive. Purebloods like the Malfoys believe in the worth of blood, breeding, and ancestry. They see Muggle-borns and "blood-traitors" such as the Weasleys as people who threaten and undermine the bloodlines that, to the Malfoys, are imperative. The Malfoys thus present a picture of cold, unfeeling aristocrats who are fighting to hold onto their own class privilege.

On the surface, Draco is easily dismissed as a common school-yard bully in Harry's first years at school. He is the only son of an extremely wealthy and pure-blooded family, and his behavior is a product of the way he was raised. Draco believes in the worth of his blood and ancestry, because this has been emphasized by his parents and most other adults in his life. He is given the best of everything and wants for nothing. For example, at the start of Draco's second year Lucius buys his son and the entire Slytherin Quidditch team Nimbus Two Thousand and One brooms, the newest and best version of the broom available on the market. In return for his life of wealth and privilege, Draco is expected to believe all that his father believes and, when necessary, to do what his family expects of him. His own personal preferences are unimportant, even when he is ordered to assassinate Albus Dumbledore.

English aristocrats in the nineteenth and twentieth centuries played a role in Muggle history similar to that filled by the Malfoy family in the Harry Potter books. Like Lucius, Draco, and Narcissa, English aristocrats lived in privileged worlds, supported by the power of wealth and tradition. They believed in the necessity of maintaining a class system that was both rigid and antiquated. The aristocracy enjoyed a period of enormous influence in Britain during the nineteenth century, until the class as a whole entered into a decline after World War I. With its wealth and power, as well as its cataclysmic fall from grace, the Malfoy family is comparable in many ways to its Muggle aristocratic counterparts. Little wonder, then, that the Malfoys are often seen by readers as being among the aristocrats of the wizarding world.

What *Is* an Aristocrat? Puzzling Out the Malfoys

It's easy to speak about the aristocracy and class in sweeping terms; however, calling the Malfoys *aristocrats* in the magical world doesn't really mean anything unless we define the term. As we shall see, in many respects the Malfoys do fit the definition of *aristocrat*: at the very least, they're the wizarding world's equivalent to the Muggle landed gentry. The wizarding world doesn't seem to have actual aristocratic titles, though, which means the word must be applied somewhat differently in the case of wizards than it is in the Muggle world.

There don't seem to be any wizarding dukes, baronets, or earls, for example. Indeed, there is no magical monarch who could have granted such titles, although it's conceivable that a wizard or a witch was granted a title by a Muggle ruler before the Statute of Secrecy was passed in 1692. The wizarding world itself apparently doesn't grant titles, apart from coveted honors bestowed by the Ministry, such as the Order of Merlin, but such orders clearly don't grant the holder any title. Even without formal titles, however, the wizarding aristocracy can be listed and defined. For starters, they have their own version of *Debrett's*, the Muggle registry of the British aristocracy: the magical social registry, *Nature's Nobility: A Wizarding Genealogy*, which lists all of the pureblood families. And wizarding "aristocrats" can be recognized not only by their inclusion in *Nature's Nobility*, but also by their ancestry, wealth, land ownership, use of house-elves, and other traits.

It is evident throughout the books that the Malfoys are accustomed to a life of privilege. Their wealth and ancestry ensure that they enjoy luxuries at home, at school, and in the public sphere. Draco takes it for granted, for example, that his family can secure the best and latest model of broom for him, even if first-years are prohibited from bringing them to Hogwarts. Lucius secures his seats at the Quidditch World Cup as Minister Cornelius Fudge's guest by making a "*very* generous contribution to St. Mungo's Hospital for Magical Maladies and Injuries." (GOF, 101)[1] Lucius has considerable influence with Minister Fudge as well. When Harry sees Lucius in the Ministry of Magic, Lucius intimates that the Minister is willing to share sensitive information with him and taunts Harry: "The Minister was just telling me about your lucky escape, Potter. Quite astonishing, the way you continue to wriggle out of very tight holes . . . *Snakelike*, in fact." (OOTP, 154) When Lucius and Fudge depart, they leave "talking in low voices." (OOTP, 155)

Lucius has Minister Fudge's ear and seems to wield influence in his government.

The Malfoys' home is huge and luxurious. There are hints in *Deathly Hallows* that the Malfoy Manor grounds are expansive. The hedge that borders the property is high and "neatly manicured" and continues into "the distance." (*DH*, 1, 2) There is no doubt that both the grounds and the manor are opulent and the hedge leads and extends beyond a "pair of impressive wrought-iron gates." (*DH*, 2) Somewhere in the distance, the manor grounds are equipped with a fountain, and peacocks strut about the grounds, leading Yaxley to comment that the mansion is also huge. It is certainly large enough to conceal Dark Arts materials from an extensive Ministry of Magic raid, as Draco tells the Polyjuiced Harry and Ron Weasley in *Chamber of Secrets*. It is also spacious enough to keep prisoners in the basement during *Deathly Hollows* and is stately and big enough to be used as the headquarters for Voldemort's forces.

The inside of the manor is also regal. Among the markers of the Malfoy family's wealth are "a magnificent carpet" and furniture and decorations that are "gilded" and "handsome" (*DH*, 2). The large drawing room where Harry and his friends are interrogated provides more evidence of the Malfoys' fortune: it's lit by a crystal chandelier and its fireplace is made of marble, not brick, and features a large gilded mirror above the mantelpiece (de rigeur in upper-class homes of the nineteenth century). Thanks to pureblood distaste for Muggle amenities, it is not, however, equipped with modern comforts.[2]

Malfoy Manor is, no doubt, a stately residence. The Malfoys' counterparts among the Muggle aristocracy in England also possessed palatial homes, basing their immense wealth and power on their land holdings. As a result, aristocratic estates were often vast. The eleventh duke of Norfolk had grounds surrounding his mansion, Greystoke in Cumberland, that totaled five thousand acres.[3] Malfoy Manor is comparable to palaces such as Blenheim, the birthplace of Winston Churchill. Blenheim is a two-thousand-acre estate with a lake and expansive formal gardens. The house is imposing, with statues adorning the area in front of the house and

Roman columns at its entrance. The rooms are sumptuously decorated with ornate furnishings and high painted ceilings.[4]

The Malfoys' estate is the only wizarding home referred to as a manor house in the entire series. This is a telling detail, if we bear in mind the comparative rarity of actual manor houses in Muggle Britain. Not every British aristocratic mansion, or even palace, can legally call itself a "manor." Manor houses are a holdover from the medieval period, when feudalism (also called the "manorial" system) assigned legal and economic power over an area to the lord of the manor; centuries after the end of feudalism, there are very few buildings left in Britain today that can legally lay claim to being a manor. Those that do exist were originally built for titled families who ruled a particular area. Manors were generally built more for aesthetics than for defense and were not fortified as castles were; still, they are always very old, with the most recent dating from the Tudor period (that is, the sixteenth century). Whether the manor has been in the Malfoys' possession since the medieval period or was acquired at some point before the wizarding world's Seclusion (perhaps under the Tudors, during the sixteenth century), their ownership of Malfoy Manor is one of their most important claims to being considered "aristocrats."

A wizarding home and an aristocratic residence of that size would have to be staffed by an army of servants. The wizarding world retains the services of house elves such as Dobby, who was likely a hereditary servant of the Malfoys. House-elves appear to have a natural urge to serve, or, as Ron baldly puts it, "They. Like. It. They like being enslaved." (GOF, 224) This is a fair statement, because the house-elf Winky reacts with horror when her master threatens to free her by giving her clothes, thereby firing her. House-elves exist under a system of slavery, however, and in households such as the Malfoys' they are treated cruelly. Yet even so, the moral guide in the series, Albus Dumbledore, argues for treating house-elves with compassion instead of freeing them.

Lacking a hereditary enslaved species, British aristocrats were and are forced to rely on servants to maintain their lifestyles. Like the Malfoys, Muggle aristocrats in the nineteenth and twentieth centuries employed servants, although they did not exert quite the level of control over the servants in their employ that wizards exert over their house-elves. In fact, working as a servant in a large home was often considered preferable during the nineteenth century to working long and dreary hours in a factory.

Wealthy employers used servants for tasks they could very well do themselves but considered demeaning, such as lighting their own fires or cleaning their own clothes. As the number of affluent people increased during the nineteenth century, so did the number of servants who worked in their households. By 1891, one in every fifteen people in London was a domestic servant. The percentage of people employed as servants in Britain declined after World War I, however, because the aristocracy grew smaller as a class and the working poor had an increasing number of other career choices.[5]

The Malfoys' marriage also resembled that of Muggle aristocrats in several respects. First and most important, neither magical nor Muggle elite families would tolerate marriages to just *anyone* whom a young family member fell in love with. Because a "pure" ancestry underlay both groups' claims to superiority, marriage outside the group would shame the whole family and "contaminate" their line of descent. Thus, when Andromeda Black married Muggle-born Ted Tonks, her pureblood family disowned her, and her name was burned off the Black family tapestry.

The Blacks were only doing what many an elite Muggle family had done before them. When Vita Sackville-West, the daughter of a baron, married the commoner Harold Nicholson, her aristocratic family was profoundly dismayed, because they felt that she was marrying beneath herself.[6] Marrying beneath one's station could cause very real problems; one example in nineteenth-century literature is the mother of Will Ladislaw, a character in George Eliot's *Middlemarch*, who fell in love with and married a Polish musician and thus (like Andromeda Black) was disinherited. The marriage of James Potter and Lily Evans must have caused a stir in families such as the Malfoys and the Blacks, because Lily was Muggle-born. Among the most traditional purebloods, such "mixed" marriages provoked derision, as reflected in the mocking laughter that erupted

at Malfoy Manor in *Deathly Hallows* when Voldemort announced
the marriage of Tonks to Remus Lupin, a werewolf whose mother
was Muggle-born:

> There was an eruption of jeering laughter from around the
> table. Many leaned forward to exchange gleeful looks ...
> so jubilant were they at Bellatrix and the Malfoys' humilia-
> tion. Bellatrix's face, so recently flushed with happiness, had
> turned an ugly, blotchy red. "She is no niece of ours, My
> Lord," she cried over the outpouring of mirth. "We—Narcissa
> and I—have never set eyes on our sister since she married the
> Mudblood." (*DH*, 16)

Yet this attitude was itself hypocritical, as Hermione Granger
explains, "The Death Eaters can't all be pure-blood, there aren't
enough pure-blood wizards left. I expect most of them are half-
bloods pretending to be pure." (*HBP*, 242) Like most Muggle
aristocrats, however, Lucius and Narcissa had conformed to their
families' expectations and married within their own class.

Lucius and Narcissa Malfoy's marriage does not appear to be
an outwardly affectionate one, although they do seem well-suited
to each other. Among upper-class families, marriages were often
seen as mutually beneficial arrangements, rather than love matches.
Elite families would seek out others from the same class with the
same values and socialization for their children. Whether Lucius
and Narcissa married for love or simply because they were from
similar backgrounds and shared values, they nonetheless managed to create a loving, if flawed, family. Lucius appears to have
affection for his son, and Narcissa asks Severus Snape to enter an
Unbreakable Vow to keep Draco from harm, watch over him, and
carry out Draco's task if Draco should fail. During the final battle at
Hogwarts, the Malfoys run through the fighting crowds, "not even
attempting to fight, screaming for their son." (*DH*, 755)

Narcissa and Lucius are indulgent parents who spoil their
only son, but they also clearly love him (certainly, this seems true
of Narcissa), and both are willing to do anything to protect him.

In this, they resemble many of their Muggle upper-class counterparts. Winston Churchill, who came from an old and prominent aristocratic British family, raised children who indulged in infamously bad behavior. His daughter Diana married a man her parents disapproved of, and her sister, Sara, became a chorus girl. Their brother, Randolph, dropped out of Oxford, took up gambling, and went heavily into debt. Despite the faults of his children, Churchill was loyal. He paid part of Randolph's debt and spoke on his behalf. Churchill's dedication to his children often led him to spoil them, and like the Malfoys, he had the resources to do so.[7]

The Malfoys, like their Muggle counterparts, expect that elite families should be able to trade on their connections to gain political influence and to build networks of supporters. Churchill used his patrician connections to build a political career. Similarly, Lucius also uses his wealth and the power it brings to gain influence in the political realm. Fudge, the Minister for Magic until after the battle at the Department of Mysteries, is influenced by Lucius so much that he leaks information to Lucius and is willfully blinded by him. Under Lucius's influence, Fudge refuses to believe that Voldemort has returned despite Harry's eyewitness account. Draco brags about his father's influence, "*My* father told me about it ages ago . . . heard it from Cornelius Fudge. But then, Father's always associated with the top people at the Ministry." (*GOF*, 169) Lucius also uses his power to ease Draco's way in school and possibly buys Draco's way onto his house Quidditch team. Like his father, Draco builds a network of supporters, including Vincent Crabbe and Gregory Goyle. He joins the Inquisitorial Squad in *Order of the Phoenix* without hesitation and proceeds to throw his weight around as a part of Dolores Umbridge's group of student police. Lucius would have done the same, one suspects.

Yet by the end of *Deathly Hallows*, the Malfoy family has been brought low, and we see them huddled in the Great Hall after the final battle. Indeed, their decline started as soon as Lucius was sent to Azkaban at the end of *Order of the Phoenix* and Voldemort moved into Malfoy Manor. Before Harry's fifth year, however, they are certainly part of the wizarding elite and consistently support a system based on a steep social hierarchy. In every respect, they lead lives that compare to those of Muggle aristocrats of the nineteenth century: they possess wealth, servants, and an ancient and impressive manor house; exert substantial political and social influence; and live in luxury. Their example offers us an understanding, general as it might be, of the lives of pureblood wizarding aristocrats who are born into privilege and who are struggling to retain their social dominance.

Keeping Up One's Standards: Class Politics and Conflict in the Wizarding World

The politics of class and the intricacies of class divisions are crucial to the struggles and conflicts in Harry's world. One of the most important differences between Dumbledore and Voldemort is in how they propose to deal with the different social strata of wizarding society. Dumbledore seems to feel that every person with magical ability (whether fully human or not) should be admitted to the wizarding world and treated as an equal. He thus rejects the idea of the supremacy of blood and heritage in wizarding society. Because magical ability would be the only prerequisite, Dumbledore's approach would mean that the wizarding world would not be stratified but, rather, inclusive. And in practice, Dumbledore does *not* discriminate, hiring staff and faculty at Hogwarts such as Rubeus Hagrid and Professor Filius Flitwick, who are only part-human; Lupin, who is a werewolf; and even Firenze, who isn't human at all.

The Malfoys and their friends would disagree, as Draco makes clear with his disdain for Hagrid as a teacher, griping, "God, this place is going to the dogs. That oaf teaching classes, my father'll have a fit when I tell him." (POA, 115) Wizards and witches who share the Malfoys' beliefs and history wholeheartedly disagree with the notion that the magical world should be open to any and all who display a degree of magical ability and talent. They believe in the significance of a hierarchy of wealth and power. As rich purebloods, the Malfoys see themselves and the families they're related to as forming the pinnacle of the social order.

The Malfoys' sense of their own importance is grounded in their wealth and their "pure" ancestry, which both go back for generations. From the Malfoys' point of view, their wealth means that they rank above families such as the Weasleys, who are purebloods but very poor. When attempting to garner Harry's friendship, Draco cautions Harry, "You'll soon find out some wizarding families are much better than others, Potter. You don't want to go making friends with the wrong sort." (SS, 135) The Weasleys are inferior, in Draco's eyes, because they have "more children than they can afford," thus associating larger families with lower-class wizards (SS, 135). By contrast, the aristocratic Malfoys have only one son. The purity of the Weasleys' ancestry is negated by the fact that they are poor.

The Malfoys also look down on the Weasleys because the Weasleys support Dumbledore and agree with his acceptance of Muggle-borns. Muggle-borns are at the bottom of what the wizarding upper classes envision to be the social hierarchy. Draco refers to Hermione as a "filthy little Mudblood," and Lucius chastises Arthur Weasley for his association with Hermione's parents, commenting, "The company you keep, Weasley . . . and I thought your family could sink no lower." (COS, 62, 112) The value that the Malfoys assign to their hierarchical class structure creates a type of class warfare that nearly destroys their society, especially in Deathly Hallows, when purebloods such as Umbridge pursue a program of vicious discrimination and impoverishment against the Muggle-born. The social stratification and divisions embraced by the Malfoys had their counterparts in nineteenth- and twentieth-century Muggle Britain as well.

Class and rank were equally important in nineteenth-century Britain, although the relations between the classes and the divisions between them were also complicated. Members of the upper classes, who were seeking to safeguard their position, often cherished the belief that being firmly subordinated led the working poor to easily accept their lower status. Acceptance of, and respect for, rank and birth, as expressed in fiction such as the novels of the

famous nineteenth-century author Sir Walter Scott, could allegedly be combined with a warm friendship between the classes,
thereby upholding a hierarchal social structure.[8] At least, this is how
wealthier Britons hoped it would work out; in reality, this idea was a
fantasy indulged in by the upper class. In spite of this (or perhaps
because of it), there is evidence that the chasm between the classes
was widening during the nineteenth century, and those of the
lower strata certainly did not accept their position as being natural and God-given. Between 1790 and 1818, there were occasional
food riots in England, and the 1830s saw a rise in demonstrations
and protest by groups of the working poor, people unsatisfied with
the social order who were hostile to the government and the aristocratic hierarchy that the government protected.

Many among the upper and middle classes, notably traditionalist Tories and Whigs, supported the old system of order because it
seemed sanctioned by tradition and custom, and they felt it must be
safe-guarded. The only way to rid Britain of social unrest, according
to those at the top of that pyramid, was to reinforce its strict social
hierarchy. They did not want so much to bridge the divide as to protect a system that gave them power and relative stability.[9] The first
duke of Wellington, a traditionalist Tory, argued that "Popular agita-
tion must be faced down and suppressed, and the time-honoured
habits of 'obedience, order, and submission' . . . must be reestab-
lished."[10] Lucius, who tolerated no knockout from his housewolves at
all, would have agreed. The Muggle-born ought to be shown their
place, too, which is why Lucius comments that Draco ought to be
ashamed for letting "a girl of no wizard family [Hermione] beat you
in every exam." (COS, 52) From Lucius's standpoint, the Muggle-
born should always be subordinate to the pure-blooded; by allowing
Hermione to surpass him in school, Draco has let down his class
as well. The affirmation of social hierarchy wasn't always pursued as
a way to maliciously keep another group of people down, although
that might have been the effect; rather, it was usually done in order
to safeguard one group's interests against another's.

Victorian society was saturated in the language of class, tightly
connected to the traditional hierarchy. For the upper classes,

the graduations of rank were distinct and plentiful, and groups that protested the social order during the nineteenth century were seen as attempted usurpers of the rightful order.[11] Discussing an 1840s proposal to extend voting rights to lower-class men, Thomas Babington Macaulay, a Whig member of Parliament, said, "I know it would be poison. . . . I should not yield to the importunity of multitudes who, exasperated by suffering and blinded by ignorance, demand with wild vehemence the liberty to destroy themselves."[12] There was a great deal of fear among the British upper classes about what would happen to their society if the lower classes were given power. Politicians, who largely represented the landed elites, sought to prevent the kind of open class warfare of the earlier part of the century from once again becoming a problem.[13]

Class in the wizarding world, at least as the purebloods see it, is based on the purity of magical lineage. Wizards such as Dumbledore and his followers use polite terms when labeling people, but even they acknowledge the existence of a social hierarchy based on blood. This is evident in their use of the term *Muggle-born*. Purebloods use the word *Mudblood* to signal, as Ron explains, "Dirty blood, see. Common blood." (COS, 116) Even the term *half-blood*, which seems to be an acceptable expression to use in the wizarding world, denotes that the wizard or the witch in question is a person with less than a completely magical lineage. Voldemort hates his Muggle blood. He says to Harry about his father, "A Muggle and a fool . . . very like your dear mother. But they both had their uses, did they not?" (GOF, 646) The word *Squib* is also used to distinguish people of magical ancestry who have no magical abilities from the population and relegate them to menial labor.

The pureblood wizards in wizarding society who seek to exclude Muggle-born wizards can be compared to elite Victorians who attempted to keep the working classes from becoming a powerful force in English society. They are safeguarding their own power base and would support a system that denies upward social mobility to both the Muggle-born and the poorer pure-blooded magical folk. In Victorian England, landed elites pursued often cruel measures that kept the lower classes where the upper classes wanted them: subordinate. When Queen Victoria asked her prime minister, Lord Melbourne, about the proposal to educate poor children, he dismissed the idea out of hand: "Why bother the poor? Leave them alone!" Melbourne also imprisoned workers who protested against their pitiful wages or demanded that factory laborers should be given (only) a ten-hour day, literally clapping them into chains and manacles for the "crime" of organizing to improve their condition.[14] Lucius and his mother-in-law, Mrs. Black, would have approved.

There was an almost comical unwillingness on the part of the Victorian aristocracy to acknowledge the hardship and the poverty endured by the lower classes. Melbourne, who oversaw the passage of the severe New Poor Laws of 1834 and the creation of workhouses that were dreaded by the working poor, refused to discuss them with a young Queen Victoria, saying, "I don't *like* these things; I wish to avoid them."[15] Indeed, most members of the gentry and the landed elites simply filtered out such harsh realities. Moreover, as the social order was threatened by reform movements—such as the groups that demanded "home rule" for Ireland (a colonial possession of Britain's at the time), which would have given limited independence to the Irish—the aristocracy became frightened. Its members ceased to be distant but sometimes benevolent colonial administrators and began to pursue more directly exploitative practices vis-à-vis the Irish. In attempting to keep their land holdings in Ireland, the landed elite in Britain acted in the spirit of narrow-minded class interest.[16]

The aristocracy's and the landed elites' dominant role in politics and society persisted through the late nineteenth century, but the landed gentry began to lose influence after 1880. A poster boy for this decline would be Henry Chaplin, first Viscount Chaplin, a squire. Chaplin came into his inheritance in 1862, acquiring a sizable rent-roll of tenant farmers, only to lose it thirty years later. The landed gentry were a dying breed, and agricultural depression, low rents, and income taxes did their part to demolish the class. Chaplin's downfall was also caused by his own lavish tastes, because he spent exorbitant amounts of money on luxuries and on his horses. Eventually, his debt reached the degree where he had to sell his estate at Blankney Hall.[17]

A parallel decline of the wizarding upper class was precisely what the Malfoys feared and was the reason they were originally drawn to Voldemort and detested Dumbledore. Dumbledore's ideal of wizarding society is one in which any wizard with magical ability has an equal chance to succeed, which would imply the dismantling of the original wizarding class system. Because this system gives the purebloods power, supporters of Voldemort demanded that their society's hierarchy be kept and indeed shored up against the influx of the Muggle-born. Elite families such as the Malfoys could respond to changes in wizarding society only by emphasizing the differences between themselves and poorer families like the Weasleys and Muggles, such as the Grangers, even more strongly.

The first half of the twentieth century witnessed the rapid evaporation of the political and social influence of the British aristocracy. Genuine fear began to grow among the upper classes that the complex hierarchal system that had long benefited them was now rapidly falling apart. In 1906, the Liberal Party won by a landslide, defeating the conservative Tories.[18] The Labour Party, which was strongly allied with the British labor unions, rose in prominence and power and became the second-largest party in Parliament after World War I. In 1911, the landed elites' bastion, the House of Lords, lost its right to veto motions passed by the House of Commons (the popularly elected part of Parliament). The loss of the House of Lords' veto represented a dramatic shift in power within Britain's class structure.[19]

The Bigger They Are, the Harder They Fall: Great Wars and the Aristocracy of Both Worlds

World War I and its aftermath shook the British aristocracy to its core, both physically and financially. The aristocracy was well represented in the armed forces and took heavy casualties during the war, losing more men, proportionately, than any other social group.

Thirteen members of the Grey-Egerton family (an aristocratic family from Chesire) alone perished in active duty.[20] The Black family, too, suffered losses during the wizarding world's wars. Its tapestry was marred by burn marks as the names of family members who went against the Blacks' pureblood ideology were removed, but the wars also cost the family many of its younger generation in other ways. Sirius's brother, Regulus, was killed in the First Wizarding War when he was only eighteen, and Sirius himself died fighting the Death Eaters at the age of thirty-five. On the other side, their cousin Bellatrix spent much of her adult life in Azkaban because of her involvement in the war and died fighting (killed by Molly Weasley), childless and at a relatively young age. As a result of these wars, the Black family tree has narrowed down considerably. By the end of *Deathly Hallows*, almost all of the descendents of Sirius's grandfather and grandmother, Pollux and Irma Black, are dead: only two great-grandchildren are recorded on the Black family tapestry (Draco Malfoy and Teddy Lupin), and the Black family name is now extinct.

The Muggle aristocracy also took a beating during the wars of the twentieth century, as estates were liquidated, and the trappings of their wealth were sold off. Death duties, inheritance taxes on the estates of deceased, often took an enormous toll on aristocrats' family fortunes during the period between the two world wars. Large estates incurred enormous death duties that already-indebted aristocrats could not meet, and they were forced to sell properties that had been in their families for generations. In the years immediately preceding and following World War I, many great estates and London mansions were placed on the market. Between 1920 and 1939, 221 mansions were destroyed across Britain, usually torn down so that they could be replaced by shops, hotels, offices, or flats. Lord Lothian inherited four grand houses in 1930, for example, yet had to sell all but one.[21]

For gentlemen who were fighting a losing battle to keep the aristocracy as it had always been, World War I began the period in which the number of true aristocrats dwindled, in part due to losses on the battlefield. As Lord Strabolgi noted in his autobiography,

"We have accomplished a silent revolution in England since 1914. A whole class, the landed aristocracy, has been wiped out."[22] Many had indeed taken losses as heavy as the Black family's.

As aristocrats declined in both numbers and wealth after World War I, they became disillusioned with the politics of democracy. Social fluidity was bad for their class because it distributed power too evenly among the classes. Moreover, middle-class suburbs, which expanded during the twentieth century, were taking more and more land away from the landed aristocracy.[23] Many aristocrats now intensely loathed politicians who pushed a democratic agenda.

Instead, some British aristocrats yearned for a system of government that was more authoritarian, flirting with extreme right-wing politics. They began to identify with the fascist systems of government that emerged across Europe during the 1920s and the 1930s. Fascism promised to recreate the paternalistic relationship between landed elites and the state and the stratified social hierarchy that aristocrats had once enjoyed. By the 1930s, some British aristocrats also longed for a decisive, authoritarian leader to move their nation out of the stagnation that had come from the consolidation of what they saw as an ineffective democratic political system. Such aristocrats admired the politics that Hitler and Mussolini had brought to Germany and Italy, for example.

Many aristocrats in Britain felt that the fascist regimes of Germany and Italy brought civility and order, where democratic government in England had bred only chaos.[24] Some came to support Sir Oswald Mosley, the son of a baronet who married Lady Cynthia Curzon, the daughter of a marquess who was the viceroy of India. Mosley broke with the Labour Party to found the British Unions of Fascists in 1932 (also known as "Mosley's Black Shirts") and went on to form close connections to fascist parties across Europe, including the German National Socialists. Despite his extremism, Mosley retained powerful admirers among the landed elites of Britain during the 1930s. Mosley's supporters clearly had counterparts among the purebloods of the wizarding world as well: a similar disillusionment with changes in wizarding society is the reason so many purebloods were receptive to Voldemort's message.

When World War II began, however, the overwhelming majority of British aristocratic men chose to fight in the war in support of their nation and therefore suffered casualties. Some of those who did not serve saw their homes destroyed in bombardment, and many estates that were not ruined were seized by the government for war-related purposes. The landed elites were also taxed heavily to support the war effort. Despite these contributions, public opinion turned against the upper classes after the war; in the new postwar Britain, the aristocracy had no real place.[25]

Fading into Obscurity

At their core, the central conflicts in Harry Potter can be seen as class conflicts. The wizards at the top of the wizarding hierarchy, the Malfoys and their associates, are fighting to maintain the world that they are accustomed to. To the elitist Malfoys, the rise of mixed-blood wizards—the most famous of whom is the Boy Who Lived—is a threat, and if the newcomers eventually came to control the Ministry and other institutions of the magical world, this would be an insult too devastating to bear. The Malfoys firmly and completely believe that their blood and wealth should put them at the top of the social pyramid. And at the start of the series, they were probably correct to see themselves that way. When Draco haughtily observes to Harry in the first book, "You'll soon find out some wizarding families are much better than others, Potter. You don't want to go making friends with the wrong sort. I can help you there," he's only telling the truth about the world as he knows it (SS, 135).

Yet like the British aristocrats of the nineteenth and early twentieth centuries, the Malfoys saw the world that they and their ancestors had built falling apart. After the First Wizarding War, the pureblood aristocracy was somewhat diminished but still very much present during Harry's childhood. Lucius, for example, was able to overcome the accusations leveled against him and maintained his contacts in the Ministry, according to Mr. Weasley. But the Second Wizarding War further weakened the power of the pureblood elite, as the old laws that favored pureblood interests came under attack.

It's possible that Draco's "somewhat receding hairline" as observed in the epilogue to *Deathly Hallows* might be the result of the increased stress of living in a world where his "pure" ancestry no longer entitles him to privilege and where the purebloods must be even more outnumbered than they were during his youth (*DH*, 755). The Hogwarts House that was most strongly dominated by purebloods—Slytherin—was discredited after almost all of its members deserted the school, rather than defend Harry and face Voldemort. The wizards and the witches who fought for Voldemort during the Battle of Hogwarts were presumably largely (or entirely) purebloods, and like the British officer corps during World War I, they must have taken heavy casualties. And as happened after Voldemort's first defeat, many of his pureblood supporters who survived must have been sent to Azkaban.

After the war, Draco is no longer the vocal snob he once was. Instead, the epilogue of *Deathly Hallows* shows him exhibiting a silent, grudging acceptance of his former enemies. If anything, the fact that Voldemort and his pureblood supporters lost seems to have turned the prewar social hierarchy on its head. Ron, however jokingly, cautions his daughter against becoming involved with Draco's son. Ron says, "Don't get *too* friendly with him, though, Rosie. Granddad Weasley would never forgive you if you married a pureblood." (*DH*, 756) Even Hermione's scolding of her husband for turning the children against one another is only "half stern." (*DH*, 756)

The British aristocracy fought on the right side of both world wars, that is, the winning side. Pureblood wizards largely fought on the losing side, the wrong side. Yet in the end, the effect was the same. After their respective wars, both groups lost power and influence, at the same time that their numbers were diminishing. In Muggle Britain, new taxation and other economic pressures forced many aristocrats to sell off parts of their land in an attempt to stay afloat. Some families were even compelled by unprecedented hard times to open their once very private homes to public visitors and sell tickets to tour groups.[26]

As far as we know, the Malfoys kept their manor and have not yet been forced to open it up to public tours. Yet they have clearly nonetheless lost a great deal. Before the war, Arthur Weasley had described Lucius's influence to Harry: "Malfoy's been giving to all sorts of things for years [. . .] Gets him in with the right people [. . .] Oh, he's very well connected Lucius Malfoy." (OOTP, 155) By the end of the series, however, Lucius has lost all political influence; he was sent to Azkaban and endured humiliation at the hands Voldemort, who even took Malfoy's wand.

The family that opposed and bedeviled Harry throughout the series—almost turning him over to Voldemort for execution when he was captured in Deathly Hallows—was lucky to escape Azkaban after the war, when all was said and done. By the end of the Harry Potter series, wizarding purebloods seem to have lost control over the seats of power, just as Muggle English aristocrats had, almost a century earlier. The decline of both groups was now complete.

Notes

1. All book quotes are taken from the American editions by J. K. Rowling as follows: Sorcerer's Stone, A.A. Levine Books, 1998; Chamber of Secrets, New York: Scholastic, 2000; Prisoner of Azkaban, New York: A.A. Levine Books, 1999; Goblet of Fire, New York: A.A. Levine Books, 2000; Order of the Phoenix, New York: A.A. Levine Books, 2003; Half-Blood Prince, New York: A.A. Levine Books, 2005; Deathly Hallows, New York: A.A. Levine Books, 2007.

2. Red Hen, "Oase in Point: Lucius Malfoy," Red Hen Publications, www.redhen-publications.com/LMalfoy.html.

3. David Cannadine, Aspects of Aristocracy: Grandeur and Decline in Modern Britain (New Haven, CT: Yale University Press, 1994), 26.

4. Blenheim Palace Web site, www.blenheimpalace.com.

5. A. N. Wilson, The Victorians (New York: W. H. Norton, 2003), 318.

6. Cannadine, Aspects of Aristocracy, 214.

7. Ibid., 136–137.

8. David Cannadine, Class in Britain (New York: Penguin, 1998), 57–62.

9. Ibid., 66–86.

10. Cannadine, Class in Britain, 73.

11. Ibid., 26–28, 98–99.

12. Wilson, Victorians, 115.

13. Cannadine, Class in Britain, 98–99.

14. Wilson, Victorians, 28.

15. Ibid., 28.

16. Cannadine, *Class in Britain*, 108.

17. Wilson, *The Victorians*, 588.

18. A. N. Wilson, *After the Victorians: The Decline of Britain in the World* (New York: Farrar, Straus, and Giroux, 2005), 48.

19. Cannadine, *Class in Britain*, 127.

20. David Cannadine, *The Decline and Fall of the British Aristocracy* (New Haven, CT: Yale University Press, 1990), 79–80.

21. Ibid., 116–121.

22. The quotation from Lord Strabolgi's autobiography is reproduced in ibid., 545.

23. Ibid., 545.

24. Ibid., 546–547.

25. Cannadine, "The Second World War," in *Decline and Fall of the British Aristocracy*, 606–635.

26. Cannadine, *The Decline and Fall of the British Aristocracy*, 637–656.

School Ties, House Points, and Quidditch

Hogwarts as a British Boarding School

Susan Hall

When *Harry Potter and the Philosopher's Stone* first appeared in 1997, boarding schools in both fact and fiction had reached a low point. The fact that boarding schools were unfashionable at the time added to J. K. Rowling's difficulties in finding a publisher and perhaps was one factor that led to a small print run for the first edition.[1]

To explain how the fortunes of these schools were Transfigured by the efforts of a green-eyed teenage wizard with a scar, readers should pick up their Time-Turners and travel back to the dawn of the nineteenth century. In 1837, Queen Victoria, an eighteen-year-old girl with a strong German accent, would ascend to the British throne. Her reign would see the face of the world change forever. By 1815, the forces of change were already gathering. The Duke of Wellington allegedly claimed that that year's Battle of Waterloo had been won "on the playing fields of Eton [College]."[2]

Eton and a handful of other British schools made up the so-called public schools, whose influence increased exponentially during the course of Victoria's reign. Somewhat counterintuitively, in British English a "public" school is one of the most exclusive privately funded schools in the country (a fuller description of the British education system appears further on).

Justin Finch-Fletchley assures Harry, "My name was down for Eton, you know, I can't tell you how glad I am I came here instead." (COS, 73)[3] Eton is considered to be la crème de la crème of the British public schools; both Prince Harry and Prince William studied there. Justin's comment establishes his upper-class status and indicates Hogwarts' own prestige.

Although King's School, Canterbury, was allegedly founded by St. Augustine in the seventh century, the small group of public schools that existed at the beginning of the nineteenth century were much later creations. Even Eton College (founded in 1440), Rugby School (1567), and Winchester College (1382) were comparative youngsters next to Hogwarts, which was founded at some point in the tenth or the eleventh century. Much about the Muggle public schools, though, seems oddly familiar to anyone who knows Hogwarts.

The British phrase "old school tie" refers to the network of connections forged between people who attended the same (prestigious) school. The Hogwarts' equivalent is the Slug Club. Yet the phrase is also a pun. Like the Hogwarts Houses in the Harry Potter films, schools such as Eton have an official, distinctive design of necktie worn by former pupils to demonstrate their school allegiance.

Even treason does not necessarily stop an Old Etonian from flaunting the "old school tie":

Moscow last week [March, 1959] was soberly ablaze with old-school ties from Eton (black and light blue). Prime Minister Harold Macmillan sported one at the Bolshoi Theater performance of the ballet Romeo and Juliet. So did one of the principal Foreign Office types he brought along. The third was worn by Guy Burgess, infamous for his 1951 flight from his Foreign

Office job to Russia with Fellow Diplomat Donald MacLean [Burgess, a covert Soviet agent who passed atomic secrets to the USSR during the Cold War, defected when on the point of arrest].[4]

Horace Slughorn's attitude to his former pupil Tom Riddle seems to have echoes of the relationship between Eton and Guy Burgess; no matter what a pupil does later, he can never absolutely sever his ties to his old school.[5]

Physical clues such as distinctive neckties are less necessary in the magical world. The population is much smaller, most of them attend Hogwarts, and all of the pureblood families are related. Yet the principle that "it's not what you know, it's who you know" affects the magical world as much as it does its Muggle counterpart.

Another point of comparison between the public schools and Hogwarts is language. Traditionally, the public schools concentrated on teaching Latin and Greek ("the classics"), and they remain a strong tradition there. Rowling drew on those languages, especially Latin, to create spells such as "Obliviate!" "Accio!" and "Crucio!"

Slytherin Ascendant: The Great Days of the British Public School

C. L. R. James, the influential West Indian historian and journalist, identified three men who, "more than all others, created Victorianism" and so gave an enormous boost to the British Empire.[6] Those three men were Thomas Arnold, Thomas Hughes, and W. G. Grace. Arnold was a headmaster who radically reformed the "public" school tradition during his time as headmaster of Rugby. Hughes wrote Tom Brown's Schooldays (1857), a best-selling school story, based on his own experiences as a pupil of Arnold's. Hughes had no hesitation in explaining that the book's purpose was to preach "muscular Christianity." This combined a vigorous, uncomplicated Christian faith with hearty athleticism. The latter quality was embodied in the cricketer W. G. Grace, a record-breaking sportsman who remained for half a century almost every (British) schoolboy's hero.

When Arnold became headmaster at Rugby in 1828, there was only a handful of public schools in the country. His example led to an explosion in new schools, which supposedly followed his lead. In many cases, they were not practicing Arnold's ideas but the mythical version of them promoted by Hughes in *Tom Brown's Schooldays*. For example, it was Hughes, not Arnold, who stressed the importance of compulsory sports in an Englishman's education.

As James emphasized, the purpose of the Muggle public schools during the nineteenth and early twentieth centuries was to create and nurture a ruling elite. Sir Charles Synge Bowen's translation of Virgil's *Aeneid*, Book VI, captures that sense of mission:

> Thine, O Roman, remember, to reign over every race!
> These be thine arts, thy glories, the ways of peace proclaim,
> Mercy to show to the fallen, the proud with battle to tame.

Schools such as Eton, Winchester, and Rugby left their pupils in no doubt that *they* were the spiritual heirs of the Roman legacy and, like the Romans, destined "to reign over every race." (Bowen [1835–1894] was himself a pupil at Rugby School; he became a senior judge.)

Albus Dumbledore and Gellert Grindelwald were born in the early 1880s. Their soaring imperial ambitions echoed those of their Muggle contemporaries. The seventeen-year-old Dumbledore's letter to Grindelwald almost seems inspired by Bowen:

> "Your point about wizard dominance being FOR THE MUGGLES' OWN GOOD—this, I think, is the crucial point. Yes, we have been given power and, yes, that power gives us the right to rule, but it also gives us responsibilities over the ruled. We must stress this point, it will be the foundation stone upon which we build. . . . We seize control FOR THE GREATER GOOD. And from this it follows that where we meet resistance, we must use only the force that is necessary and no more." (*DH*, 357)

Rudyard Kipling, a Nobel Prize–winning author and "the prophet of British imperialism in its expansionist phase," also wrote an influential school story, *Stalky & Co*, set in a thinly disguised version of his own school, the United Services College, located in the Devon village of Westward Ho![7] In its final chapter, "Slaves of the Lamp, Part II," Kipling's schoolboy characters, now grown up, reminisce about how the lessons they learned at school—outside the classroom—stood them in good stead in the wilder parts of the British Empire. The narrator, Beetle (Kipling himself), states,

> "India's full of Stalkies—Cheltenham and Haileybury and Marlborough chaps—that we don't know anything about, and the surprises will begin when there is really a big row on."
> "Who will be surprised?" said Dick Four.
> "The other side. The gentlemen who go to the front in first-class carriages. Just imagine Stalky let loose on the south side of Europe with a sufficiency of Sikhs and a reasonable prospect of loot. Consider it quietly."[8]

There is something scarily reminiscent of Dumbledore and Grindelwald's plotting "for the greater good" about Kipling's quiet assumption that it was only a matter of time before "the south side of Europe" lay open to be looted by English public schoolboys, just as they had already looted India and large swathes of Africa.

Cheltenham, Haileybury, and Marlborough are public schools created in the latter nineteenth century, after the model developed by Arnold. Yet the "big row" to which Kipling looks forward with naive optimism in *Stalky & Co* turned out to be World War I, in which a generation of public schoolboys, reared on Elgar's patriotic anthem "Land of Hope and Glory" and its associated myths of imperial invincibility, were slaughtered in the Flanders mud. An older Kipling, devastated by the loss of his only son, John, in the Battle of Loos, observed in *Epitaphs of the War*:

> "If any question why we died,
> Tell them, because our fathers lied."[9]

C. L. R. James himself attended Queen's Royal College, Trinidad.[10] Schools such as his, located in the outposts of the British Empire, modeled themselves on the principles embodied by Hughes, Arnold, and Grace and served up an intensely anglophile curriculum of classics and cricket. In contrast to Kipling, James observed the "mother-country's" public school system from the perspective of those it classified as inherently inferior: the colonized, not the colonizers. He noted,

> It was only long years after that I understood the limitation on spirit, vision and self-respect which was imposed on us by the fact that our masters, our curriculum, our code of morals, *everything* began from the basis that Britain was the source of all light and leading, and our business was to admire, wonder, imitate, learn; our criteria of success was to have succeeded in approaching that distant ideal—to attain it was, of course, impossible.[11]

The insights James gained from having been *in* but not *of* the public school system were crucial in his later career. He joined the Pan-African movement and became a leading figure in the campaign for West Indian independence. He was instrumental in dismantling the empire that Arnold, Grace, and Hughes had done so much to build up.

In a not dissimilar way, Harry also possesses an outsider's perspective. His experience living in a Muggle household and being the victim of the Dursleys' snobbery at first makes the magical world seem like a place of refuge, much as it had been years earlier for Tom Riddle. Unlike Riddle, however, Harry possesses an ability to draw parallels between evils he has experienced in the Muggle world and their equivalents in the magical one. He rejects both the corrupt Ministry of Magic and the seductive imperialist fantasies of the Death Eaters.

The sun setting on the British Empire after World War II also seemed, at first, to herald the decline of the public schools. Enrollment numbers dwindled, those with "posh" public school speech patterns adopted instead regional or working-class accents, and publishers purged their catalogues of school stories. George MacDonald Fraser enjoyed massive popular success with a series of historical novels, beginning with *Flashman* (1969).

The Flashman Papers are an impeccably researched, witty, and subversive reinterpretation of *Tom Brown's Schooldays*. Flashman, the first-person narrator of the stories, is Tom Brown's principal enemy in Hughes's original nineteenth-century novel. He is a vicious bully with much in common with Draco Malfoy, including cowardice, snobbery, and a tendency to buy favors using lavish gifts sent to him from home.[12]

MacDonald Fraser does not soften a single one of Flashman's original traits but still turns him into one of the funniest characters in fiction. "Flashy" cheats, embezzles, seduces, and deceives his way through most of the major events of the later part of the nineteenth century, including the Charge of the Light Brigade, the Battle of Little Big Horn, and John Brown's attack on Harper's Ferry. As a result, he becomes a popular hero and a much-decorated soldier, the embodiment of Victorian double standards and a symbol of the seamy underbelly of the empire.

This subversive approach to the previous idealization of public school values continued with Lindsay Anderson's surreal 1968 film *If . . .* (the title is an ironic take on another Kipling poem). In this cult classic, three disaffected senior students at an exclusive public school become increasingly alienated from the values it stands for. In a climactic scene that is even more chilling post-Columbine than when originally filmed, the three seize semiautomatic weapons and carry out a massacre of staff and pupils against the hauntingly beautiful backdrop of the school's Gothic buildings.[13]

The next few years saw even this degree of interest in the public schools wane. Grange Hill, a rough state-run comprehensive school in a blue-collar neighborhood, became the country's favorite fictional school. The BBC children's TV series *Grange Hill* ran from 1978 to 2008, and the fictional school's swearing, drinking, drug-taking, and truanting pupils drew numerous complaints from viewers who shared Uncle Vernon's prejudices. Nevertheless, *Grange Hill* won many awards for realism.

Back to the Future: Harry Potter and
the Return of the Boarding Schools

When *Philosopher's Stone* first appeared in 1997, the boarding school story genre begun by Hughes in 1857 seemed wholly outdated. The success of the Potter series did not simply revive the boarding school in fiction. As this 2003 news story from Rowling's native Edinburgh shows, even some of the most prestigious schools in the country turned to magic to improve flagging enrolments:

> FETTES College is attempting to cash in on the Harry Potter phenomenon by staging a themed open day.
>
> The exclusive establishment's prep school [in English usage, the junior department of the school, for ages seven through thirteen] is targeting children who dream of attending a real-life Hogwarts by offering a "spell-making" course in a chemistry lab and the chance to handle owls like the schoolboy wizard's feathered friend Hedwig. Teachers at the school will even don robes for the occasion.
>
> The £13,000-a-year [$19,057] boarding school hopes the one-off event will capitalise on the overwhelming success of the best-selling books and blockbuster films, which has turned author JK Rowling into one of Britain's richest women. . . . School chiefs plan to bring in South Queensferry magician Scott Lovat and four owls from the Edinburgh Bird of Prey centre for a demonstration. The event will also feature a torchlit tour of the school grounds, and teachers in fancy dress will emulate characters including Harry's headmaster Professor Albus Dumbledore.[14]

In addition to former prime minister Tony Blair, Fettes College (founded in 1870) can also claim fictional super-spy James Bond as an alumnus. Clearly, neither of them possesses the drawing power of Harry Potter.

Fee-paying schools are now increasing their share of the education sector in the United Kingdom, and English-style boarding schools are being built in places such as Cyprus to deliver the benefits of a UK public school education at a lower cost than the original. Harry Potter cannot be responsible for all of it, but at the very least, Rowling can claim to have taken full advantage of a previously unsuspected change in public mood.

Unfogging the British Education System

As indicated earlier, the term *public school* in British English denotes a fee-paying establishment, under the control of a board of governors and not subsidized by the local or national government. Most British public schools have the legal status of charities and enjoy significant tax exemptions as a result.

Public schools take pupils from ages eleven (or thirteen) to eighteen; for more junior children, "prep" or preparatory schools, taking children from age seven (or younger), are the equivalent. As shown earlier with Fettes College, it is common for a public school to have an associated prep school, which acts as a "feeder" to it. Oddly, there is no prep school equivalent to Hogwarts, implying that magical children must be educated at home until attending Hogwarts at age eleven.

The public schools, properly so called, are only the tip of the independent school iceberg. Below them in the status hierarchy sits a bewildering mixture of fee-paying schools of various types, relatively free of outside oversight.

The murkier aspects of private education in Britain were satirized in Evelyn Waugh's 1928 novel *Decline and Fall*. After a disastrous hazing incident at his Oxford college, disgraced student Paul Pennyfeather is consoled by a college servant: "I expect you'll be becoming a schoolmaster, sir. That's what most of the gentlemen does, sir, that gets sent down for indecent behaviour." Pennyfeather, accordingly, applies to an agency that places staff in private schools. They tell him, "We class schools, you see, into four grades: Leading School, First-rate School, Good School, and School. Frankly . . . School is pretty bad."

Dudley Dursley's school, Smeltings, appears to hover on the borderline between Good School and School. Because independent schools operate in an extremely competitive market, academic success is highly important. More prestigious schools insist that applicants are capable of reaching a prescribed minimum standard, embodied in the Common Entrance (CE) examinations of the Independent Schools Examination Board. It seems impossible to believe that Dudley, who at the age of eleven has trouble adding 2 to 37, could possibly have reached CE standard in English, mathematics, classics, or history.

Whatever its academic deficiencies, Smeltings compensates for them with the sheer preposterousness of its uniform: "Smeltings boys wore maroon tailcoats, orange knickerbockers and flat straw hats called boaters. They also carried knobbly sticks, used for hitting each other while the teachers weren't looking. This was supposed to be good training for later life." (PS, 29) Smeltings seems to be trying a bit too hard to look like an ancient establishment.

Even if the school lacks prestige, Smeltings' fees must absorb a large percentage of the Dursleys' income. This may explain — although it does not excuse — Vernon and Petunia's paranoia about incurring any additional expense with respect to Harry.

Had Harry not received his Hogwarts letter, he would have attended Stonewall High, the local state (that is, "public," in the American usage) comprehensive school. At the current date (2010), approximately 90 percent of state schools are comprehensive; that is, they have nonselective criteria for entry. Recent political changes have sought to increase parental choice about which comprehensive school a child attends. Incentives have been given for schools to become "academies" (centers of excellence), while sanctions have been brought in against "failing" schools. None of these measures were in place during the early 1990s — when Harry would have attended Stonewall High — when state education was suffering from a prolonged period of underinvestment.

One reason for the comparatively poor state of government-funded education at the time when Harry faced his move to Stonewall High was the bitter political infighting that accompanied the change to comprehensive education from the previous selective system, remnants of which still apply in a small number of places in the United Kingdom.

The 1944 Butler Education Act required local education authorities to provide free secondary education in accordance with the "tripartite" system; grammar schools for the academically inclined who were likely to go into clerical positions or on to higher education, technical secondary schools for those with a technical bent, and "secondary moderns" for everyone else. In practice, few technical schools were built, so the system became bipartite, with about 80 to 85 percent of state school pupils attending secondary modern schools. Most pupils at secondary modern schools left at the minimum school-leaving age of fifteen (raised to sixteen in 1972) without any formal qualifications.

Whether a child attended a grammar school or a secondary modern was determined by a public competitive examination, taken at the age of eleven and known, with startling originality, as the "11-plus." The 11-plus results largely determined a child's entire future career. As a result, Muggle children waited to know whether they had passed or failed the 11-plus as anxiously as magical children await their Hogwarts' O.W.L.s.

In self-conscious mimicry of the public schools, grammar schools featured teachers who taught in gowns, the division of pupils into different "houses," a narrow academic curriculum, and a severely formal style of architecture. Grammar schools were, however, usually day schools, although "direct grant" grammar schools might have limited boarding accommodations.

Direct grant grammar schools were a group of schools that enjoyed specific status within the grammar school hierarchy. In general, they consisted of those schools that had been founded in the sixteenth century or earlier and that had prestige and traditions equivalent to those of the great public schools.

The Protestant Reformation created an increased emphasis on the ability of individuals to be able to read the bible for themselves, although Latin remained the language of educated discourse. Edward VI (1547–1553) was particularly active in founding free

grammar schools to educate poor but talented boys. King Edward's
School, Birmingham, which educated J. R. R. Tolkien, among a
host of other distinguished pupils, including two Nobel Prize winners, is one of Edward VI's foundations.[15]

When the 1944 Act came into effect, many of these older grammar schools became direct grant grammar schools, in which the
majority of their places were allocated free of charge to pupils who
passed the 11-plus, but some places were reserved for fee-paying
pupils.

Although the grammar schools gave an excellent, if narrowly
focused, education to the 15 to 20 percent of pupils who passed the
11-plus, there were major difficulties with this system. First, there
were fewer grammar school places for girls than for boys. Most
grammar schools were single sex, and the vast majority of the direct
grant grammar schools were for boys only. As a result, a girl had to
score higher on the 11-plus than a boy did to be offered a grammar
school place. Girls' grammar schools also tended to be less well-
equipped, especially with regard to laboratory and sports facilities.
Second, the system made no provision for "late-developers" or for
those whose primary schools (state junior schools; for pupils ages
five to eleven) failed to prepare them for the 11-plus. Finally, as
children's fantasy writer Alan Garner observed from his experience as a working-class boy arriving at the prestigious Manchester
Grammar School (founded in 1515), the experience could produce
cultural dislocation for first-generation grammar school pupils.[16]

Garner came from a family of Cheshire stone-masons who had
inhabited the same piece of land for more than three hundred years.
They spoke "North Mercian Middle English," the dialect used in
the fourteenth-century poem "Sir Gawain and the Green Knight," a
beautiful but difficult work. Garner reported that although his father
and uncles could read "Sir Gawain" with ease, his own attempt to
speak its dialect as a child at school led to him having his mouth
washed out with carbolic soap.

Grammar schools sought to ensure that their pupils abandoned hobbies and reading materials that were seen as lower class.
Grammar schools also preferred that pupils played rugby football,
rather than the far more popular soccer, which was dismissed as

"common." Some parallels can be seen with Muggle-borns arriving at Hogwarts, where Quidditch is expected to replace their old soccer allegiances and where pureblood kids such as Ron Weasley know about Muggle culture only from caricatures such as *The Adventures of Martin Miggs, the Mad Muggle*. In the case of both Muggle-borns at Hogwarts and working-class children in grammar schools, this must cause resentment between such pupils and their families.

Petunia Evans's difficult relationship with her sister, Lily, as a result of Petunia's failure to enter Hogwarts may be set within a fantasy framework, but it is a realistic depiction of the kind of simmering resentment that often occurred when one sibling passed the 11-plus and others did not. Severus Snape's touchiness when confronted with the arrogant assurance of James Potter and Sirius Black (both from wealthy pure-blood families) and his exaggerated pride in his own intellectual attainments are also characteristic of working-class pupils who attend grammar schools.

To alleviate these concerns, the first comprehensive schools were introduced in 1949, with the United Kingdom gradually converting to comprehensive education during the sixties and the seventies. Comprehensive schools were automatically despised by Conservative voters, such as Uncle Vernon, who has passed his prejudices on to Dudley. Ignoring the institutionalized nature of bullying at Smeltings, symbolized by the stick, Dudley jeers at Harry, "They stuff people's heads down the toilets first day at Stonewall." (*PS*, 28) Dudley, it seems, has been watching *Grange Hill*.

Sorcery and Certification

Pupils do not "graduate" from British schools. They are entitled to leave once they have attained the minimum school-leaving age. Mrs. Weasley's anger at Fred and George Weasley's abrupt departure from Hogwarts is not because they have "dropped out" but because they have passed only a few O.W.L.s and will not go on to take the N.E.W.Ts, which are entry-level qualifications for most Ministry departments.

O.W.L.s (taken during the fifth year) and N.E.W.T.s (taken during the seventh year) were established long before their Muggle equivalents. Dumbledore himself took N.E.W.Ts in 1899. Griselda Marchbanks, who examined him, claimed that he "did things with a wand I'd never seen before." (*OOTP*, 627)

At that time, the Muggle world had no standardized tests, but this changed about a generation later. From 1918 to 1951, the Muggle world used the "School Certificate" (taken at sixteen) and the "Higher School Certificate" (taken at eighteen), in which pupils were examined in a variety of subjects and had to pass all of them. In 1951, the School Certificate and the Higher School Certificate were replaced, respectively, by the GCE Ordinary ("O") and Advanced ("A") Levels, where pupils were examined in individual subjects. Each pass in each subject was graded from A to E (with A* for exceptional performance).

As a result, British Muggle students describe their school performance in terms of numbers and grades of O Levels and A Levels achieved, for example, "Nine O Levels, eight at grade A, grade B in maths; four A grades at A Level," not as a grade point average. The magical world does the same. The tradition of sending out examination results in the school holidays and having different standards of not only passing but of failing grades is also common to both worlds.

Like O.W.L.s and N.E.W.Ts, O Levels and A Levels are almost entirely examination-based. Hogwarts seems never to have allowed course work to count toward the final O.W.L.s and N.E.W.Ts results. The essays that Ron and Harry complain about (and that they usually copy from Hermione Granger) are assigned simply to demonstrate to their teachers' satisfaction that they understand the subject, in preparation for later examinations.

Tom Riddle's Schooldays: Poor Pupils at Hogwarts

Hogwarts is a very unusual school. As obvious as the comment seems, the strangest thing about Hogwarts is not that the Deputy Headmistress often turns herself into a cat. Hogwarts' accessibility makes it stand out, from a British Muggle point of view.

All children with magical talent in Great Britain (and possibly in Ireland; the political relationship in the magical world between Britain and Ireland is unclear) receive an invitation to study at Hogwarts at the age of eleven. It appears that financial reasons are not permitted to stand in the way of their accepting that place. Tom Riddle, for example, is told by Dumbledore, "There is a fund at Hogwarts for those who require assistance to buy books and robes." (*HBP*, 256)

How this works in practice is vague. Pre-Hogwarts, children do not seem to have their education supervised in any way by the Ministry for Magic. There is no attempt to make sure they are educated up to a standard that will ensure they can cope when they arrive. That applies not merely to magic but to factors such as basic literary and numeracy.

Although Dumbledore expresses doubt about whether his brother, Aberforth (who attended Hogwarts), can read, this reflects the antagonistic relationship between the two brothers, rather than being a serious claim. From what we see of the curriculum, it seems impossible that anyone illiterate could attend Hogwarts.

The magical underclass may include those from magical backgrounds who were eligible to attend Hogwarts but who, despite the financial assistance offered, were unable to take advantage of the opportunity because of their lack of basic skills. The Gaunts, Tom Riddle's mother's family, seem to be in this position.

Through many centuries, the literacy requirement probably also filtered out peasant or working-class Muggle-born students. In any event, such children were too important to their family's economic survival to be spared for education.

Until child labor was limited by various acts of Parliament in the nineteenth century, children as young as four or five were employed in mines and factories. During the Napoleonic Wars in the early nineteenth century, children no older than six were employed as "powder-monkeys" aboard Royal Naval vessels, engaged in the dangerous task of bringing gunpowder from the powder magazine, where they were stored aboard ship, to the gun crews during sea battles. Children too young for paid employment were still occupied in tasks such as bird scaring (if the family had a vegetable patch), looking after younger siblings, and watching pots on the stove. By the time these Muggle children reached eleven, they would have been significant contributors to the family income.

The cost of equipping a child for Hogwarts is substantial. Tuition, board, and food seem to be provided free of charge, even though meals at Hogwarts are on a lavish scale unknown to any other school in fact or fiction. Yet robes, wands, books, and potion ingredients have to be paid for. Gilderoy Lockhart takes advantage of this captive market by assigning significant quantities of his own books for his courses, which threatens to cause serious financial embarrassment to the hard-up Weasleys.

Again, the close parallel is with twentieth-century grammar-school children. Tom Riddle, whatever his character defects, possesses outstanding intelligence. If he had remained in the Muggle school system, he would have had good prospects of qualifying for one of the limited free places that existed at schools such as King Edwards, Birmingham. As a penniless orphan, though, he would have experienced great difficulty in accepting that place because of the extra expense involved. He would probably have been forced to settle for elementary education and would have left school at age fourteen.

Grammar school uniforms were a major cost (elementary schools did not usually require uniforms) and required items such as tennis racquets, an unheard-of luxury. The intense embarrassment this could inflict on sensitive children from poor families is explored in children's books such as Eve Garnett's *The Family from One End Street* (1937) and Hester Burton's *In Spite of All Terror* (1968). Echoes appear in Ginny Weasley's self-consciousness about arriving at Hogwarts in *Chamber of Secrets* with secondhand robes and books. When she confides her distress to Tom Riddle, who inhabits her diary, he offers pretended sympathy.

Whatever the practical difficulties, however, the wizarding world can only be applauded for having sought, for more than a thousand years, to give all of its children an education, irrespective of finances, gender, or social standing. Muggle experiences were very different.

"Christianise It or Crush It": Religion and Education in Muggle Britain

Until the early to mid-nineteenth century, British educational options had been limited for boys and virtually nonexistent for girls. Class and religion were the main factors in determining educational chances.

Poor children were dependent first on a patchy and voluntary provision of Sunday schools and later on the National Schools run by the National Society for Promoting Religious Education (a Church of England body founded in 1811) and the competing British Schools run by the British and Foreign Schools Society (founded in 1808), which promoted nondenominational education.

Conflict over religion dominated attempts to provide free, compulsory education to all children in England and Wales. (Scotland had a different and far superior public education policy, which is why the eighteenth and nineteenth centuries produced many Scottish engineers and scientists from working-class backgrounds.) The chief debate was between the biblical party and the secular party. In the biblical corner were the likes of the Salford preacher Canon Hugh Stowell. His view of education for the poor was simple and direct: "Either Christianise it or crush it." The secular party, which objected to compulsory religious education and worship in schools, included Methodists, Baptists, Quakers, Unitarians, and Roman Catholics. Their objection was essentially that compulsory religious education privileged the Established Church (the Church of England) above other denominations.

Compulsory education for children in England and Wales was finally introduced by Foster's Education Act in 1870. This act provided for the establishment and the inspection of elementary schools to educate children from ages five through twelve, although only the very poorest children attended free of charge. In areas where there were existing National or British schools, the act provided for grants to bring such schools into the elementary school network.

The elementary schools maintained under the act became known as "board schools," because their establishment and the education provided within them were under the control of school boards elected by the local "rate-payers" in the relevant district. Rate-payers eligible to vote were people who were registered and paid property taxes on their homes. Dependants of rate-payers, such as grown-up children or wives of rate-payers, did not get a vote, nor did people who simply rented a room or who lived in lodging houses.

Many proponents of women's suffrage sought election to school boards, because it offered an opportunity for women to show that they could be competent and effective in public life. Yet board schools still offered different types of education to boys and girls, with girls' education concentrating on sewing and domestic skills. Playgrounds were segregated between the sexes, and schools typically had separate entrances for boys and "girls and infants" (these practices lingered into the 1960s). Minerva McGonagall would no doubt have snorted in disgust at the very idea (before using the cat-flap).

Board school is used as a term of scorn by Kipling in *Stalky & Co*, but Sir Arthur Conan Doyle put a ringing eulogy of board schools into the mouth of Sherlock Holmes in *The Memoirs of Sherlock Holmes*: "The Board Schools! Lighthouses, my boy, beacons of the future! Capsules with hundreds of bright little seeds in each, out of which will spring the brighter, better Britain of the future."[17] The 1944 Education Act, referred to earlier, required state schools to participate in a "daily nondenominational act of collective worship," known to generations of bored schoolchildren as "Assembly." This requirement is still in force today. Many state primary schools (for children from four to eleven) are associated with local churches, as are some state secondary schools. There are also a limited number of state-supported schools explicitly categorized as "faith" schools, which have a more marked denominational character to their teaching.[18]

Although independent schools are free of the constraints with regard to religion that the state sector imposes, the Arnold legacy meant that in practice, religious worship, including compulsory chapel attendance, formed a very large part of school life at public schools during the nineteenth and early to mid-twentieth centuries.

Ironically, religious writers such as Dorothy L. Sayers and C. S. Lewis cited negative experiences with school religion as a barrier to the development of their own personal faiths.

The secular character of Hogwarts, which has no Assembly, no school chapel, no Christian Union, no grace before meals, and no R.E. (religious education) classes, is another factor that marks it as odd, compared to the general experience of British schoolchildren. Although Christmas and Easter are mentioned in the Harry Potter books—Sirius sings carols, and Mrs. Weasley sends the Trio chocolate eggs—these holidays lack any form of religious element. The only character who appears definitely Christian is the Fat Friar, and he appears to take the traditionally British approach that it is bad manners to discuss religion in public.

"Miss! Please, Miss!"

It was "Co-educational," a school for both boys and girls—what used to be called a "mixed" school; some said it was not nearly so mixed as the minds of the people who ran it.

—C. S. Lewis, *The Silver Chair*[19]

Hogwarts was founded more than a thousand years ago by Rowena Ravenclaw, Helga Hufflepuff, Salazar Slytherin, and Godric Gryffindor. Paradoxically, at that date, the idea of two women cofounding a major educational institution and of boys and girls being educated under the same roof was not so shocking as it later became. Rowling has a far keener sense of history than she is often given credit for. Long before Rugby was founded, schools had become strictly segregated on gender lines. There were very few schools for girls, and boys' schools excluded girls as pupils and women as teachers.

In the relatively recent past, women struggled to gain entrance to educational institutions on equal terms with men. The girls' boarding schools of the eighteenth and early nineteenth centuries existed, in Jane Austen's magnificently dismissive phrase, to be places "where girls might be sent to be out of the way, and scramble themselves into a little education, without any danger of coming back prodigies."[20] In fact, the girls' schools of Austen's day concentrated on instilling "accomplishments" into their pupils (to the detriment of any other studies). Accomplishments were, nominally, music, art, posture, foreign languages, and dancing, but the core accomplishment such schools were intended to teach was the ability to attract a husband of suitable wealth and status.

Only when reformers such as Frances Buss and Dorothea Beale, the mid-nineteenth-century headmistresses of, respectively, the North London Collegiate School for Girls and the Cheltenham Ladies College, insisted on applying rigorously academic standards could girls' education move past shallow accomplishments. Yet the process of having women's educational aspirations taken seriously continues to be a slow one, and coeducation remains a battleground.

For example, girls are still not admitted today to the premier British public school, Eton College. As mentioned earlier, Eton's strengths lie not only in its educational standards (although these are exceptionally high) but in the connections forged through the "old school tie." In fact, Eton functions much as Horace Slughorn's Slug Club does, except that the latter has equal opportunity entry standards.

Many other influential public schools either remain single-sex or are coeducational only in the sixth forms (at ages seventeen to eighteen). Oxford and Cambridge colleges were single-sex until the 1970s, and the progress toward coeducation was slow and reluctant. Commentators noted that the former women's colleges seemed more willing to offer student places and faculty posts to men than the former men's colleges were to offer such places to women.

Proponents of single-sex education come both from certain strands of feminist thinking, which put forward the arguments that boys tend to dominate the discussions in mixed-sex classes, and from social conservatives, who fear that educating boys and girls together is likely to lead to sexual experimentation.

It is fatally easy to assume that resistance to coeducation must have been even worse in the remote past. Yet to do so would be to fall into the fallacy sometimes called the "Whig" view of history.[21]

During the violent upheavals in the Muggle world between the eighth and the tenth centuries, the monastic houses of Ireland were crucial in preserving learning and literacy in Western Europe. Nuns were no less important than monks in this essential academic work. Under the Celtic tradition, "double" monasteries, containing both monks and nuns, were not uncommon; they included the Abbey of Kildare, founded by St. Brigid in the fifth century. In France, the twelfth-century double monastery of Fontrevaud remained presided over by an abbess until the French Revolution, with a number of French princesses taking the job. Female mystics such as the musician and writer Hildegard von Bingen (1098–1179) were celebrated; Hildegard went on preaching tours and corresponded with the pope and foreign dignitaries.

Outside the monastic arena, however, educational opportunities for women were limited. In the lower classes, there were few practical differences between the sexes as far as scholarship was concerned, because literacy was rare and (outside the Church) little valued. The guilds controlling access to skilled trades were overwhelmingly male, although there are documented examples of widows or daughters entering trades such as gold-smithing, following a husband or a father. Chaucer's Wife of Bath is a renowned weaver. Most skilled trades (for example, working as a carpenter or a bookbinder) were closed to women, however, unless they worked in the business of a male relative.

Hogwarts, from the point of view of women's education, draws on the best aspects of the medieval period without its drawbacks and continues its traditions unbroken to the present day. Furthermore, in promoting female education it has always had one great advantage.

During the Muggle world's great witch panics of the sixteenth, seventeenth, and early eighteenth centuries, a woman practicing healing skills or appearing to be too assertive risked being condemned as a witch. Accusations of being a witch or a "scold" (a woman considered too vocally assertive) were powerful mechanisms of social control during the period. As discussed in Birgit Wiedl's chapter on the Statute of Secrecy, witch trials occurred across Europe, as well as in Salem, Massachusetts, and resulted in widespread executions. A woman trained at Hogwarts, such as Dilys Derwent (Healer, St. Mungo's, 1722–1741; Headmistress, Hogwarts, 1741–1768), would, of course, have been able to meet such accusations with a calm "Yes. And your point is?" before Disapparating in short order.

Female Muggles were less fortunate. Furthermore, even when women started to enter professions such as teaching, they were often required to resign when they got married. Virginia Nicholson's *Singled Out* looked at the two million British women whose hopes of marriage were destroyed by the carnage of World War I. She told the tragic story of Lizzie Rignall who, in 1925, fell deeply in love with Bob, the headmaster of her Kensington school. Because Lizzie was supporting her elderly parents with her earnings and Bob also had financial commitments to his family, they could not afford to live on Bob's wages alone. Had Lizzie married Bob, she would have been forced to resign her post. As a result, they began a secret affair that lasted until Bob's death from cancer in 1935.[22]

Again, coeducation may not have been invented in the magical world, but, like free, undifferentiated education for everyone, the magical world's take on it has substantial improvements over our own, and has always been available to witches.

Why Now, Why Hogwarts?

Hogwarts is clearly a fantasy environment but one that strikes deep resonances with its readers. In the same way, Hughes's Rugby—the Rugby of *Tom Brown's Schooldays*—had more of an effect than the historical school that it purported to reflect.

George Orwell, himself an old Etonian, discussed in his essay "On Boys' Weeklies" (1940) the *Gem* and the *Magnet*, boys' weeklies that concentrated on the adventures of a small group of boys at the fictional Greyfriars and St. Jim's public schools. The *Gem* and the *Magnet* lasted from 1908 to 1940 (when World War II paper rationing proved fatal), but similar papers continued on into the 1970s in various guises.

Orwell noted in particular that for the readers, they provided an entire fantasy world. He observed, "I have seen a young coal-miner . . . a lad who had already worked a year or two underground, eagerly reading the *Gem*. Recently I offered a batch of English papers to some British legionaries of the French Foreign Legion in North Africa; they picked out the *Gem* and the *Magnet* first."[23] For him, the strength of the *Gem* and the *Magnet* picture of school life was the uncomplicated security the background provided, even if the events within the story were hair-raising. He summoned up the picture as follows:

> The year is 1910—or 1940, but it is all the same. You are at Greyfriars, a rosy-cheeked boy of fourteen in posh tailor made clothes, sitting down to tea in your study on the Remove passage after an exciting game of football which was won by an odd goal in the last half-minute. There is a cosy fire in the study and outside the wind is whistling. The ivy clusters thickly round the old grey stones. The King is on his throne and the pound is worth a pound.[24]

Rowling's strength is that she still manages to convey the essential comfort and security of that picture, while adding a modern edge. Hogwarts is coeducational; some of the students had to buy their robes secondhand, rather than having them made to measure; Lord Voldemort is just around the corner; and maybe—just maybe—the howls of Fenrir Greyback are mingling with the whistling of the wind. Yet the sense of cozy belonging, which Orwell highlighted with regard to St. Jim's and Greyfriars, is just as much true of Hogwarts:

> The portrait swung forwards to reveal a hole in the wall, through which they all climbed. A crackling fire was warming the circular common room, which was full of squashy armchairs and tables. [. . .] Harry, Ron and Neville climbed up the last, spiral staircase until they reached their own dormitory which was situated at the top of the Tower. [. . .] Harry, Ron

and Neville got into their pyjamas and into bed. Someone—a
house-elf, no doubt—had placed warming pans between the
sheets. It was extremely comfortable, lying there in bed and
listening to the storm raging outside. (*GOF*, 169)

School comes close to being a universal experience, and anyone who attends school spends time daydreaming about how it
could be made more interesting, as at Hogwarts. What Rowling
achieves with Harry Potter is a fantasy but one that has sufficient
roots in her readers' lived experiences and in the body of works set
in other fictional schools to strike deep and lasting resonances. Like
Hughes, the likelihood is that Rowling will continue to be read and
to inspire for a very long time.

Notes

1. The initial British print run of *Harry Potter and the Philosopher's Stone* was five
hundred copies. If you happen to find one, hold onto it! Think of it as a trust fund you can
read.

2. Charles Montalembert in *De l'Avenir Politique de l'Angleterre* (Paris, 1856) was the
first to attribute the quotation to him.

3. All book quotes are taken from the British editions by J. K. Rowling as follows:
Philosopher's Stone, London; Bloomsbury, 1997; *Chamber of Secrets*, London; Bloomsbury,
1998; *Goblet of Fire*, London; Bloomsbury, 2000; *Order of the Phoenix*, London;
Bloomsbury, 2003; *Half-Blood Prince*, London: Bloomsbury, 2005; *Deathly Hallows*,
London; Bloomsbury, 2007.

4. "Lonely and Ruined Man," www.time.com/time/magazine/article/0,9171,825653,00
.html#ixzz0r3dk1jz2.

5. Captain Hook from Peter Pan is another (fictional) Etonian old boy; in the original
stage version, his dying words are "Floreat Etona!" the Eton school motto.

6. C. L. R. James, *Beyond a Boundary* (Yellow Jersey Press, London, 2005), 212.

7. George Orwell, "Essay on Rudyard Kipling's Verse," in *Horizon: A Review of
Literature and Art* (London, 1942). *Stalky & Co* was published 1899, just as Dumbledore
was taking his N.E.W.T.s. Westward Ho! is both the only place in the United Kingdom to
have an integral exclamation point in its place name and to be named after a children's
book, Charles Kingsley's saga about the Spanish Armada's attempted invasion of England in
1588. Kingsley, like Hughes, was an advocate of "muscular Christianity."

8. Rudyard Kipling, *Stalky & Co* (Oxford: Oxford University Press, 1987), 296.

9. *Rudyard Kipling: The Complete Verse* (London: Kyle Cathie Limited, 1990).

10. Institutions such as Queen's Royal College, Eton College, and the United Services
College took pupils ages thirteen to eighteen. This can cause confusion with the Oxford
and Cambridge colleges and other higher-education "colleges" that take pupils from eighteen years old upward.

11. James, *Beyond a Boundary*, 39.

12. Perhaps in a concession to modern sensitivities, Draco does not imitate Flashman's drinking habits, which eventually lead to his expulsion.

13. Cheltenham College, one of the three schools mentioned earlier in the *Stalky & Co* extract, somewhat oddly allowed Anderson, a former pupil of the school, to use its buildings for location filming.

14. "Fettes Says Potter Can Cast Spell on Pupils," http://edinburghnews.scotsman.com/latestnews/Fettes-says-Potter-can-cast.2395255.jp.

15. Education for girls lagged well behind, a point addressed at more length further on.

16. Alan Garner, *The Owl Service* (London: Collins, 1973), *The Weirdstone of Brisingamen* (London: Puffin Books, 1963), and the *Moon of Gomrath* (London: Puffin Books, 1965), Garner's use of language is discussed at www.elimae.com/interviews/garner.html.

17. Sir Arthur Conan Doyle, "The Naval Treaty" reprinted in *The Penguin Complete Sherlock Holmes* (Penguin, London, 1988), 456.

18. There are Jewish and Islamic faith schools in the British state sector, in addition to Roman Catholic, Church of England (Anglican), and others.

19. C. S. Lewis, *The Silver Chair* (London: Puffin Books, 1965), 11. Lewis is particularly scathing about the fact that the head of the disastrous "Experiment House" School, which two of his characters attend, is a woman. Experiment House may be based on real-life Dartington Hall, a free-form boarding school that existed from 1926 to 1987 and had a very similar educational philosophy to the school Lewis satirized.

20. Jane Austin, *Emma* (London: Penguin Books, 1996), 20.

21. Herbert Butterfield, *The Whig Interpretation of History* (New York: W. W. Norton 1965), criticized the theory that presented history as a constant progression toward enlightenment and social justice.

22. Virginia Nicholson, *Singled Out* (London: Penguin Books, 2007), 130–131.

23. George Orwell, *Boys' Weeklies* included in *Selected Essays* (London: Penguin, 1957), p. 183.

24. Ibid., 189.

Of Marranos and Mudbloods

Harry Potter and the Spanish Inquisition

Ruth Abrams

As [Mr. Dursley] sat in the usual morning traffic jam, he couldn't help noticing that there seemed to be a lot of strangely dressed people about. People in cloaks . . . He supposed this was some stupid new fashion . . . *He* didn't see the owls swooping past in broad daylight, though people down in the street did.

—*Sorcerer's Stone*, 3[1]

From the beginning of the Harry Potter series' popularity, Jewish readers have seen in its magical world a parallel to their own historical experience as a tiny cultural minority. Like the wizards in the Potterverse, Jews have an entire way of life that most people don't know much about, even today—though the sense of secrecy that wizards maintain in Harry Potter is a thing of the past for Jews in North America. Yet for many Jewish readers, there is still something awfully familiar about being part of a small, invisible culture.

219

In one witty essay, "There's Something about Harry: Call Me Parochial, but Doesn't Hogwarts Seem Jewish?" Jewish journalist Andrew Silow-Carroll told his wife,

> "Harry is going to yeshiva!"
> "You mean Harry Potter is Jewish?" she asked.
> "No, but he might as well be. Because if you strip away the magic and the fantasy, the Harry Potter books are really lessons in how to negotiate between your religious, ethnic particularity and the wider, universal world. Jews are experts at this."[2]

Because wizards and witches keep their magical culture a secret from the wider Muggle culture, they seem like the crypto-Jews of late medieval Spain: people who were outwardly Christian but who secretly retained Jewish practices. Although the majority of Jews in the United States are Ashkenazim (people whose ancestors lived in Germany and France under Christian rulers) and not Sephardim (people descended from the Jews of medieval Spain), the story of these secret Jews, sometimes called Marranos, has been an important cultural myth for North American Jews. In the late nineteenth and the twentieth centuries, stories of the Marranos maintaining a secret Jewish identity were an important part of Jewish cultural life in a period when Jews weren't sure how safe they were to practice Judaism or behave in an identifiably culturally Jewish way in public.

The Marranos are remembered today because the popular imagination of nineteenth- and twentieth-century readers was captured by a period in Spanish history that began in the 1390s, when mobs forced large numbers of Spanish Jews to convert to Catholicism, and continued to the founding of the Spanish Inquisition in 1480 and the final expulsion of unconverted Jews in 1492. Modern readers are also interested in accounts of inquisitorial torture in the late fifteenth and the sixteenth centuries. These torture sessions may have been more unusual for what they were supposed to uncover than for their brutality, in a time and a place where secular law enforcement used torture as a matter of course.

Although the Catholic Church developed many different versions of the Inquisition during earlier centuries, the Spanish Inquisition was a separate phenomenon, operating only in territories under Spanish control. Only in Spain, and in Portugal and Southern Italy under Spanish rule, did the Catholic Church interrogate prisoners in order to uncover whether they had participated in the Jewish rituals of their parents and grandparents even though they had been baptized as Catholics, a crime that the church called "judaizing." The paradox of first compelling people to convert to Catholicism and then punishing them for supposed insincere conversion looks like a precursor to the racial anti-Semitism that faced Jews in the nineteenth and twentieth centuries.

This period in Spanish history also presents itself as something appropriate to study after reading the Harry Potter series, because the parallels are striking. When we look at the position of Muggle-born wizards sent to Hogwarts while Lord Voldemort controlled the school and the Ministry of Magic, we can't help thinking of the people whose Jewish parents or grandparents were pressured into conversion to Catholicism, leaving them permanently suspect, neither Jewish nor Catholic. The "Old Christians" called them Marranos. Like the young witches and wizards who were cut off from their Muggle relatives, yet still not fully accepted into wizarding society, Marranos were stuck.

The origins of the term *marrano* are mysterious. No one knows exactly what it means—it probably came from an old Spanish word for "pig"—and no one knows how it became an insulting name for the *conversos*, or Jewish converts to Catholicism. Most Jews called those who had been forced to convert to Christianity *anusim*, "forced ones," although some referred to them as *meshumadim*, "heretics"—it depended on how much they sympathized with or blamed those who had converted because of outside pressure or the threat of violence. Today, some use the neutral term *conversos*, rather than the term that outsiders had used to insult the converts, while others use *Marranos* as a way to reclaim the peculiar cultural experience of people whose persecutors defined their identity. The difference between conversos and Marranos is similar to the different implications in using "Muggle-born" and "Mudblood."

Because of their fear and resentment of the Inquisition, Marranos in late medieval Spain and Portugal, where many Spanish Jews had fled, developed their own beliefs and practices, characterized by the public eating of nonkosher food and the secret observance of Jewish religious rituals. There are still people who identify as Marranos or conversos, who learned about their Jewish roots only late in life when a parent or a grandparent told them to reject Catholicism because only through Judaism could they be saved. One historian has pointed out how Catholic the very emphasis on salvation is, because it's not a term that Jews use in the same way.[3] There is evidence that a small group of people persists to this day whose religious culture was permanently shaped by the fear of the Spanish Inquisition—even though the institution was abolished in 1834. Their beliefs about the secret Judaism they practice may have come from the signs that the Inquisition used to identify "judaizing" heretics—the term *judaized* was used for Catholics who continued to practice the Judaism of their ancestors.

Some families of crypto-Jews maintained secret Jewish practices for only a generation and left the Iberian peninsula in the 1500s for places where it was safe to return to the public practice of Judaism. The Jewish heroine Doña Gracia Mendes, who smuggled conversos out of Portugal in the 1500s, is one example. The family of the philosopher Baruch Spinoza is another. Although Jews around the world have been more public about their beliefs and culture since the 1960s, the myth of the secret Jews still has a hold on the Jewish imagination.

In the early Harry Potter books, it was easy for the Jewish reader to think of the entire wizarding population of Britain as secret Jews who were hiding their true culture from a majority who wouldn't understand. *Deathly Hallows* shifts that view, however. In the last book of the series, when Harry and his friends race against the Death Eaters to defeat their evil leader Voldemort, all of the protagonists and antagonists are wizards. Wizards aren't hiding from Muggles but from one another, and all of the action is internal to the wizarding subculture.

In this all-magical setting, the Death Eaters are like the Spanish Inquisitors. Muggles are absent, but people of Muggle heritage, the

Mudbloods and the half-bloods, are persecuted—just as the Spanish Inquisition went after converted Jews and their descendents. The Death Eaters take control of the Ministry of Magic, Hogwarts, and other wizarding institutions, forcing the people of Muggle heritage into hiding. The Death Eaters even use exactly the same terminology that the Spanish did in their pursuit of a unified nation—*blood purity* or, in Spanish, *limpieza de sangre*.

On Blood Purity

"You realize that I am on my way downstairs to interrogate your wife, Cattermole? In fact, I'm quite surprised you're not down there holding her hand while she waits. Already given her up as a bad job, have you? Probably wise. Be sure and marry a Pureblood next time."

—Yaxley, *Deathly Hallows*, 243

The Spanish Inquisition was a Roman Catholic institution, and it was about religion, but it was also something that Spain's monarchs invented in part to unify the country by defining the racial characteristics of a "true" Spanish identity. In a country like Spain, with many regions and dialects, Catholicism was a good candidate to solidify Spanish identity—and former Jews could be cast in this process as a cultural enemy, a permanent racial Other. The Spanish Inquisition was officially a religious institution, but it worked to reinforce some Spanish cultural values that were anti-Christian—the panic over "blood status" and the sense that having Jewish or Muslim ancestors was a form of "infamy," akin to how Death Eaters see Muggle-borns. Under the Inquisition, these prejudices overrode normal Christian beliefs about baptism and repentance, just as the Death Eaters override previous wizarding understandings of how Muggle-born witches and wizards gain magical power and become part of the wizarding community, when Dolores Umbridge and others claim that the Muggle-borns have somehow "stolen" magical ability and wands.

Christian theology actually asserts that baptism is a rebirth in Christ, that ethnic accidents of birth should not matter, and that repentance is effective against sin. The Spanish church, or at least the members of the Inquisition itself, chose to ignore these principles in the case of baptized Jews and their children. Conversos were permanently suspect Jews, and the children of anyone who had been accused by the Inquisition could be ritually humiliated for generations afterward. The differences between Jews (and later on, to some degree, Spanish Muslims) and Christians seemed to be impossible to overcome—even for people who had never practiced Judaism and whose parents and grandparents hadn't, either. By creating an institution to regularize their prejudice, the Spanish Crown ensured that conversos could not become true Christians—like Mudbloods among pureblood wizards, they retained the stigma of their Jewish origins for generations.

Although the Spanish Inquisition eventually branched out to look for other forms of heresy, the Holy Office, as the Inquisition was called, was originally formed to deal with popular suspicions that conversos were still practicing Judaism while pretending to be Roman Catholic. Their neighbors were alert to ways that people who were currently Catholic might retain Jewish practices. They might notice that their converso neighbors still ate differently, for example. Jews have a set of rules about food, called *kashrut*, which excludes pork, whereas Catholics in many parts of Spain relied on pork as a major item in their diet. Jewish traditional dishes were different from the food of Christian Spaniards, and when the Inquisition publicized the eating of Jewish foods as a sign of difference, their neighbors came to see certain dietary practices as signs of conversos' religious deviation. Simply continuing to eat your mother's recipes was enough for you to be suspected of still being secretly Jewish—even if what you were really expressing was a preference for the taste of bread made with olive oil instead of lard.

These differences between Jews and Christians may seem trivial in our present society, where we don't see anything all that odd about eating different food or resting on a different day. Jews and Christians believe in the same God, and both hold the Hebrew Scriptures sacred. In the United States, where alliances between religious Christians and Jews are strong, people blur the differences between the two religions by referring to our "Judeo-Christian culture"—emphasizing similarities, rather than differences, in beliefs and positive, rather than negative, aspects of common history.

Certainly, the differences between Christians and Jews in the medieval period, as today, were nowhere near as significant as the differences between wizards and Muggles in J. K. Rowling's fictional world—although some medieval European cultures had stories and ideas of Jews as weird, magical, or monstrous. Difference is important only when societies make it important. In his book *The Formation of a Persecuting Society* R. I. Moore argued that European society changed profoundly in the eleventh and twelfth centuries when discrimination and violence against groups of people who were different became part of European culture.[4] It is the decision that differences are significant and negative that made such a cultural shift possible, one whose legacy continues to affect Western culture.

The Inquisition claimed that it was preventing the continuation of Jewish religion among converts to Catholicism. Historians disagree about the extent to which large numbers of conversos were secretly practicing Judaism. Several have suggested that the Inquisition itself was responsible for forging a Jewish identity in the descendants of converts who, after the expulsion of Spain's unconverted Jews in 1492, would otherwise have had no exposure to Jewish life at all

One of the most interesting aspects of the Spanish Inquisition for those of us whose governments are participating in the war on terror is the role of torture, which is the subject of political scandals and heated debate today. The very fact that church officials were involved in torture as a religious matter is shameful to many Catholics and contradicts their religious beliefs. Liberal Catholic intellectuals, including Andrew Sullivan, have written extensively about how U.S. interrogation practices resembled those of the Spanish Inquisition, including the use of what we today call *waterboarding* and *stress positions*.[5] Another parallel to the war on terror was that the Inquisition "outsourced" torture to secular authorities. The Inquisition also used secret arrests and secret tribunals, which came uncomfortably close to the practices of the war on terror in the United States.

Rowling has both worked for, and given large donations to, the human rights organization Amnesty International; clearly, torture is an issue that concerns her.[6] When we compare the Unforgivable Curses of the Potterverse to the torture practices of the Inquisition and those of present-day governments, we can learn a lot about the motivations for torturing people and what they say about the radical evil that Rowling indicts in her novels. What is the relationship between how we figure out which cultural, ethnic, or political difference really does make a difference and the decision to intentionally inflict pain for its own sake? Which comes first—believing that suspects deserve pain and humiliation, or torturing them?

The Spanish Inquisition

> And as he reached the foot of the stairs and turned to his right he saw a dreadful scene. The dark passage outside the court-rooms was packed with tall, black-hooded figures, their faces completely hidden, their ragged breathing the only sound in the place. The petrified Muggle-borns brought in for questioning sat huddled and shivering on hard wooden benches. Most of them were hiding their faces in their hands, perhaps in an instinctive attempt to shield themselves from the dementors' greedy mouths. Some were accompanied by families, others sat alone. The dementors were gliding up and down in front of them, and the cold, and the hopelessness, and the despair of the place laid themselves upon Harry like a curse.
>
> —*Deathly Hallows*, 257

The habit of the Inquisitors of keeping detailed records of every aspect of each arrest and interrogation, along with meticulous lists of the property that Inquisitors confiscated from prisoners on arrest, gave a large set of sources to historians and a chance for us today to learn about daily life in the 1400s and the 1500s. The period of the Inquisition that most closely resembles the Death Eater–dominated Ministry of Magic that Rowling creates in *Deathly Hallows* was the earliest period of its existence, from 1480 to 1575, when the Inquisition was most focused on the heresy of judaizing and on individual conversos and their children and grandchildren. The secret accusations by unknown accusers and the long detention without trial that we see in *Deathly Hallows* were also real practices of the Spanish Inquisition.

One difference between fiction and history is that in fiction you can cut right to the chase and in history you need some background to understand the scene. The background of the Spanish Inquisition is the political attempt of the Christian rulers of late-fifteenth-century Spain to unify the country through the church. It's worth examining this background.

In the medieval period, Spain was not a single country but consisted instead of many small kingdoms, some only the size of a single city and its surrounding territory under the rule of either Christian or Muslim heads of state. The Golden Age of Spain, the age of *convivencia*, of Muslims, Christians, and Jews living together side by side, is associated mainly with the period from the late 800s to the late 1000s, when the southern region of al-Andalus, or Andalucia, was under relatively weak Muslim rule. It was there that scholars of the three religions exchanged scientific knowledge, perfected the astrolabe, introduced the concept of the number zero into mathematics, and wrote poetry and music.

At the end of the eleventh century and the beginning of the twelfth century, Muslim invaders from North Africa, the Almoravids and the Almohads, changed the culture of southern Spain from one that tolerated a Jewish minority to one that did not. Jews fled north to Christian Spain in the 1200s, and the Christian rulers encouraged this. This was a sort of Silver Age for Spanish Jewry—the tolerance in Christian Spain allowed a second flowering of Sephardi culture.

The majority of Spanish Jews were relatively poor, working inside their own communities as artisans or shopkeepers, and there were a small number of wealthy Jews. Because of medieval Christian rules about usury (charging interest on loans) and money-lending, only Jews could lend money at interest, and this is an essential method of fueling trade. Rulers could also outsource the task of tax collection to Jews. You can guess that this was not a means of making Jews popular but of diverting public attention away from the rulers' own responsibility for taxation. The taxes still went into the pockets of landowning nobles, even when they passed through Jewish hands first, and even in periods when the tax burden fell more heavily on Jews as a class than on people from the majority religion.

Both Islamic and Christian societies had medieval statutes that reduced Jews to a second-class status, but rulers and people alike chose not to enforce all of these regulations. This is a very common narrative in Jewish history. Rulers invited Jews to play a certain role in the economy, effectively importing a whole community of Jews of all economic statuses in order to have the benefit of the financial skills and the capital of a few wealthy Jews. It was also not uncommon in Jewish history for the entire community of Jews to become targets of persecution as the visible outsiders associated with taxation and lending money at interest.

The economic and social turmoil that followed the pandemic of the Black Death (the plague) in the 1340s changed the status of Jews in Christian Spain. During the 1300s, there were gradual signs of the erosion of tolerance toward Jews. This was capped in 1391 by major anti-Jewish riots in Castile and Aragon. A large number of Jews were forcibly converted to Christianity during these riots. Some speculate that more than half of the original Jewish population of Aragon and Castile chose to convert to Christianity rather than face continued persecution. In the first half of the 1400s, former Jews were absorbed into Christian culture relatively readily, but this gradually changed.

For nearly a century after these forced conversions, conversos or New Christians continued to live in the same homes where they had lived before, in the midst of their still-Jewish neighbors and extended family members. In the century between the massive forced conversions of 1391 and the official expulsion of the Jews from Spain in 1492, both Christians and Jews considered it likely that most conversos were still Jewish in private, when they were out of the public eye.[7] Although there seems to have been a diversity of beliefs and practices among individual conversos, some may well have continued to keep the Sabbath in Jewish ways and to continue not to eat pork—it's not clear to what extent these were cultural practices they retained because their families had always done them and which were things that held religious significance. Whether they were remaining Jewish in secret doesn't matter; family ties and traditional ways of life were more important than theology.

Whatever the reasons were for it, individual cities and academic and church institutions began to enact *limpieza de sangre* ("blood purity") statutes to exclude conversos and their children from public positions beginning in Toledo in 1449. As economic conditions worsened, conversos were targets of violence, particularly in 1473, when Old Christians—people with no Jewish heritage—attacked conversos in several cities in Andalucia, in southern Spain. When King Ferdinand of Aragon and Queen Isabella of Castile came to power in 1474 and merged their two kingdoms, creating a unified Christian Spain, they may have been motivated to establish an official Inquisition in part to quell ongoing riots against conversos, which disrupted the maintenance of public order in their new unified country. The queen, who was known for her piety, may have been persuaded by religious arguments. Her confessor was Tomás de Torquemada, who became the first Grand Inquisitor, and he seems to have pushed her both to establish the Inquisition and to expel the unconverted Jews from Spain in 1492. The rulers petitioned Pope Sixtus IV for permission to establish the Inquisition specifically to scrutinize the religious practices of converted Jews.

In the early years of the Inquisition, beginning in 1480, neighbors, relatives, and members of converso households denounced conversos to the Inquisition for the crime of judaizing, or reverting to Jewish religious observance. Sometimes these conversos were actually children of converts and had always been Christian. Denouncers gave as evidence that conversos had put on clean clothing in honor of Shabbat on Friday evening. They mentioned when conversos cooked only with olive oil instead of with lard.

When the officers of the Inquisition arrested people suspected of heresy, much as Umbridge does, they did not tell these people who had accused them or what they were accused of. The prisoners were interrogated, and if they did not confess, the inquisitors could choose to have them tortured until they did. Confessions extracted under torture did not count, however, and the prisoner had to confess again when he or she was not under pressure or being tortured.

Some heresies were not punishable by death, but all required public humiliation at an auto-da-fé, literally "an act of faith," a public ritual involving a Mass (a religious service) and the public confession of sin. Although artistic and fictional depictions of autos-da-fé involve torture and burning at the stake, these were never part of the actual ceremony. The prisoners would appear in public in *sanbeitos*, special garments that identified them as heretics, and would publicly confess to the crimes of which they had been accused. Then the officials of the Inquisition would read the sentences, which might involve corporal punishment or death. Secular authorities carried out these sentences when the Inquisition "relaxed" the prisoners to the custody of the Crown. After the prisoner had been released or executed, the garment with the person's name on it would be hung in his or her local church. The *sanbeitos* were displayed in public for generations, and some parishes would refresh them when the fabric of these garments eventually disintegrated. Death was not the final punishment—the family of the Inquisition's prisoners could be stigmatized for generations afterward.

By 1492, the Spanish Crown had burned hundreds of conversos at the stake. Like a wizarding court in the Potterverse consigning prisoners to be kissed by dementors, Inquisition tribunals needed to distance themselves from the harm they inflicted on their prisoners. Those early years were the most violent.

Why, if the Inquisition was directed solely at conversos and not at practicing Jews, did the Crown choose to expel the remaining Jewish population? Apparently, it was reluctant to do so. The Inquisition had a role in the final expulsion, because it influenced partial expulsions of Jews from local municipalities where the Inquisition had tribunals.[8] On March 31, 1492, immediately following the fall of the last Muslim stronghold in Granada, the

Crown issued a decree giving Jews who refused Christian baptism four months in which to leave Spain or face the death penalty. The expulsion was therefore also another invitation to conversion, bringing a second wave of reluctant converts from Judaism to Catholic Christianity into Spanish society.

How Were the Inquisitors Like the Death Eaters?

Half proofs and torture. Next if the crime appears half proven, the inquisitors, in consultation with the ordinario, shall consider putting the accused to the question of torture. If the accused confesses the crime under torture, and afterward ratifies or confirms his confession on the next or third day, he shall be punished as convicted. If, after torture, he revokes his confession and retracts it (and if the crime is still not completely proven), the inquisitors must order him to publicly abjure the error of which he is defamed and suspected, on account of infamy and the presumption that results against him. The inquisitors shall give him some arbitrary penance and treat him mildly. They must follow this process whenever a crime is half proven. The aforesaid does not deny that the inquisitors can repeat the question of torture in a case where they must and can do so by law.

— Instructions of the Holy Office of the Inquisition" (1627)[9]

Inquisitorial tribunals seem to have been less likely to use torture than medieval criminal courts were, but they still used torture as an important part of their judicial process. They did not torture every prisoner, as most criminal courts seem to have done, but had a deliberative process before they ordered prisoners tortured. The one category of prisoner the Inquisitors were most likely to order tortured were alleged judaizers—Marranos. Although the Inquisition broadened its focus over time to include other groups, including *moriscos* (descendents of former Muslims) and practitioners of other heresies, Marranos were still the main focus of Inquisitorial violence.

What terrified contemporary Spaniards about the Inquisition was the sense of secrecy: people disappeared into Inquisition prisons, and the process was mysterious. Some feared the possibility that they were guilty of crimes they themselves didn't understand or even know they had committed, for which they could be suddenly arrested. Generally, the rule was to isolate the prisoners from the outside world and from one another.

The Inquisition, unlike Spanish royal courts, permitted secret denunciation. Accused heretics could not confront their accusers. The Holy Office (the official name of the part of the church that oversaw the Inquisition) would immediately confiscate the property of the accused on arrest, but the inquisitors might wait months or even years to present the accused with an actual accusation. Sometimes this was because the inquisitors had not examined the evidence for arrest before they sent bailiffs to arrest the suspect. The prisoners' children could be left without support or sometimes were brought with them to the prison. Like the Death Eaters, the Inquisition could make people simply disappear.

The inquisitorial tribunals operated systematically, and the use of torture was guided by specific rules. A panel of theologians had to decide whether torture was appropriate for each individual suspect, because it wasn't used in all cases. Religious tribunals such as the Inquisition's could not kill or shed blood, and they weren't allowed to torture a suspect more than once. Therefore, the inquisitors hired executioners from the secular courts to perform torture for them so that their hands stayed clean. If they believed that a suspect might crack under additional physical pressure, they would declare a torture session "suspended" so that they could reserve the right to resume torturing that suspect later on.

Torturers were not part of the inquisitorial squad and were sent from the room when prisoners were ready to confess so that the confidentiality of the confessional would not be breached.[10] The three most common tortures used in inquisitorial interrogations were the *garrucha*, which involved hanging the suspect by his or her wrists from a pulley attached to the ceiling; the *potro*, or rack; and the *toca*, or water torture. The *toca* was what we today call waterboarding—the torturers tied the suspect down and forced a cloth down the throat to keep the mouth open, and then poured water onto the cloth to simulate the sensation of drowning.

These weren't creative or bloody or exciting tortures; they were simply things that hurt a lot and were frightening. Like Crucio and other Unforgivable Curses from the Potterverse, the point of using these tortures was—and is, when governments use them in the present—to break the will of the victim, not to harm him or her physically. (That they did cause physical, as well as psychological, harm was documented by the inquisitors themselves, however.) One thing that made torture psychologically damaging to the victims was being stripped naked before the inquisitors and the torturers, when many had never appeared naked even before their own spouses.[11]

Hanging by the wrists from the ceiling with heavy weights attached to the feet dislocated people's arms and legs. The rack hurt because the cords that tied the victim bit into the body when they were tightened. The inquisitors requested that the torturers adjust the torture devices or pour more water, and then they recorded the prisoner's screams for mercy as part of the transcription of the interrogations. The coldness of these transcriptions is remarkable.

What was the point of doing this? The Inquisition did not permit confessions extracted under torture to be used as evidence for sentencing. Nevertheless, they did value the process as a means to persuade the heretics to confess. Presumably, the process was meant to break the will of the accused, so that they would be willing to confess when they were no longer under physical and psychological duress. Afterward, the prisoners would be truly repentant.

To put this into a present-day context, confessions obtained under torture are never admitted as evidence in a U.S. court. In December 2009, a U.S. judge in the Binyam Mohamed case determined that torture invalidates information obtained without coercion. The district judge concluded that uncoerced statements taken in U.S. government interrogations at Guantanamo were unreliable because the detainee had previously experienced torture.[12] The Spanish Inquisition's loophole has thus been closed in U.S. law—once the interrogators have used torture, have intentionally inflicted physical and emotional pain, the testimony of the prisoner is no longer reliable.

Why Do Death Eaters Use Torture?

"Pain," said Moody softly. "You don't need thumbscrews or knives to torture someone if you can perform the Cruciatus Curse . . . That one was very popular once, too."

    —*Goblet of Fire*, 215

In Rowling's books, we have evidence of Death Eaters using physical and psychological torture, and it's not clear why they do so, when Voldemort has mastered Legilimency and can enter others' minds at will. Only Severus Snape is apparently capable of resisting the force of Voldemort's mental invasion. If the Dark Lord doesn't need confessions, why extract them through torture? Yet Voldemort tortures the wand maker Ollivander for information, although he could have used Legilimency.

If Snape knows how to perform Legilimency, why don't other Death Eaters also use it? We don't know whether they all can. They can all cast Crucio, the torture curse that causes terrible pain, but even this seems not to be the first resort. Rowling gives the reader a scene of very-low tech torture when Harry and his friends are captured and brought to Malfoy Manor, and Bellatrix Lestrange interrogates Hermione Granger using a combination of Crucio and physical cuts with an ordinary sharp knife, even though she presumably can use Legilimency, because she taught her nephew Draco Malfoy how to Occlude. Other prisoners in Malfoy Mansion show bruises and welts from beatings.

The three Unforgivable Curses are good candidates for magical methods of torture. The Cruciatus Curse, whose sole purpose is to cause severe pain, could be nicknamed the "torture curse." Most of the times that characters in the Potterverse wield this curse, they aren't seeking information from the person they are torturing. Harry observes Voldemort's reactions when he uses the curse as "an explosion of anger"—wielding power over another person for its own sake (*DH*, 85). This is not the cold torture of the Inquisition or even the torture of present-day data aggregation, although such a possibility does exist in this magical world.

The scene in Umbridge's Muggle-Born Registration Commission has more in common with the Inquisition's tactics. Umbridge questions wizards and witches who have Muggle backgrounds with the assumption that they are guilty, just as the Inquisition chose its victims on the basis of ancestry, in the cases of the conversos and the moriscos. Like the Inquisition, Umbridge's tribunal keeps a bureaucratic record of everything that is said during the hearings. The Inquisitorial Instruction required that a scrupulous record of interrogations should be kept in all cases, with the macabre results that included fully documented screams of anguish and begging from the prisoners. A similar picture of Umbridge's tribunal emerges when Umbridge gives Hermione, temporarily transformed into a Ministry functionary by Polyjuice potion, the task of taking notes on the interrogations, although we don't know whether the notes in front of Hermione record the screams of the prisoners as the Inquisitors so carefully did.

In the Potterverse, there are many analogies to real-life torture and human rights violations, both historical and modern. At the very least, there is the violence of many painful, nonfatal hexes that the students at Hogwarts use on one another—the stinging hex, the tickling jinx, and so on. It seems strange that Rowling chose to show her wizarding characters torturing others by using the most pedestrian Muggle methods—beatings and stabbings—when she also created magical means of coercing people and violating their human rights.

Another Unforgivable Curse exists that could (in theory) magically compel the cursed person to tell the truth—the Imperius Curse. This could have been another alternative to both Muggle and magical methods of torture. Imperius is never mentioned as a means for gathering information, however, only for compelling other behavior, although it should theoretically work for intelligence gathering. Why don't the Death Eaters use this instead of torture when questioning prisoners?

The answer might be because in the world of *Deathly Hallows*, part of the purpose of the Cruciatus is its effect not only on the target of the curse, but also on the caster. Voldemort insists that Draco cast the curse, threatening him with it if he fails to cast it: "Draco, give Rowle another taste of our displeasure . . . Do it, or feel my wrath yourself!" [. . .] He sat up. Malfoy's gaunt, petrified face seemed branded on the inside of his eyes. Harry felt sickened by what he had seen, by the use to which Draco was now being put by Voldemort." (*DH*, 174–175)

Neville Longbottom defies the Carrows when they demand that all Hogwarts students learn to cast Cruciatus on children who are being punished. The Death Eaters could have forced students to Cruciate one another by using the Imperius Curse on pupils like Longbottom but chose not to do that. They wanted their students' full voluntary participation—to implicate the students in their crimes and to change the students into the kind of wizards who can cast these curses.

The Spanish Inquisition did not demand that the inquisitors themselves perform acts of torture, although, like the Carrows, they ordered others to torture. The inquisitors did not torture every person who was accused. They did try to get full participation from conversos and their families in denunciations of heretics, such as by torturing prisoners until they gave up the names of family members. Before their expulsion from Spain, Jewish family members of conversos denounced them to the authorities, driving a wedge between conversos and unconverted Jews. Afterward, conversos denounced other conversos, including their close relatives, in order to escape further torture. In *Deathly Hallows*, we see wizards and witches doing the same.

Although they made use of it, it's not clear how inquisitors felt about torture as a means of gaining confessions. They employed it more sparingly than did the royal criminal courts, they didn't want to be directly involved in it, and they refused to use confessions obtained under torture that weren't later repeated in less violent interrogatory conditions. What's odd is that some Death Eaters seem to believe in torture's efficacy to reveal information—at least,

Bellatrix Lestrange, who tortures Hermione, believes in it. They use it instead of other methods that might be more reliable, such as Legilimency, the impressionistic mind reading that Snape tries to teach Harry during his fifth year, or Veritaserum, the truth serum that both Snape and Umbridge threaten to use on Harry. And they apparently never even consider using Imperius to force their prisoners to tell the truth.

Psychologists know a great deal about the psychological impact of torture on victims who experience it—see, for example, the reports of Physicians for Human Rights and other human rights organizations.[13] They have also examined the impact of torture on torturers, most famously in the Milgram Experiments. (Stanley Milgram, a Yale University psychologist, conducted a series of experiments in the early 1960s on whether subjects would willingly inflict pain on others if ordered to do so.) More recently, a psychological study showed that the more tortured prisoners suffered pain, the more likely it was that observers of their torture would judge them to be guilty.[14] This is the role that inquisitors took in torture—they observed while others inflicted it, and they allowed the suffering of those accused to confirm their prejudgment of guilt.

Jews and Muggles, Mudbloods and Conversos

One strange aspect of Rowling's Potterverse is the way the walls between the wizarding and the Muggle worlds seem somewhat porous and easily breached. Nowhere is this more evident than when Voldemort and his evil minions take over the wizarding world. Although we are alerted to some effects on the Muggle world of the internal struggle between the good and the bad wizards in the first chapter of the book, the fallout for Muggles mainly seems to manifest itself in the form of smog, automobile accidents, bad weather, and bad moods. For all of the power that wizards could exert over Muggles, by enslaving them through mind control or by targeting them with evil curses, most of the Death Eaters direct their violence toward other wizards. The closest that most Death Eaters come to harming Muggles is turning them upside down and laughing at their underwear. Voldemort, who kills many people, both wizard and Muggle, is, of course, a different story.

It's here that we find the greatest similarities between the Spanish Inquisition and the Death Eaters. Although Tomás de Torquemada, the first Grand Inquisitor, was involved in the expulsion of the Jews from Spain, the Inquisition itself never arrested or tortured Jews who did not convert. Its focus was originally solely on conversos and later expanded to moriscos and other suspect groups within the Catholic population. All of the work of the Inquisition was internal to the church, but the Spanish Inquisition was not an instrument of the Church of Rome so much as an instrument of the Spanish church and even more of the Spanish civil authorities.

Like the Inquisitors, Voldemort is most concerned with cementing his ideological position *within* wizarding institutions: at the Ministry of Magic and, most especially, at Hogwarts School. This, too, is one of the similarities between the Spanish Inquisition and the Potterverse. Most of the *limpieza de sangre* statutes were enforced on people within church institutions, such as university faculty or students and members of religious orders. This was a way of singling out a population for never really being Catholic enough and attaching to descendents the stigma of Jewish practice or essential nature for generations after the Inquisition had arrested a family member. It seems possible that Voldemort, too, wanted to create a permanent class of persecuted people whose perceived threat would continue to justify his seizure of power—this is the model that nearly all repressive regimes that came after the Inquisition seem to have followed.

Racism in a Pre-modern Society: Inflicting the Mark

> He let out a gasp of pain. The words had appeared on the parchment in what appeared to be shining red ink. At the same time, the words had appeared on the back of Harry's right hand, cut into his skin as though traced there by a scalpel—yet even as he stared at the shining cut, the skin healed over again, leaving

the place where it had been slightly redder than before but quite smooth.

Harry looked around at Umbridge. She was watching him, her wide, toadlike mouth stretched into a smile.

"Yes?"

"Nothing," said Harry quietly.

—*Order of the Phoenix*, 267

Are the Death Eaters like the Inquisitors? In many ways, they aren't. They can't sustain a movement in wizarding Britain for more than a few years, and the Inquisition was able to maintain itself as an institution in Spain for nearly four centuries by changing its focus over time, from the issue of judaizing to other heresies. One thing the Death Eaters have in common with the Inquisition, however, is using the mechanisms of the state to make an entire society believe in the permanent inferiority or difference of a particular group.

In the fictional world of Harry Potter, in the real historical world of the Spanish Inquisition, and in our own time, torture is used in part to mark and damage people, in order to justify the torture. Torturers use torture to change their victims so that the torturers can see their victims as deserving what they suffer. In *Order of the Phoenix*, Umbridge tortures Harry with a quill that inscribes his "crime" into his hand. With the words "I must not tell lies," she marks him as someone who might tell lies, who has an inherent tendency to tell lies.

The very fact of having been arrested and tortured by the Inquisition was marked into the lives of the conversos and their families by the process of the ritual public humiliation of the autos-da-fé. The long-term public display of the *sanbeito*, inscribed with the names of converso ancestors who had been tried, is similar in effect to the inscription on Harry's hand. Torture is a means of making a suspected difference in its victims more real, more permanent, more *marked*—which is why the treatment of suspected judaizers by the Inquisition has so many parallels to the treatment Death Eaters mete out to suspect Muggle-borns in the world of Harry Potter.

In Rowling's magical world, the differences between magical beings are metaphors for differences in our world. Which differences matter? We believe we are past the kinds of bias that the history of the Spanish Inquisition displayed. The truth is, many governments in the present are apparently still just as likely as the fictional Death Eaters and the real-life inquisitors to employ torture as a means to break the will of others. We allow these practices to continue because we don't see the danger that they will create a society in which populations are permanently suspect because of their national or religious origins. We also don't think they are that bad. After all, we aren't really drowning people or breaking their bones—these are practices that leave no marks—except, of course, they do, as Alastor Moody knew very well: "'Now, if there's no countercurse, why am I showing you? Because you've got to know. You've got to appreciate what the worst is. You don't want to find yourself in a situation where you're facing it. CONSTANT VIGILANCE!' he roared, and the whole class jumped again." (GOF, 217)

Notes

1. All book quotes are taken from the American editions by J. K. Rowling as follows: *Sorcerer's Stone*, A.A. Levine Books, 1998; *Goblet of Fire*, New York: A.A. Levine Books, 2000; *Order of the Phoenix*, New York: A.A. Levine Books, 2003; *Deathly Hallows*, New York: A.A. Levine Books, 2007.

2. Andrew Silow-Carroll, "There's Something about Harry: Call Me Parochial, but Doesn't Hogwarts Seem Jewish?" www.clal.org/coc1601.html.

3. Yirmiyahu Yovel, *The Other Within: The Marranos, Split Identity and Emerging Modernity* (Princeton, NJ: Princeton University Press, 2009).

4. R. I. Moore, *The Formation of a Persecuting Society* (Cambridge, MA: Blackwell, 1987), 5.

5. Andrew Sullivan, "Comparing Tortures," February 9, 2010, from his blog at the *Atlantic Monthly*, http://andrewsullivan.theatlantic.com/the_daily_dish/2010/02/comparing-tortures.html.

6. See, for example, the text of Rowling's Harvard commencement address delivered on June 5, 2008, http://harvardmagazine.com/commencement/the-fringe-benefits-failure-the-importance-imagination.

7. Michael Albert, *Crypto-Judaism and the Spanish Inquisition* (Hampshire, UK: Palgrave, 2001), 19–26.

8. Helen Rawlings, *The Spanish Inquisition* (Malden, MA: Blackwell, 2006), 63.

9. Lu Ann Homza, *The Spanish Inquisition, 1478–1614: An Anthology of Sources* (Indianapolis: Hacket, 2006), 61–79.

10. Albert, *Crypto-Judaism and the Spanish Inquisition*, 120.

11. Ibid., 117.

12. Jamie Doward, "Torture Claims by British Resident Are Given Credence by American Judge," *Observer*, December 20, 2009.

13. "Broken Laws, Broken Lives Discussed on Thom Hartmann Show," http://brokenlives .info/.

14. Kurt Grey and Daniel Wegner, "Torture and Judgments of Guilt," *Journal of Experimental Social Psychology* 46 (2010): 233–235.

PART THREE

Women and Witches, Werewolves and Muggle-Borns

Magical Hierarchies

"Oh, this is Crabbe and this is Goyle," said the pale boy carelessly, noticing where Harry was looking. "And my name's Malfoy, Draco Malfoy. [. . .] You'll soon find out some wizarding families are much better than others, Potter."

—*Sorcerer's Stone,* 108

The creature slipped off the bed and bowed so low that the end of its long, thin nose touched the carpet. Harry noticed that it was wearing what looked like an old pillowcase, with rips for arm- and leg-holes.

"Er—hello," said Harry nervously.

"Harry Potter!" said the creature in a high-pitched voice Harry was sure would carry down the stairs. "So long has Dobby wanted to meet you, sir. . . . Such an honor it is. [. . .]

The wizard family Dobby serves, sir . . . Dobby is a house elf—bound to serve one house and one family forever."

—*Chamber of Secrets,* 12–14

Witches vs. Women

What Muggles Could Learn from Wizarding History

Janice Liedl

"ARE YOU A WITCH OR NOT?" Ron Weasley impatiently demanded of Hermione Granger as they desperately struggled against the hold of the Devil's Snare (*PS*, 202).[1] Hermione, already much celebrated for her cleverness and respected by both Harry and Ron for her bravery in facing the troll alongside them earlier in the first year, had been unable to react to the plant's threat as she struggled to remember the appropriate techniques to do so. But Ron's question jolted her out of that indecisiveness: Hermione used her wand to force the dangerous plant to release them. The three young students were free to carry on with their quest to retrieve the Philosopher's Stone. A short while later, Hermione's intellectual prowess helps save the day when she puzzles her way through a logic problem and helps Harry get past that obstacle to the final confrontation with Voldemort.

Was Hermione simply behaving as one would expect any other young modern Muggle woman to do? In other words, was she stopping to think too long before her brave and powerful response simply because she was a product of her upbringing in the senior Grangers' Muggle household? Hermione is, even in her first year at Hogwarts, exploring her identity as both a powerful magic user and a Muggle-born woman. Surprisingly enough, given so much of the quaint old-fashioned flavor of the wizarding world, Hermione's active and powerful character isn't just an artifact of her Muggle background. From the earliest histories of the wizarding world, we learn of powerful witches who played an important role in their society, schools, and government.

Throughout the Muggle history of Britain, women were denied rights to inherit property or position, to work in many jobs, and to vote, until decisive advances were made in women's rights during the nineteenth and twentieth centuries. Virginia Woolf famously summarized women's limited freedoms in her 1929 publication *A Room of One's Own*, arguing that without access to money and a little private space, it was impossible for women to compete with men for jobs or public recognition. In the book, Woolf painted a sad picture of the unknown history of "Shakespeare's sister" and listed all of the obstacles such a gifted woman would have faced in pursuing a playwright's career during Shakespeare's lifetime: "She could get no training in her craft. Could she even seek her dinner in a tavern or roam the streets at midnight? —At last . . . she found herself with child. . . [and] killed herself one winter's night."[2]

The wizarding world, for all of its seemingly conservative traditions, was an environment where magical ability, not gender, determined members' choices and status. Many generations before Hermione enrolled at Hogwarts, witches participated fully in the wizarding world in areas such as politics, sports, and education, even while their Muggle sisters could never have dreamed of such opportunities. Women held public positions and power in the wizarding world centuries before they enjoyed such privileges in the Muggle world, but other evidence shows that their society retained many prejudices regarding women's abilities and duties.

The Monstrous Regiment of Women

The English were never comfortable with the idea of women wielding power or even claiming equality with men until very recently in historical terms. Although women could inherit power and position, the practice of primogeniture (where the oldest son inherited all or most family property on his father's death) meant that a younger brother would inherit before an older sister would and, in some cases, a male cousin instead of a daughter had the right to the inheritance. This tradition, which preferred male heirs, sparked a crisis in Henry VIII's reign when he had no son to inherit his throne, only a daughter, Mary Tudor. Henry and his peers couldn't easily imagine England being governed by a woman. The only historical precedent that the country had with a female heir to the throne had led to the disastrous twelfth-century civil war between Matilda (the daughter of Henry I, whose sons had died early on) and Stephen (her cousin).[3]

In part motivated by his desperate desire to have a male heir, as well as by his love for Anne Boleyn, Henry VIII famously took England out of the Roman Catholic Church when the pope refused to annul his marriage to Catherine of Aragon. (Of course, Anne may have had some magical assistance in courting the king, if rumors of her Squib status are true.)[4] Henry was soon married to Anne, but his second wife provided him only with a daughter, the future Queen Elizabeth I. It wasn't until his third marriage, to Jane Seymour, that Henry had a son, Edward, who survived the dangerous first months of childhood and secured the Tudor lineage (at least until his own untimely death in 1553). It's no wonder that Jane, who died from complications in childbirth, was memorialized as Henry's favorite wife.[5] Henry's son Edward ruled after him, but died as a teenager, and then was succeeded by Henry's two daughters: first Mary, and then (after Mary's death), Elizabeth I.

In 1558, John Knox published *The First Blast of the Trumpet against the Monstrous Regiment of Women*, contending that divine displeasure was the only explanation for the elevation of three Catholic women (Marie de Medici, the queen-mother of France;

Mary Tudor, the queen of England; and Mary Stuart, the queen of Scotland) who now ruled in their respective nations. While the Presbyterian Knox was chiefly upset with the Catholic beliefs and policies of these queens, he also argued that women, by their very nature, were unfit to rule. Although refuted by John Aylmer's *An Harborowe for Faithfull and Trewe Subjects* the following year, Knox's prejudice against women in power was a conventional wisdom not easily countered by even a queen's most fervent supporters.[6]

To be honest, few people of the time would have argued for women's merits, let alone their equality with men. Martin Luther, the sixteenth-century religious reformer who promoted the marriage of churchmen, also held that women were, by their very nature, inferior to men: "Men have broad chests and narrow hips; therefore they have wisdom. Women have narrow chests and broad hips. Women ought to be domestic; their creation reveals it, for they have broad backsides and hips, so that they should sit still [and stay at home]."[7] Even Elizabeth I, when rallying her troops against Philip of Spain's Spanish Armada in 1588, downplayed her feminine nature in asserting her power as a proper monarch in the style of her male peers: "I may have the body of a weak and feeble woman, but I have the heart and stomach of a king."[8]

Not only queens, but ordinary British women struggled with a society that denigrated their worth and ability. In 1543, for fear of their simple minds being confused on religious matters, Parliament passed a law forbidding bible reading by some lower-class men and *all* women, except for gentlewomen (that is, more affluent and educated women) and noblewomen in their own homes. The law was repealed a few years later, but suspicion remained about women as readers and thinkers.[9] Some women responded directly to that suspicion and hostility in print. Jane Anger's *Protection for Women*, published in 1589, asserted that women should be considered superior to men as the later creation (by God) and argued that women were more given to fidelity and constancy.[10] Still, in the latter seventeenth century, a man could claim that it was the "usual work of women either to spin or knit, not to meddle with State Affairs" and could ignore or disregard the continuing, even growing, presence of women in a public, political sphere.[11] The right to vote was restricted to property-owning men until well into the nineteenth century: women and dependent men (such as servants) were categorized as "passive citizens" whose subordination to their male relatives, especially in the case of wives and daughters, meant that they were not suited to having an active voice in the political future of the nation.[12]

Although Muggle women lived under rules that restricted women's political participation and independence, the position of witches during this period may well have been much better. We don't know whether witches were able to vote in early wizarding elections, although the letter of Modesty Rabnott in 1269, protesting how the Chief of the Wizards' Council, Barberus Bragge, had abused a Golden Snidget by making it a stake in the match, ended with a comment that suggested otherwise: "Chief Bragge would have lost my vote if I'd had one." (*QTTA*, 11–12)

In 1792, in the wake of the French Revolution, Mary Wollstonecraft published *A Vindication of the Rights of Woman* to passionately demand that women's equality be recognized in British society and politics. The work became instantly notorious—a well-known politician and aristocrat, Horace Walpole, referred to Wollstonecraft as "a female hyena in petticoats"—criticized by some, read by many, translated immediately into French and German.[13] Wollstonecraft's controversial private life, especially the fact that she bore a child out of wedlock, made her work all the more sensational, but no real change resulted from her arguments.[14]

Yet Wollstonecraft's arguments apparently applied only to the Muggle world: whether or not witches had the right to vote during the thirteenth-century Quidditch dispute discussed earlier, they had certainly achieved political equality with wizards long before the French Revolution convulsed the Muggle world. In the wizarding world in 1798, just a few years after Wollstonecraft's *Vindication* appeared in print, Artemisia Lufkin took the highest office in the wizarding world as Minister for Magic, a position she held until 1811. Lufkin was the first female Minister for Magic but hardly the first woman to figure prominently in the wizarding world.[15]

Nevertheless, her elevation apparently inspired a protest: "Several of the oldest Wizengamot wizards walk[ed] out in protest at Minister's appointment."[16] We can only assume that the protest was at the Minister's being a woman.

Was Lufkin's appointment so revolutionary? By some standards, it wasn't. Elfrida Clagg had served as Chieftainess of the Wizengamot in the seventeenth century (equivalent to the Speaker of Parliament), which shows that women had a presence in the wizarding world's parliamentary system well before Lufkin's ministry.[17] In contrast, Muggle women had to wait at least two hundred years longer, until 1918, for the passage of the Parliament (Qualification of Women) Act, which only permitted women to stand for parliamentary election. Before 1917, they could not even observe the workings of Parliament directly but had to peer from behind an obtrusive grating concealing a "ladies' gallery" above an open viewing area for reporters.[18]

A separate parliamentary act also permitted women to vote at long last in 1918, although at first this was allowed to women only if they were taxpayers older than age thirty. This was eventually relaxed in 1928 so that any woman twenty-one and older had the right to vote on the same basis as men.[19] Women soon entered the House of Commons as members of Parliament, but it wasn't until 1992 that Betty Boothroyd became the first female Speaker of the British House of Commons. This was some time after Margaret Thatcher led the Conservative to victory in the 1979 general elections, making her Muggle Britain's first female prime minister.[20]

A Galleon of Her Own

Going back to the Middle Ages, British women were subject not only to the authority wielded by monarchs and church leaders, but also to the power of their male relatives. As with most of the rest of the European world, women were assumed to be naturally dependent on the men in their lives. The legal system simply reinforced this by forcefully upholding men's power within the family. Women were born into a world dominated first by fathers, later by husbands, and eventually even by sons, who wielded the power of a pater-familias as heads of their households, especially if they controlled a family's property or business; in effect, most women were placed under the legal guardianship of male relatives.

As Henry Howard, a sixteenth-century nobleman, explained in A *Dutiful Defense of the Lawful Regiment of Women*, unmarried women owed obedience to their fathers and married women owed obedience to their husbands.[21] A generation later, Thomas Edgar similarly asserted that it was only natural that women had few independent rights and no voice in Parliament because "All of them are understood either married or to be married and their desires are subject to their husband, I know no remedy though some women can shift it well enough."[22]

English women were legally considered to be "one with their husbands" on marriage: a status described as *femme couverte*. A married woman could not hold a job, sign a contract, testify in court, or make important decisions about her children without her husband's consent; he controlled all property that she might own or inherit during the marriage as well. This legal situation was characterized by some legal scholars as making England "the Paradise of Women" because coverture also demanded married men to provide economic support for their wives, offered wives protection against extreme physical violence, and also mitigated the punishments that could be levied against women if their husbands could be seen as responsible.[23]

Theoretically, an adult unmarried woman, or *femme sole*, could own and sell property, make contracts, and sue or be sued in courts. In reality, few women had the resources to do so. Hester Pinney left her deeply religious family's household in 1682 to set up shop in London, selling lace from a small stall in the market or working door-to-door. As a spinster (a common occupation of unmarried women was to spin wool into thread, hence the term being used to describe single women), Hester faced severe criticism from her family for what they saw as her unnatural choices in deciding to live alone and independently. Her brother demanded that she return to the countryside when their sister Rachel married. When Hester later returned to London, her father wrote in frustration,

"What purpose you would furnish a room in London where you have no business, I do not at all understand."[24]

Some cities, such as Bristol and London, allowed married women to set themselves up as femmes sole in a limited sense (for example, they could make relatively small purchases and economic agreements on their own) for the purpose of running a business separate from their husbands. This tradition went back to the Middle Ages, as the 1305 case of Mabel the innkeeper illustrates. Mabel was sued in a London court by Gilbert le Brasour for repayment of a debt. The court case went unresolved on the technical question of whether she was trading as a femme sole, as Gilbert's charge would suggest, or as a *femme couverte*, legally "covered" by her marital relationship as little more than an extension of her husband.[25] A married woman working as a femme sole faced serious penalties, just as any male entrepreneur would have done at the time, and unlike most married women, she could be sued or even imprisoned for debt if her business failed to prosper.

In reality, few married or unmarried women had the wherewithal to act independently in financial matters: land, the main source of wealth and prestige, was customarily passed from father to oldest son, based on the concept of primogeniture. Fathers had to make a conscious decision to leave any property to a daughter, if they had sons as well, or the daughters would inherit no property at all. In the case of "entailed" estates, they often were prohibited from leaving real estate to daughters, as the famous fictional example of Elizabeth Bennett in Jane Austen's *Pride and Prejudice* shows: the Bennett daughters had no financial security because they knew that when their father died, the house and the land had to pass to a male cousin, Mr. Collins. If a landowner whose property was not entailed died without any sons to inherit it, the property either passed on to the next most closely related male relative (a brother, a nephew, or a cousin) or was divided equally among the daughters. Such women became targets for marriage or remarriage, as indicated by the 1185 *Register of Rich Widows and of Orphaned Heirs and Heiresses*, which considered these people profitable assets to exploit, and which listed their names for fortune-hunting men.[26]

In the wizarding world, witches apparently did much better when it came to property rights and acting independently. Two of the founders of Hogwarts were women, and at least one of them, Rowena Ravenclaw, had a daughter who later became the Grey Lady. If Ravenclaw was married while she participated in Hogwarts' creation, the fact that her husband's name is never mentioned in association with the founding of the school suggests that the wizarding world might well have recognized married women's property rights and freedom to act on their own—a revolutionary stance compared to the Muggle world's laws of the period. Of course, Rowena Ravenclaw and Helga Hufflepuff might have been widows and thus in a position where even Muggle laws recognized their right to dispose of land and possessions.

We have no evidence that either wizards or witches enjoyed an advantage in the wizarding world when it came to the inheritance of property or social standing. The infamous Black family tapestry that Sirius interprets for his godson gives no hint that witches labored under any disability when it came to status or recognition within a wizarding family. What mattered most to the ferociously pureblood-minded Blacks was blood purity and magical ability. Across wizarding Britain, magical ability, not gender, was the key to your status. Muggle-born witches and wizards automatically gained entrance to the wizarding world through the manifestation of their abilities and their admission to Hogwarts.

But what of children born to wizarding parents who failed to develop magical powers? Squibs, when they failed to develop their own abilities, became effective nonentities in the wizarding world; being male was apparently no help in such a case. Like Arabella Figg, most Squibs were shunned in the wizarding world (Argus Filch is an interesting exception, but the way in which he was frequently mocked suggests that his position was far from secure or enjoyable). Unlike other Squibs who were marginalized or forced out of the wizarding world, Mrs. Figg, at least, managed to retain some connection to her birth culture through her position watching over young Harry and her membership in the Order of the Phoenix. But Cornelius Fudge dismissed her testimony as coming

from "not a very convincing witness" because of her Squib status
(*OOTP*, 133). Witches had the advantage that their undeniable
magical ability reinforced their role in the wizarding world, whereas
Squibs of either sex were essentially excluded from political, educational, and social advancement in ways that women in the historical Muggle world would have understood. Like Squibs, before the
twentieth century, Muggle women were considered a lesser sort of
person, socially and legally, in their world.

Blue Stockings and Broomsticks

Witches are integral to the wizarding world's educational system.
Hogwarts was founded in the tenth century by four powerful magic
users: Godric Gryffindor, Helga Hufflepuff, Rowena Ravenclaw,
and Salazar Slytherin. That two women were among the founders
is not unprecedented: in the Middle Ages, women from well-to-
do families, especially widows, donated property and possessions
to the church (and most educational foundations were linked with
the church), as might any faithful Christian.[27] Yet these founders
did more than merely grant lands, books, and building materials to
the new school: Gryffindor, Hufflepuff, Ravenclaw, and Slytherin
all contributed to the creation and development of Hogwarts as an
educational institution open to both boys and girls.

The wizarding world thus approached women's education far
differently than conventional English culture had in earlier periods.
Muggle women had few educational options before the eighteenth
century, almost all of them segregated from men. A few well-to-do
women were educated privately by tutors, as was the case with the
great twelfth-century scholar and nun Heloise. Peter Abelard, hired
to tutor the young woman, entered into a romantic relationship
with her that ended badly, at least for the scholar: her relatives cas-
trated him in revenge after she bore a son out of wedlock.[28] Witches
enjoyed an equal education with wizards for more than a thousand
years, centuries before their Muggle sisters could even hope to get
equivalent formal schooling.

In 1787, Mary Wollstonecraft was fired from her job as governess in no small part for publishing *Thoughts on the Education of Daughters*. By modern standards, her statements in favor of women's education are bland and conventional, but Wollstonecraft argued for the cultivation of reason and rationality in women to counteract the Gothic romance and frivolity that were fashionable among eighteenth-century elites. Nevertheless, Wollstonecraft felt that women's education should supplement, not replace, their domestic training: "No employment of the mind is a sufficient excuse for neglecting domestic duties, and I cannot conceive that they are incompatible. A woman may fit herself to be the companion and friend of a man of sense, and yet know how to take care of his family."[29]

The contemporary Muggle Bluestocking Society, founded in the mid-eighteenth century by three influential women, Elizabeth Vesey, Elizabeth Montagu, and Frances Boscawen, attempted to improve women's education along with the rest of society by hosting meetings devoted to sober intellectual study. Their lack of interest in fashion and style, famously indicated by allowing the botanist Linnaeus to attend an event wearing his everyday blue stockings, led some to mock educated women with the label "bluestocking," an insult that was soon applied to all studious (and allegedly unfashionable) women. Yet no witch of the period would have thought that being interested in reading was something to be ashamed of; after all, by the time of the Muggle Bluestockings, witches had been encouraged to read and study for more than seven hundred years.[30]

A few separate schools for women flourished in the eighteenth and nineteenth centuries, but some of these were criticized for the very limited education they provided, because they focused mostly on domestic skills that women would need to manage their households and not for any higher purpose or profession. In 1840, Queen's College and Bedford College were founded to train women as elementary school teachers with a challenging curriculum. A few decades later, though, the Taunton Commission, established by Parliament, reported that most girls were not being educated in any way equivalent to boys. Their investigation characterized most female education across the nation as domestic and frivolous. Especially at the universities, women faced stern opposition during the early twentieth century. Women's colleges, such as Girton at Cambridge (founded in 1869), struggled for recognition of their courses, degrees, and basic accreditation, let alone equal opportunities for their graduates. It wasn't until 1947 that Cambridge University awarded women students degrees on the same terms as men.[31] Even so, Woolf's A *Room of One's Own* pointed out that women's colleges and institutions in the early twentieth century lagged far behind men's in terms of finances, property, and influence because women had, for so long, little right to earn and dispose of money.[32]

The fact that Hogwarts had provided equal educational opportunities for witches and wizards in the same institution since the Middle Ages shows that women's education in the wizarding world was a more equitable affair. Perhaps it was a lack of resources, as much as anything else, because the wizarding population of Britain was much smaller than the Muggle, making it difficult to finance separate schools for boys and girls. Yet other wizarding communities on the continent similarly supported one integrated wizarding school for each culture or region (Beauxbatons in the French-speaking world, Durmstrang for central Europe), suggesting that integrated education was a value shared among all magic-using populations.[33]

Women continued to play a key role in magical education long after the founding of Hogwarts. Magical schools were led by women and men, seemingly without any great outcry or upset, as had happened with the Minister's position. We know that at least one eighteenth-century witch served as Headmistress of Hogwarts: the celebrated Dilys Derwent, whose portrait also adorned St. Mungo's Hospital. Minerva McGonagall is Deputy Headmistress of Hogwarts when Harry first arrives and eventually becomes Headmistress after Voldemort's defeat (*TOBTB*, xiv). When the Beauxbatons contingent arrives to participate in the Triwizard

Tournament, it is Madame Olympe Maxime's unusual size, not her sex, that causes remark, suggesting that women are equally integrated into wizarding education worldwide.

Nevertheless, many of the women on staff at Hogwarts fulfill what might be considered women's roles in education (although only since the nineteenth century). Poppy Pomfrey fills a traditionally feminine role as Hogwarts's school matron (nurse), ruling over her infirmary with strict efficiency that Florence Nightingale would have admired (and Pomfrey has much more independence than a nineteenth-century nurse would have enjoyed).[34] Similarly, Irma Pince is a librarian, another occupation closely associated with women. Professor Pomona Sprout, in Herbology, seems akin to the nineteenth-century tradition of indomitable women naturalists who published books and studies on their botanical specialties.[35] A negative stereotype of the woman "teacher type" current in the early twentieth century as "a 'cross-hatch' who was bossy, overbearing, domineering, aloof and who carried an instantly recognisable trademark of the 'certificated air'" might stand as well for someone like Dolores Umbridge, except for her magical abilities, of course![36]

Quidditch, whether at Hogwarts or professionally, is another area where witches compete and appear to be on an equal footing with wizards. From early on, women appear in the accounts of Quidditch as an organized sport. A letter from the twelfth century showed Gunhilda Kneen of Yorkshire as a regular Catcher, the medieval term for today's Chasers in the local game of Quidditch enjoyed in her wizarding community (QTTA, 9). No student is surprised that a woman, Madam Xiomara Hooch, serves as Hogwarts' broom instructor and Quidditch trainer when Harry starts broom instruction in his first year. Witches' athleticism isn't confined only to the Quidditch field, because it was a witch, Jocunda Sykes, who first flew a broom across the Atlantic in 1935 (QTTA, 48).

Women and men both played in professional Quidditch for some time at least, with star players such as Catriona McCormack, who led the Pride of Portree as Captain and Chaser during the 1960s. The Holyhead Harpies, the team that Ginny Weasley eventually plays for in her professional career, stands out as unique across the wizarding world for being the sole witches-only team: no mention is made of wizard-only teams in the leagues (*QTTA*, 34–36). In contrast to the acceptance of women in sports shown in the wizarding world, when the newly formed Muggle British Ladies' Football Club ventured to play exhibition games in 1895, they were mercilessly mocked in the popular press. It took a determined effort for Muggle women to be accepted as having the right to play vigorous sports, let alone compete in public, and such Muggle female teams and leagues still have not won the public support and the audiences that witches have apparently enjoyed in their sports for a very long time.[37] Overall, in education and sports, witches appear to have had seemingly equal access with their male counterparts for centuries.

Muggle-born witches who entered Hogwarts during its first thousand years must have been dazzled by the contrast, as suddenly the doors to education, sports, and politics were thrown wide open to them. Before the twentieth century, it must have been almost painful for them when they returned to their homes for the holidays or summer and saw how their Muggle mothers and sisters were confined to lives without educational or professional opportunities and indeed without the most basic legal rights. Return to Hogwarts, in such circumstances, perhaps appeared as a bittersweet escape.

A Different Sort of S.P.E.W.

In 1859, a Lincolnshire woman, Jessie Boucherett, founded the Society for Promoting the Employment of Women, or S.P.E.W. The unfortunately named society sought to train Muggle women, mostly from the lower middle class, for work beyond governessing and dressmaking. S.P.E.W. founded the first bookkeeping, typewriting, and shorthand classes for women in the early years of its existence. The society also provided a registry service for women workers but found itself overwhelmed at times with the number of requests it got from Muggle women for information about job training and for help with work placement. Men protested S.P.E.W.'s mission (rather as Ron protested Hermione's similarly named organization promoting Elfish Welfare more than a century later), fearing that an influx of women into these occupations would lower wages and prestige.[38]

Historically, Muggle women frequently worked in or owned family businesses: taverns were often family-owned ventures to which the entire family contributed and that a widow might carry on with after the death of her husband. Madam Rosmerta's ownership of the Three Broomsticks in Hogsmeade wouldn't have seemed unusual in the Muggle world, even in centuries past. Social custom and legal restrictions made it difficult for British women to train in and pursue many occupations outside the home, although medieval employers were advised to hire women if they wished to save on their labor costs, because women would work "for much less money than a man would take."[39]

Most British women had to work for a living, just as men did, but much of "women's work" was unpaid or underpaid labor conducted at home. Molly Weasley, even for all of the magical spells she knew to help her conquer housework, worked hard raising seven children and keeping the Burrow as intact as she could through the family's many troubles.

Although many British women traditionally worked as part of a family business, such as a farm or in their own households, by the nineteenth century some women earned wages working as household servants, dressmakers, or governesses. Unmarried women could keep their earnings, and they worked in a variety of occupations, according to the census of 1851, including smithing and mining. Women from the lower and middle classes increasingly aspired to serve as governesses in a well-to-do household or work in a retail store as a shop assistant.[40] Married women were discouraged by law and social pressure from taking on work outside the home. Even if they did, unlike unmarried women, they had no right to their own wages. Before the 1882 passage of the second Married Women's Property Act, married Englishwomen's property rights were nearly nonexistent, due to the doctrine of coverture that held that a married woman was legally "covered" by her husband. Therefore, a married woman couldn't own property as an individual, even if she had inherited that from her family: her husband was free to do what he wanted with the income of that property and any other goods his wife brought to the marriage. Charles Dickens was one of many Victorians who criticized the old laws that let abusive husbands spend their wives' earnings and their children's inheritance.[41] As no mention is made of the marital status of women workers in the wizarding world, however, it's possible that this was only ever an issue for Muggles and not among magic users. Certainly, the many witches we know who pursued careers long before the twentieth century, such as Artemisia Lufkin, may well have been married.

World War I took many British men out of the ordinary working world, as the army recruited soldiers to fight in Europe. This opened up more employment options for British women, although war's end meant the loss of those same choices, because returning soldiers were given first priority for many jobs. During the interwar period, Muggle women were employed not only in traditional domestic jobs, but increasingly in a range of clerical and light manufacturing positions.[42] The twentieth century saw an enormous increase in the employment of women outside the home, as well as in the range of jobs that women could pursue, but in 1938 Virginia Woolf noted that jobs in the church or the diplomatic corps weren't open to women. Woolf campaigned for women's rights to hold jobs in such male-only or male-dominated professions, something that didn't happen before her death in 1941.[43]

In the wizarding world of Harry's day, we also see women employed in a variety of positions: some traditional for women (from a Muggle point of view, that is), and others anything but. Madam Rosmerta and Madam Puddifott, respectively, keep their inn and tea shop as other women might across Muggle Britain. Nymphadora Tonks is not the first woman working as an Auror, the elite of the magical world's defenders against the Dark Arts, because Alice Longbottom had earlier been employed in this dangerous job. Amelia Susan Bones rose through the Ministry ranks and headed the department of Magical Law Enforcement until her death. Other wizarding women worked in a variety of jobs, such as Rita Skeeter's career as a journalist or the more magically flavored employment of Gladys Boothby as a Quidditch broom manufacturer (*QTTA*, 48).

Potions, Pills, Bodies, and Wands: Domestic and Private Life

Ideas and laws are one thing, but how different, really, were women's daily lives in the wizarding and the Muggle worlds? We have to go beyond the story of a few outstanding women to try to see what the ordinary experience was like for witches. Despite the ease with which Hermione and other Muggle-born witches traveled back and forth between the two communities, it seems clear that witches' private lives differed drastically from those of Muggle women.

One interesting possibility about the wizarding world is that magic could have liberated witches from household drudgery and uncontrolled childbearing centuries before their Muggle counterparts were able to finally obtain effective forms of birth control. Although we have much evidence that European women had tried for centuries to control how often they became pregnant, they lacked any reliable devices or potions to prevent conception before the nineteenth century. At that time, Muggle medicine hadn't even discovered that women ovulated.[44]

With so little information available, regulating family size was difficult. Well-to-do Englishwomen of the seventeenth century rarely breast-fed their children, for example, and Dorothy McLaren noticed that these same wealthy women had many pregnancies, closely spaced, while less well-to-do families had children spaced three to four years apart. This was a consequence of the natural contraceptive effect of prolonged breast-feeding.[45] Still, rich or poor, all Muggle women lacked reliable forms of birth control.

Nineteenth-century advertisements for (largely quack) methods of contraception suggest that some Muggles still struggled to control their fertility, but it wasn't until the nineteenth century that the vulcanization of rubber made both bicycle tires *and* condoms technically possible; even so, condoms were too expensive for most

Muggle families. Rubber cervical caps and diaphragms followed in the early twentieth century, but (like condoms) these were both expensive and outlawed in many Western nations.[46] The development of the birth control pill during the 1960s finally provided a reliable and widely accessible way for Muggle women to reduce the risk of pregnancy and was soon followed by a plethora of other improved devices.[47]

Yet with magical concoctions such as Polyjuice Potion able to literally reshape bodies, maybe the wizarding world had magical solutions for this age-old problem? Given the long history of witches who were active in wizarding politics and public life, it's likely that some such magical pregnancy prevention existed for witches and wizards, allowing them to manage their fertility in ways that Muggles might envy. A culture in which bored adolescents spent their days dreaming up new charms and hexes to use for pranks would surely not have overlooked women's fundamental need to control their own childbearing, although such matters apparently weren't discussed in front of Harry. It's possible, however, that the book that Ron gave Harry for his seventeenth birthday, *Twelve Fail-Safe Ways to Charm Witches*, contained some advice along these lines.

Another way in which witches' lives were easier than those of Muggle women was in housework. Molly Weasley magically managed the Weasley household, directing knives to chop potatoes for dinner and conjuring sauces with her wand. Muggle women used elbow grease and appliances to achieve the same effect. Eighteenth-century homes commonly featured open hearths belching smoke and earthen floors, which were impossible to clean. Women, whether householders or servants, prepared food, cleaned clothes, and cared for children, and these tasks involved quantities of sheer labor that are striking for historians today:

> What above all else strikes one is the amount of time, preparation, and energy, that went into the provision of even these basic necessities. Take, for example, the provision of water for cooking, drinking, washing, and cleaning. Except for the

houses of the very rich, a piped water supply was rare. There was no system of drainage, no sewerage, and before 1770, no water closets [toilets]. Water had to be drawn and carried from the water source.[48]

Inventions such as washing machines and vacuum cleaners transformed modern Muggle home life in the twentieth century. This didn't always make life easier. Even when modern appliances became affordable, they didn't always free up women's lives. After World War II, historians found that women who stayed at home often couldn't afford these appliances, while women who worked outside the home to afford such devices spent long hours on weekends and evenings catching up on domestic chores.[49] Ideals of housewifery promoted in society and the media overwhelmed and depressed some Muggle women, an insight eloquently expressed in Betty Friedan's *The Feminine Mystique*.[50]

Despite the improvements that magic offered when it came to birth control and housework, in other respects the wizarding world is only a slightly distorted mirror of our own. Although some opportunities were open to women much earlier than in the Muggle experience, many other aspects of wizarding life suggest a depressing similarity between our world and theirs. Prejudice still had power in the wizarding world, especially in the private lives of witches and wizards.

Particularly when we look at the attitude toward women demonstrated in some pureblood families such as the Gaunts, some witches seem no more empowered than the most downtrodden of Muggle women from their own time. Even though Merope Gaunt had magical ability enough to charm a Muggle into marriage, she was physically and emotionally abused by her father, Marvolo, who put great stock in his family's pureblood status, even as they lived in filth and poverty. Merope eventually fled her wizarding family's abusive treatment, only to be served even worse when her love potion wore off Tom Riddle and he abandoned her, leaving her to die after bearing their unfortunate son, the future Voldemort.

While the Gaunts personified dysfunctional relationships in the wizarding world, the marriage bonds and the family relationships in Britain's magic-using culture could also be quite strong and supportive. The Weasley family, for all of their quarrels and lack of funds, came together in times of need, such as when Arthur Weasley was attacked by Nagini and rushed to St. Mungo's for treatment. Such family solidarity wasn't characteristic only of Harry's friends. Narcissa Malfoy passionately defended Lucius Malfoy against her sister, Bellatrix, while pleading with Severus Snape to assume Draco's assigned duty of killing Albus Dumbledore. Muggle or magical, anyone could have a good or a bad family experience.

Magical relationships between the sexes weren't automatically easier or more equal than in the Muggle world, either. At Hogwarts, Hermione resorted to an application of Sleekeazy's Hair Potion in order to tame her hair for the Yule Ball. Witches and wizards, just as much as ordinary men and women, thus still struggled with fears of rejection and hoped to find love. In many of the most ordinary ways, when it came to matters of emotion and the heart, it wasn't any easier to be a magic user. Yet witches seemed to enjoy earlier and more equal access to political position, education, and employment, perhaps because the wizarding world was more interested in magical ability than in whether the magic user was male or female. In the end, the fact that Hermione *was* a witch (as Ron reminded her) could matter quite a bit.

Notes

1. All book quotes are taken from the British editions by J. K. Rowling as follows: *Philosopher's Stone*, London: Bloomsbury, 1997; *Order of the Phoenix*, London: Bloomsbury, 2003; *Tales of Beedle the Bard*, London: Bloomsbury, 2007; *Quidditch through the Ages*, London; Bloomsbury, 2001.

2. Virginia Woolf, *A Room of One's Own* (New York and London: Harcourt Brace and Jovanovich, 1929), 50.

3. Charles Beem, *The Lioness Roared: The Problems of Female Rule in English History* (London: Palgrave Macmillan, 2008), 25–30.

4. The W.O.M.B.A.T. examination on J. K. Rowling's Web site is now closed, but the questions and answers were transcribed at the Harry Potter Lexicon, including 5.d.: "The second wife of King Henry VIII, Anne Boleyn, was accused by Muggles of being a witch, but was actually a Squib." "The W.O.M.B.A.T. Grade 3," www.hp-lexicon.org/wizworld/wombat/wombat3comments.html.

5. Janice Liedl, "Above the Rest of Ladies: Celebrating the Life of Jane Seymour," in *Constructions of Death, Mourning and Memory Conference Proceedings 2006* (Woodcliff Lake, NJ: WAPACC, 2006), 117–120.

6. Natalie Mears, *Queenship and Political Discourse in the Elizabethan Realms* (Cambridge, UK: Cambridge University Press, 2005), 222–225.

7. Susan C. Karant-Nunn and Merry E. Wiesner, eds., *Luther on Women: A Sourcebook* (New York: Cambridge University Press, 2003), 28.

8. Carole Levin, *The Heart and Stomach of a King: Elizabeth I and the Politics of Sex and Power* (Philadelphia: University of Pennsylvania Press, 1994), 1.

9. Suzanne W. Hull, *Chaste, Silent and Obedient: English Books for Women, 1475–1640* (San Marino, CA: Huntington Library, 1982), 100–101.

10. Jane Anger, *Jane Anger, Her Protection for Women* (London: Richard Jones and Thomas Orwin, 1589), C1^{r-v}.

11. Lois G. Schwoerer, "Women's Public Political Voice in England: 1640–1740," in *Women Writers and the Early Modern British Political Tradition*, ed. Hilda L. Smith (Cambridge: Cambridge University Press, 1998), 56–58.

12. Margaret Thornton, "The Judicial Gendering of Citizenship: A Look at Property Interests during Marriage," *Journal of Law and Society* 24, no. 4 (December 1997): 487.

13. Walpole's charges and the contemporary response to her work are explained in R. M. James, "On the Reception of Mary Wollstonecraft's *A Vindication of the Rights of Woman*," *Journal of the History of Ideas* 39, no. 2 (1978): 294.

14. Barbara Taylor, "Wollstonecraft, Mary (1759–1797)," in *Oxford Dictionary of National Biography*, ed. H.C.G. Matthew and Brian Harrison (Oxford: OUP, 2004); online edition, ed. Lawrence Goldman, May 2007, www.oxforddnb.com/view/article/10893.

15. J. K. Rowling, "Wizard of the Month Archive," www.jkrowling.com/textonly/en/wotm.cfm.

16. "The W.O.M.B.A.T. Grade 3," www.hp-lexicon.org/wizworld/wombat/wombat3 comments.html.

17. There is some confusion as to the date of Clagg's tenure in the Wizengamot. See J. K. Rowling, "Wizard of the Month Archive," www.jkrowling.com/textonly/en/wotm.cfm.

18. Claire Eustance, "Protests from behind the Grille: Gender and the Transformation of Parliament, 1867 1918" *Parliamentary History* 16, no. 1 (1997): 107 108.

19. Michael S. Smith, "Parliamentary Reform and the Electorate," in *A Companion to Nineteenth-Century Britain*, ed. Chris Williams (New York: Wiley-Blackwell, 2004), 167–170.

20. For Boothroyd, see John L. Irwin, *Modern Britain: An Introduction* (London: Routledge, 1994), 35. On Thatcher's rise to PM, see Eric J. Evans, *Thatcher and Thatcherism*, 2nd ed. (London: Routledge, 2004), 13–19.

21. Linda A. Pollock, "Rethinking Patriarchy and the Family in Seventeenth-Century England," *Journal of Family History* 23, no. 3 (1998): 5.

22. Thomas Edgar, *The Lavves Resolutions of Womens Rights: Or, the Lavves Prouision for Woemen a Methodicall Collection of Such Statutes and Customes, with the Cases, Opinions, Arguments and Points of Learning in the Lavv, as Doe Properly Concerne Women* (London: John More, 1632), 6.

23. Joanna Bailey, "Favoured or Oppressed? Married Women, Property and 'Coverture' in England, 1660–1800," *Continuity and Change* 17, no. 3 (2002): 351–352.

24. Pamela Sharpe, "Dealing with Love: The Ambiguous Independence of the Single Woman in Early Modern England," *Gender and History* 11, no. 2 (July 1999): 211–214.

25. Marjorie K. McIntosh, "The Benefits and Drawbacks of *Femme Sole* Status in England, 1300–1630," *Journal of British Studies* 44, no. 3 (July 2005): 419.

26. Henrietta Leyser, *Medieval Women: A Social History of Women in England, 450–1500* (London: Phoenix, 1996), 170–172.

27. Lisa M. Bitel, *Women in Early Medieval Europe, 400–1100* (Cambridge, UK: Cambridge University Press, 2002), 123–125.

28. For the full story of Abelard and Heloise's lives in their own words, see Betty Radice, ed., *The Letters of Abelard and Heloise* (Harmondsworth, UK: Penguin, 1974).

29. Mary Wollstonecraft, *Thoughts on the Education of Daughters, with Reflections on Female Conduct in the More Important Duties of Life* (London: J. Johnson, 1787), 56.

30. Paula R. Backscheider "Bluestockings," *The Oxford Encyclopedia of Women in World History* (Oxford: Oxford University Press 2008), www.oxford-womenworldhistory.com/entry?entry=t248.e117.

31. Jane McDermid, "Women and Education," in *Women's History: Britain, 1850–1945*, ed. Jane Purvis (London: University College of London Press, 1995), 109–112.

32. Woolf, *A Room of One's Own*, 20–23.

33. Although the Harry Potter movies suggest that Beauxbatons and Durmstrang were single-sex schools, Rowling describes the delegations as including both boys and girls.

34. Carol Helmstadter, "Building a New Nursing Service: Respectability and Efficiency in Victorian England," *Albion* 35, no. 4 (Winter 2003): 606–609.

35. Jeanne Kay Guelke and Karen M. Morin, "Gender, Nature, Empire: Women Naturalists in Nineteenth Century British Travel Literature," *Transactions of the Institute of British Geographers*, New Series, 26, no. 3 (2001): 312–313.

36. Wendy Robinson, "Frocks, Frills, Femininity and Representations of the Woman Teacher in the Woman Teacher's World: Reconstructing the Early Twentieth Century English 'Schoolmarm,'" *Journal of Educational Administration and History* 35, no. 2 (2003): 90.

37. Lee James, "As Natural a Game for Girls as for Boys," *International Journal of the History of Sport* 24, no. 11 (2007): 1411–1412.

38. Michelle Elizabeth Tusan, "'Not the Ordinary Victorian Charity': The Society for Promoting the Employment of Women Archive," *History Workshop Journal* 49 (2000): 222–224.

39. Judith M. Bennett, *History Matters: Patriarchy and the Challenge of Feminism* (Philadelphia: University of Pennsylvania Press), 92–103.

40. Ellen Jordan, *The Women's Movement and Women's Employment in Nineteenth Century Britain* (London: Routledge, 1999), 65–70.

41. Mary Lyndon Shanley, *Feminism, Marriage, and the Law in Victorian England* (Princeton, NJ: Princeton University Press, 1993), 60.

42. Selina Todd, "Poverty and Aspiration: Young Women's Entry to Employment in Inter-War England," *Twentieth Century British History* 15,:no. 2 (2004): 122–123.

43. Lyndall Gordon, "Woolf, (Adeline) Virginia (1882–1941)," *Oxford Dictionary of National Biography* (Oxford: Oxford University Press, 2005), www.oxforddnb.com/view/article/37018.

44. Angus McLaren, *Birth Control in Nineteenth Century England* (Teaneck, NJ: Holmes & Meier, 1978), 203.

45. Dorothy McLaren, "Fertility, Infant Mortality and Breast Feeding in the Seventeenth Century," *Medical History* 22, no. 4 (1978): 377–378.

46. Angus McLaren, *Twentieth-Century Sexuality: A History* (Malden, MA: Blackwell, 1999), 69–73.

47. Hera Cook, "The English Sexual Revolution: Technology and Social Change," *History Workshop Journal* 59 (2005): 112.

48. Bridget Hill, *Women, Work and Sexual Politics in Eighteenth-Century England* (Montreal & Kingston: McGill-Queen's University Press, 1994), 107–108.

49. Louise A. Tilly and Joan W. Scott, *Women, Work and Family* (New York: Routledge, 1989), 221.

50. Betty Friedan, *The Feminine Mystique* (New York: Dell, 1963).

Marx, Magic, and Muggles

Class Conflict in Harry Potter's World

Susan Hall

The early-nineteenth-century city was squalid, overcrowded, violent, and disease-ridden. Matters like sewers, clean water, and street lighting received little attention and less funding. In 1830s Great Britain, three in ten children never reached their fifth birthday.

Early public health reformers such as Dr. James P. Kay drew attention to the dangers of urban living: "In Parliament-street there is only one privy [outhouse] for three hundred and eighty inhabitants, which is placed in a narrow passage, whence its effluvia infest the adjacent houses, and must prove a fertile source of disease."[1] The conditions under which the urban poor lived were so appalling, it seemed to many, including Karl Marx and his fellow communist Friedrich Engels, that the only possible outcome must be a bloody revolution.

The revolution they actually got was powered by steam. The development of steam-powered trains and the resulting spread of the railroads created a far more profound change in society on both sides of the Atlantic than any angry mob storming the White House or Windsor Castle could have managed.

On September 15, 1830, the world's first scheduled, steam-powered passenger railroad opened between the English industrial cities of Manchester and Liverpool, some thirty-five miles distant from each other. By the time night fell, a British cabinet minister lay dying, the victim of the world's first fatal rail accident. The Duke of Wellington, the conqueror of Napoleon, had been prevented from leaving the train at Manchester station by a stone-throwing mob. Speculators were already buying up crucial packages of land where they hoped the next tracks would be laid. The Railroad Age had begun.[2] For Muggles, nothing would ever be the same again.

In the magical world, one imagines that the date passed without note. Witches and wizards could already travel significant distances almost instantaneously. With limited exceptions (for example, 12 Grimmauld Place), witches and wizards live outside major urban centers, commuting to work using the Floo Network or Apparition.[3]

Dark Lord problems aside, the work-life balance for most witches and wizards is an enviable one. It also seems to have lasted largely unchanged for many centuries.

Mass transit at last made it possible for Muggles to come close (although not equal) to the magical world's freedom of movement. Or, as Ralph Waldo Emerson put it, more poetically: Railroad iron is a magician's rod, in its power to evoke the sleeping energies of land and water.[4]

Once commuting became possible, those Muggles who could afford it moved out of the city. Many did not move very far; the limits of omnibus and train speeds limited the range within which commuting was practical. The cost of fares was a significant factor, increasing in proportion to a journey's length. Distant suburbs became, in general, more prestigious than inner ones. Once the middle classes left the city centers, the once-elegant townhouses they had occupied were broken up into small apartments or single rooms for multiple occupancy, making the slum phenomenon worse. The "flight to the suburbs" is often seen as a post–World War II phenomenon. Yet as early as 1845, Friedrich Engels observed,

> With the exception of [the] commercial district, all Manchester proper, all Salford and Hulme . . . are all unmixed working people's quarters, stretching like a girdle, averaging a mile and a half in breadth, around the commercial district. Outside, beyond the girdle, lives the upper and middle bourgeoisie, the middle bourgeoisie in regularly laid out streets in the vicinity of the working quarters . . . the upper bourgeoisie in remoter villas with gardens . . . in free, wholesome country air, in fine, comfortable homes, passed once every half or quarter hour by omnibuses going into the city. And the finest part of the arrangements is this, that the members of this money aristocracy can take the shortest road through the middle of all the labouring districts to their places of business, without ever seeing that they are in the midst of the grimy misery that lurks to the right and to the left.[5]

The pattern of the modern city, with its downtown business district, virtually deserted at night, its violent and dilapidated innercity slums, and its outer commuter belts, was created by the mass transit revolution of the mid-nineteenth century. At the same time, the railroad lines carved into existing cities, turning previously prosperous districts into slums crippled by urban blight. Such districts became, almost overnight, on "the wrong side of the tracks."

Even without the railroads, magical society also has its own run-down, dangerous districts where middle-class magical children never set foot:

> "Where did you come out?" Ron asked.
>   "Knockturn Alley," said Hagrid grimly.
>   "*Brilliant!*" said Fred and George together.
>   "We've never been allowed in," said Ron enviously.
> (COS, 46)[6]

Knockturn Alley, "a dingy alleyway that seemed to be made up entirely of shops devoted to the dark arts," lies only a short walk from Gringotts Bank, with its flight of white stairs, burnished bronze doors, and uniformed door-wardens (COS, 45). Engels's "grim misery that lurks to the right and the left," which the bourgeoisie pass their lives "without ever seeing," remains a fact of life in the wizarding world. It can, in fact, be seen as a metaphor for the core conflict of the series. Dark alleys breed Dark Lords.

Little Whinging and Much Angst

The railroads had an equally profound effect on the rural environment. They stimulated a flow of ideas and tangible goods from the wider world. Small-town businesses were forced to compete against mail-order goods delivered by rail. Their customers could now opt to shop in nearby urban centers. Dairy farmers and fishing communities, however, received (at least initially) an enormous boost, because it became practicable to transport perishable products quickly to a far wider range of markets.

The social mix of villages and towns within easy commuting distance of the major urban centers changed most dramatically. The Home Counties, those bordering London but not including the capital city itself, were particularly affected. In the film version of *Half-Blood Prince*, Harry is shown chatting up a waitress in a railroad station café, and he later meets Dumbledore on the railroad platform. Those scenes were filmed in Surbiton, Surrey, a town that exists purely because a railroad junction happened to be built there in the nineteenth century. In discussions of the British class system, Surbiton has become synonymous with affluent, white Middle England, characterized by narrow-minded conformity and self-policed by an obsession with "what will the neighbors think?"

Surbiton has much in common with the fictional Surrey town of Little Whinging, the home of the Dursleys and of Harry until his seventeenth birthday. The Dursleys, predictably, are obsessed with status and with conformity to what they see as middle-class norms. Although, as we will see later in Rowling's treatment of Stan Shunpike and Rubeus Hagrid, Rowling is not free of class prejudice herself; some of her best comedy arises in her treatment of the snobbish, social-climbing Dursleys.

This ties into the serious themes of the series. Harry, having been himself the victim of class prejudice, can immediately recognize it in the magical world. When, in *Philosopher's Stone*, Draco Malfoy (then unaware of Harry's identity) dismisses Hagrid as "a sort of savage" and asks Harry whether his parents were "the right sort," he is speaking pure Dursley (*PS*, 61). Harry rejects Draco's overture of friendship with outright scorn and sides with Ron Weasley, whose large, loving family he envies and whose money troubles he has nothing but sympathy for.

Transfiguring the Class System

The magical world appears to have been in a government-proclaimed state of emergency since 1692. That date saw the enactment of the Statute of Secrecy, which requires all witches and wizards to conceal evidence of their powers from the Muggles. To achieve this, the Ministry of Magic has been given sweeping control over all aspects of magical life. These powers are extended further on Lord Voldemort's return.

The fact that the wizarding world's government is so powerful means that ministry influence is, as a result, the chief basis for status and power in the magical world. It is as important for a wizard or a witch who wishes to rise in magical society to keep on good terms with the Ministry as being "a good Party comrade" used to be in the former USSR.[7]

Anyone who upsets senior Ministry figures may be denied promotion (such as Arthur Weasley), be "disappeared" to Azkaban, or be forbidden to practice magic at all. Harry's trial for the use of underage magic in *Order of the Phoenix* is an example of ministerial muscle flexing. Cornelius Fudge, the Minister for Magic, intends to send a message to Albus Dumbledore and the Order of the Phoenix that challenging the official Ministry line is a very unwise thing to do.

Harry is saved only by his personal reputation and by the intervention of Dumbledore. He owes his continued ability to live in the magical world not to what he is, but to who his friends are.

Class conflict is fueled by unjust treatment of various groups in any society based not on inherent merit but on external factors such as wealth or family connections. The magical world is no exception to this rule, as we see in the case of Severus Snape, a pupil from the "wrong side" of the wizarding tracks. Snape's poor treatment at the hands of more affluent purebloods like James Potter and Sirius Black was certainly one of the factors that drove him into the arms of the Death Eaters.

Magical society is a very stable society, which does not provide any clear avenues through which change can be effected. The Ministry does not appear to be subject to any form of democratic oversight; when at the start of *Half-Blood Prince* we learn that Fudge has been replaced by Rufus Scrimgeour, there is no suggestion that an election has occurred. It is fair to assume that the Wizengamot played some role in the events, but becoming a member of the Wizengamot is probably itself dependent on "being in with the right sort." Most likely, only an elite group of witches and wizards possesses any real political power.

The small size of the magical community means that most pureblood wizarding families are related, a point Sirius Black makes when showing Harry the tapestry depicting the Black family tree: "The pure-blood families are all inter-related. [. . .] If you're only going to let your sons and daughters marry pure-bloods your choice is very limited; there are hardly any of us left." (*OOTP*, 105) The power of "connections" is thus very great, so that any outsider to the magical world, such as Tom Riddle, is immediately placed at a profound disadvantage.

At the date of that epic first rail journey in 1830, ordinary Muggles also lacked any real influence over how their society was run. At the time, few men and no women were entitled to vote. The secret ballot was unheard of; those qualified to vote had to announce their choice openly. Unsurprisingly, electoral bribery and intimidation were rampant. Furthermore, Great Britain in the aftermath of the Napoleonic wars had almost magical levels of censorship and government oppression. In 1834, the Tolpuddle Martyrs were sentenced to seven years' transportation (banishment to the British colony of Australia to carry out forced labor there) simply for swearing an oath to one another to work to oppose further reductions to the already pitiful wages of agricultural workers, although as a result of popular protest against the move the sentence was never carried out. In 1842, George Holyoake was imprisoned for six months simply for declaring himself to be an atheist.

During the course of the nineteenth century, Muggle society began to change and become more egalitarian, with a much wider range of people beginning to have a voice in how society was run. How that was achieved is examined in the next section. Until the very end of *Deathly Hallows*, by contrast, not only has the magical world avoided such change, it seems unaware of the need for it.

Engineering Social Change

A scarlet steam engine was waiting next to a platform packed with people.

— *Philosopher's Stone*, 71

Rowling uses the Hogwarts Express as a bridging device. When Harry first crosses the invisible barrier that separates Platform 9 3/4 from the rest of King's Cross Station, he finds himself in a strange world, where all rules have changed. The Express itself, a very old-fashioned vehicle—but still one that a Muggle-born would recognize—is used to convey outsiders like Harry to Hogwarts.

As disoriented as Harry feels, it is the Hogwarts Express that is the true interloper on the scene. The steam train must have been obtained by theft or trade from the Muggles or, most probably, must be a magical counterfeit of a Muggle original.

To explain why, we need to investigate the society that produced the railroads, which were the Great Pyramids of their day. Their construction could not have been achieved without the sweat—and, in many cases, the lives—of a faceless multitude of laborers: men, women, and children. Nor could they have been produced without highly skilled engineers who solved a vast array of problems by the application of logic, inspiration, and the scientific method. Finally, they represented an enormous financial investment. Railroad companies raised money for construction and operation by issuing bonds or by the sale of shares (stock). Speculation in railroad shares proved to be a major factor in stock market booms and crashes during the nineteenth century, on both sides of the Atlantic.

The Railroad Age rested on a three-legged stool of labor, technology, and capital, each of which played a part in the development of the class system. These remain the threefold supports of modern industrialized society. As the global financial crisis of 2008 amply demonstrates, once one of the three legs starts to wobble, it threatens the entire structure.

Magical Capital

In 1694, two years after the International Statute of Wizarding Secrecy had forced the magical world underground, the Muggles founded the Bank of England. The Bank of England issued paper money from the start, with the bank making a pledge to redeem the paper money from its gold reserves if anyone requested. The words "I promise to pay the bearer on demand the sum of [denomination]" appears on UK bank notes to this day. Yet the right to be repaid in gold was suspended on numerous occasions and was ended in 1931.

Gringotts Bank, by contrast, appears to be a glorified safety deposit box. Its vaults contain heaps of precious metals that are withdrawn physically by investors. Paper money seems unknown.

Another contrast between the two banks lies in the Bank of England's key role as banker to the Crown (the British government). On its foundation in 1694, it raised an initial loan for the government of £1.2 million ($1.824 million) by public subscription. Subscribers ranged from enormously wealthy aristocrats investing thousands to small-town merchants having a modest flutter with a spare ten or twenty pounds. Given that the loan paid 8 percent per annum, their investment was a shrewd one. The first loan (and its numerous successors) was spent, largely, on national defense.

The Royal Navy facilitated Great Britain's ruthless imperial expansion, thus creating a cycle. The money the government raised by selling bonds went to build warships, which aided aggressive expansion into further territories, which in turn required building yet more warships. Other European powers, such as France, Spain, and the Netherlands, followed similar patterns, leading inevitably to war as competing colonial ambitions clashed. War, in turn, increased these governments' need for money. The pattern of modern government debt finance was laid. For individual investors, profits gained from sales of coffee or sugar produced on slave-worked plantations in Jamaica could be safely reinvested in government bonds, divorcing it (in class terms) from the degrading taint of "trade."

Despite the murky underpinnings of national finance, owning "something substantial in the four-per-cents" (that is, bonds) became the touchstone of middle-class respectability.[8] In the terms familiar to Karl Marx and Friedrich Engels, the "bourgeoisie" are those whose income derives from their ownership of capital assets, such as rental income or income from investments. The "proletariat" are the employed classes, who depend on selling their labor. National debt finance facilitated the rise of the bourgeoisie.

With the exception of Voldemort's and Grindelwald's activities, the only wars we hear about in the Harry Potter books are the Goblin Rebellions of the eighteenth century. These wars would hardly have been financed by war bonds issued by Gringotts Bank, yet no alternative financial institution seems to exist. Whatever the sources of wizarding wealth, some form of magical military-industrial complex seems improbable.

Because Gringotts hires "curse-breakers" for a "challenging career involving travel, adventure and substantial, danger-related treasure bonuses," at least one source of the magical world's wealth is grave robbing (OOTP, 579). Perhaps magical society is living on inherited capital, which is now running out.

Magical Technology

Any sufficiently advanced technology is indistinguishable
from magic.

> —Arthur C. Clarke

The Hogwarts Express is probably the least efficient way the magical world could have chosen to send its children to school. Even Harry's uncle Vernon, who is not overburdened with brains, draws that conclusion: "Funny way to get to a wizard school, the train. Magic carpets all got punctures, have they?" (PS, 67)

Although magic carpets are currently the subject of an embargo, at least by the British Ministry of Magic, Uncle Vernon's basic point is sound. One hundred thousand witches and wizards from all over the world attended the Quidditch World Cup in the fourth book, most of them traveling by Portkey or, if old enough and licensed, by Apparition. Floo Powder is used to hop through a network of connected fireplaces. Which fireplaces are connected to the network is under the control of the Ministry. Ministry control is a recurring theme in the Harry Potter books.

All of the previous forms of transport are practically instantaneous. Muggles, bound by physical laws, such as Heisenberg's uncertainty principle and the speed of light, seem unlikely ever to achieve this.[9]

Broomsticks, carpets, flying horses, and the Durmstrang ship (which emerges from under the Hogwarts lake) are all forms of noninstantaneous magical transport that are equal to or superior to the railroads and have existed for many centuries.[10]

The Hogwarts Express thus represents technology superseded by magic centuries earlier. Yet it is also old-fashioned by Muggle standards. By September 1, 1991, when Harry caught the Hogwarts Express for the first time, it was the only scheduled passenger steam train operating in Britain.[11] Furthermore, even when Tom Riddle boarded it in 1938, when British-built steam engines were breaking speed records, continental Europe had already turned to electric trains as the way of the future.

The choice of inefficient Muggle technology to transport young witches and wizards to Hogwarts may reflect an implied assertion of the magical world's technological superiority. More charitably, it perhaps represents a "soft landing" for Muggle children going to Hogwarts for the first time, because even outdated Muggle technology is less alien than the magical world. This latter explanation, though, needs one to accept that magical families would be willing to suffer inconvenience in order to make Muggle-borns feel at home, which seems inconsistent with what we see of the Malfoys, the Crabbes, the Goyles, and so forth.

At the date of the Statute of Secrecy, the magical world could be pardoned for seeing Muggle technology as a pale imitation of its magical counterpart. Nowhere was this more apparent than in medicine. Seventeenth-century Muggle medical treatments included blood-letting and dosing with potions that contained mercury, earthworms, and powdered, mummified corpses. Treatment was based on a detailed horoscope cast by the physician. Madam Pomfrey's treatments appear superficially similar — except that magical treatments work, and their Muggle equivalents usually did more harm than good.

Prior to the Statute of Secrecy, some wizards appear to have moonlighted as Muggle physicians. For example, Harry finds a card of Paracelsus among his first batch of chocolate frog cards. Paracelsus, a Swiss physician born around 1493, founded a school of medicine that laid heavy emphasis on chemical analysis.[12]

During the late seventeenth and the eighteenth centuries, science started to assume its modern form. It enjoyed royal patronage; Charles II founded the Royal Society (a prestigious scientific body) and instituted the Royal Observatory. Other European monarchs were equally interested. "Natural philosophers" (the term *scientist* was not coined until 1833) developed the scientific method of empirical research and observation. Furthermore, although the so-called Age of Reason was marred by almost continuous wars between European powers, scientists insisted on the principle that science was universal and owed no national allegiances.

The impact of these changes on the Muggle class structure was complex. First, theoretical science ceased to be the preserve of aristocratic dabblers and became more formalized. Universities expanded their curricula to incorporate "natural sciences." This increased professionalism had downsides. In the older, less formal days, women such as Caroline Herschel, Mary Somerville, and Ada, Countess of Lovelace, were given a chance to display their scientific talents; their upper-class connections mattered more than their gender did. Once scientific institutions became formalized and, often, attached to universities, such women lost out. For example, in 1897, Beatrix Potter was prevented from presenting an important paper on lichens to the Linnaen Society and was denied access to the Royal Botanical Gardens at Kew solely because of her sex.

Yet a new class of university-trained scientists and technicians ("boffins") arose, who during the nineteenth and twentieth centuries carved themselves a place in "the corridors of power."[13] C. P. Snow, himself a physicist, became a member of the House of Lords. Chaim Weitzmann started as a chemistry professor but became the first president of the State of Israel. His brilliant scientific work during both world wars was a crucial factor in the Allied victories and helped build political support for the Zionist movement.

Second, as the Industrial Revolution progressed, patented inventions founded the fortunes of many industrialists on both sides of the Atlantic. Although only a miniscule percentage of those industrialists came from the working classes, the stories of "self-made" men such as Richard Arkwright and Andrew Carnegie, who rose from modest beginnings to wealth, served as an inspiration for many.

Samuel Smiles's book *Self Help*, published in 1859, preached the virtues of individual effort, study, thrift, and self-improvement as the means of improving one's social status. He, too, praised the steam engine as the pinnacle of technological and collaborative achievement:

> The steam-engine was nothing, however, until it emerged from the state of theory, and was taken in hand by practical mechanics; and what a noble story of patient, laborious investigation, of difficulties encountered and overcome by heroic industry, does not that marvellous machine tell of! It is indeed, in

itself, a monument of the power of self-help in man. Grouped around it we find Savary, the military engineer; Newcomen, the Dartmouth blacksmith; Cawley, the glazier; Potter, the engine-boy; Smeaton, the civil engineer; and, towering above all, the laborious, patient, never-tiring James Watt, the mathematical-instrument maker.[14]

Smiles's philosophy of self-improvement through innovation and industry offered ordinary Muggles a chance of upward class mobility otherwise lacking at the time. The notion that hard work and ingenuity could lead to social and financial improvement acted as a safety valve, diffusing class tensions.

The author George Orwell went further, suggesting (in 1941) that technological advances and the new jobs they brought with them were crucial in breaking down rigid pre–World War I class distinctions, and that "the technicians and the higher-paid skilled workers, the airmen and their mechanics, the radio experts, film producers, popular journalists and industrial chemists . . . are the indeterminate stratum at which the older class distinctions are beginning to break down."[15]

By contrast, witches and wizards have been shielded from the technological advances and the upward class mobility of the Muggle world behind the Statute of Secrecy and their own invincible sense of superiority. Unsurprisingly, their world treats science and technology in a very different manner, and opportunities for upward mobility through technological innovation are therefore more limited.

We do hear of witches and wizards who carry out research. Albus Dumbledore "discovered the twelve uses of dragon's blood." (*PS*, 77) Fred and George Weasley, despite very modest academic achievements, are first-class research wizards, even if their experimental methods, which include testing dangerous substances on child subjects, would have any ethics committee howling in outrage. Yet such individuals are precisely that: individual, and few in number. There seems to be no framework within which their research endeavors can be recognized and rewarded. We learn of a "Ludicrous Patents Office" within the Department of Magical

Games and Sports but not of magical inventors using their discoveries to change society.[16] There is no magical equivalent of splitting the atom or landing on the moon. Indeed, the overriding objective of secrecy would prevent projects with such global scope.

Given the absence of magical universities, the only place for structured, funded research is through the highly secretive Department of Mysteries within the Ministry of Magic. Yet there is no suggestion that magical experimentation is carried out on a footing that Muggles would regard as scientifically valid. Indeed, when the Ministry falls to Voldemort in *Deathly Hallows*, scientific integrity is one of the first victims. The *Daily Prophet* publishes a claim that "[r]ecent research undertaken by the Department of Mysteries reveals that magic can only be passed from person to person when wizards reproduce. Where no proven wizarding ancestry exists, therefore, the so-called Muggle-born is likely to have obtained magical power by theft or force." (*DH*, 172) This pseudoscience forms the spurious basis for persecution of Muggle-born witches and wizards under the Voldemort regime.

Muggle science can also suffer from this kind of manipulation for political ends. During Stalin's domination of Russia, Trofim Denisovitch Lysenko's claims that acquired characteristics could be inherited became the party line.[17] Those who challenged his science lost their jobs. Many simply disappeared. So strong was the emphasis on "the scientific method," however, that the international scientific world created an outcry against Lysenkoism. Even scientists within the USSR challenged his dominance, at considerable personal risk. Eventually, Lysenko was ousted from his state positions and died in disgrace.

Magical control of technological innovation, via the Ministry and the International Council of Wizards, facilitates intellectual stagnation, resisting useful cross-fertilization from Muggle or other scientific traditions. Research by goblins (who possess skills in metalworking and craftsmanship unknown to wizards) is artificially restricted by the rule that no nonhuman magical being may carry or use a wand. Goblins, understandably, also refuse to share metalworking secrets with wizards, creating further artificial barriers to technical advance. In addition, there is no independent tradition of magical research, so this state of affairs is not subject to challenge.

Far from being a mechanism of social change, technology in the magical world is the agent of conformity and state control. This is reinforced by the Statute of Secrecy and by popular ignorance of, and contempt for, Muggle technology; Ron, for example, refers to doctors as "those Muggle nutters who cut people up." (*OOTP*, 428) Unlike the promise held out by Smiles or the real-life stories of people such as C. P. Snow, technology does not offer a magical avenue for class mobility.

Magical Labor

Despite the supposed glamour of steam, facilitated today by railroad preservation societies and the "steampunk" movement, the steam age rested on the exploitation of the lowest classes in society.

To function, a steam engine requires water, coal, and unrelenting physical labor. Shoveling coal into the boiler to keep steam pressure up is a full-time and very laborious job, almost as strenuous as mining the coal in the first place. As various analysts have pointed out, without a large pool of low-paid labor, traditional capitalism would find it impossible to function. This remains true to this day, as demonstrated by the decisions of various companies to relocate their manufacturing facilities to what are euphemistically termed "low-cost manufacturing jurisdictions" overseas, with scant regard to working conditions there.

Although the use of powered tools, instead of brutal physical labor, has improved the position of the laboring classes in many respects, skilled artisans have found themselves increasingly without a role in modern society. In Flora Thompson's memoir, *Lark Rise to Candleford*, she describes her shoemaker uncle as representing "a class which is now extinct."[18] Thompson, writing in 1939, recalled the Oxfordshire of the late 1880s and the 1890s. Her eulogies of the little market town of Candleford and the associated village of Candleford Green at times have echoes of Hogsmeade and Godric's Hollow.

By contrast, the magical world still seems attuned to the small craftsman. Wand makers such as Ollivander and Gregorovitch seem justly celebrated for their talents, as are skilled tailors such as Madam Malkin. There are close parallels with the Candleford society of skilled craftspeople and small shopkeepers, answerable to no one but themselves and their customers.

In these respects, therefore, magical society reflects an idealization of a bygone society, that of the English country town before the impact of the railroads. Yet there is one crucial difference.

According to the 1901 census, approximately 1.4 million people in Britain and Ireland worked as domestic servants, out of a total population of about 44 million. The total resident female domestic workforce (including people working in hotels, lodging houses, and so forth) was 1,330,783. In cities such as Bath, one in five of the female population above the age of ten was a domestic servant; in London, it was one in seven.[19] Thompson herself comments that in the hamlet of Lark Rise, there were no girls above the age of twelve; they had all been sent out to work as maids in better-off households.[20]

The magical world is very different. Despite claims by groveling Death Eaters to be "his most loyal servants," not even Lord Voldemort seems to possess domestic staff. Furthermore, the situation seems to have been unchanged for years. The only people we see in servant roles are Rubeus Hagrid (expelled from Hogwarts under circumstances where he was apparently forbidden "ter do magic, strictly speaking") Argus Filch (a Squib), and assorted house-elves (PS, 48). Peter Pettigrew angrily tells Severus Snape, "I am not your servant!" (HBP, 29)

Household tasks are performed largely by magic, although this still does not explain the magical world's arrangements for food production. In Lark Rise, when the girls of the village go out into service, their brothers go into the fields as farm laborers. In the magical world, it is impossible to conjure good food out of thin air, although it is possible to increase the quantity if one already has some.

The need for human physical labor seems to have been reduced practically to nothing in the wizarding world. Reg Cattermole, from the Ministry's maintenance team, carries out janitorial duties, but they also include selecting the appropriate weather for the Ministry's subterranean levels. This argues for some level of magical skill. No doubt, he carries out the heavy lifting by using Summoning charms or clearing charms of other sorts. It also seems likely that no one (except possibly a house-elf) is actually required to either mine or shovel coal to keep the Hogwarts Express running.

We have no real evidence as to how magical food is produced, how fuel to cook it is provided, or how it reaches the market. Certainly, there is no evidence that the (presumably considerable) magical population whose members fail to finish their education at Hogwarts are engaged in either domestic service or agricultural labor. Nor are there magical factories to absorb this presumed underclass. What do they do for a living?

All Wizards Are Equal . . . but Some Are More Equal Than Others

The magical underclass certainly exists; one key representative is Stan Shunpike. We meet Stan first in *Prisoner of Azkaban*, when he is the conductor of the Knight Bus. The following is a representative sample of his dialogue:

> "Yeah," said Stan, still rubbing his chest, "Yeah, that's right Very close to You-Know-'Oo, they say. . . anyway, when little 'Arry Potter put paid to You-Know-Oo . . . all You-Know-'Oos supporters was tracked down, wasn't they, Ern? Most of 'em knew it was all over, wiv You-Know-'Oo gone, and they came quiet. But not Sirius Black. I 'eard he thought 'e'd be second in command once You-Know-Oo 'ad taken over." (*POA*, 34)

By depicting Stan's accent visually, Rowling clearly labels him as "other." It is a technique she uses only with working-class characters (such as Hagrid) or "comic foreigners" (such as Fleur Delacour or Viktor Krum). The Hogwarts staff and pupils speak largely grammatical English, conventionally spelled, except for occasional regionalisms such as "me mam." This applies even to characters such as Professor McGonagall or Seamus Finnigan, whom one might expect to have regional accents at least as marked as Stan's.

Stan appears briefly in *Goblet of Fire*, when, to impress some Veela, he asserts that he is about to be named the youngest-ever Minister for Magic. His fantasizing subsequently lands him in Azkaban when he is overheard boasting of knowing the Death Eaters' secret plans. In *Deathly Hallows*, he is one of the mob of Death Eaters attacking Harry, although Harry notes his "strangely blank" face and concludes that he is acting under the Imperius Curse (*DH*, 55).

Stan's life follows a depressing pattern, one that is familiar in the Muggle world. We first see him trapped in a dead-end job, limited by his class and educational disadvantages. Joining Voldemort's gang of extremist thugs offers a chance of excitement and glamour that his life lacks otherwise. The criminal justice system fails him; unlike Harry, he is not the sort of accused whom the likes of Professor Dumbledore exert themselves to defend. He is pushed further into the extremist camp. They regard him as cannon fodder.

Mundungus Fletcher is, in some respects, Stan's counterpart in the Order of the Phoenix. He is initially presented as subhuman, barely animate: "The thing Harry had taken to be a pile of rags gave a prolonged, grunting snore, then jerked awake." (*OOTP*, 77) He also suffers from the dialogue hex: "And if you'll believe me, lads, the gormless gargoyle buys all 'is own toads back orf me for a lot more'n what 'e paid in the first place—" (*OOTP*, 82) His nickname of "Dung" gives a fairly clear hint of how the reader is supposed to regard him. He scrapes out a living as a petty criminal and a con man.

In her portraits of the previous characters, Rowling can be seen not simply depicting working-class characters, but showing a degree of class prejudice in how she does so. This is not wholly surprising. The genre in which she is working—the boarding school story—is one imbued with class issues. As is discussed more fully in a chapter on Hogwarts in this book, only approximately 6 to 7 percent of British children are educated privately. Of those, only a minority attend boarding schools. Yet representatives of the most exclusive private schools are disproportionately represented in politics and in the upper reaches of law, in finance, and in the universities.[21] Attending a "good" school—and displaying the accent and the mannerisms associated with that background—opens a vast range of doors that would otherwise remain resolutely shut.

Class, particularly in Great Britain, is not simply a question of relative wealth. The source of that wealth is important, with "old money" (inherited wealth) conferring more status on its possessor than money acquired through business. One British politician from an aristocratic background used the term "the kind of people who *buy* their silver" (instead of inheriting it) as a put-down of the *nouveaux riches*. Furthermore, nonmonetary considerations outweigh purely financial ones when assessing someone's class status.

This principle was demonstrated during the late nineteenth century, when American heiresses with substantial fortunes derived from industry, such as Consuela Vanderbilt and Jenny Jerome, married impoverished English aristocrats. Swapping a fortune for a title was presented as either an equal trade or one where the aristocrat conferred the favor.

The magical world seems to have no aristocracy as such, although connections with ancient pureblood families such as the Peverells or with the Hogwarts founders are celebrated. Families such as the Blacks, the Potters, and the Malfoys possess substantial inherited wealth, although the source of that wealth is left vague. The Weasleys are poor (in comparative terms), but their class status within the magical world is second to none.

The Weasleys are pureblood; Ron mentions vaguely that "Mum's got a second cousin who's an accountant, but we never talk about him."(*PS*, 75) Arthur Weasley's promotion at the Ministry is blocked because of his unpopular political opinions, but in *Chamber of Secrets* we learn that he is behind a Muggle Protection Bill, making him influential as a lawmaker. In *Goblet of Fire*, he has no problem mingling in the Top Box with dignitaries such as the Minister for Magic and the Bulgarian Minister, who treat him as an equal. Even the Weasleys' boom-and-bust spending habits (where sudden windfalls are spent on exotic foreign holidays, rather than saved for emergencies) suggest that Molly and Arthur were brought up in affluent families and have never gotten used to the economic management needed to bring up seven children on a small income. The idea that there is wealth somewhere in the family is reinforced by the Weasleys' Great-Aunt Muriel, who owns a priceless goblin-made tiara that has been in her family for generations and who threatens to cut Fred and George out of her will. Arthur's clash with Lucius Malfoy in Flourish and Blotts's bookshop is therefore the clash of social equals, one of whom believes the other is betraying his class.

Rowling uses the idea of "pureblood" status to explore issues such as racism and anti-Semitism. Her exploration of pureblood status is also peculiarly relevant to class, as can be seen from the case of the Gaunts. Although the Gaunts live in squalor, they treasure Slytherin's locket and a ring alleged to bear the Peverell coat of arms. Tellingly, although Marvolo Gaunt is aggressive and apparently illiterate, his speech is not depicted using any of the class markers that Rowling uses for Stan or Mundungus.

The Gaunts' story has many parallels with Thomas Hardy's *Tess of the D'Urbervilles*. In this 1891 novel (which was considered very scandalous when first published), Hardy deals with sexual double standards and the corrupting effect of urban values on country life. The novel tells the tragic story of a village girl, Tess, who is seduced, disgraced, and eventually hanged for the murder of her lover.

Tess's father, the village peddler Jack Durbeyfield, cherishes "a wold [old] silver spoon, and a wold graven seal" handed down by his great-grandfather. The local vicar tells him that "Durbeyfield" is a corruption of "D'Urberville" and marks his descent from a Norman knight who came over to England with William the Conqueror.[22]

Durbeyfield's newfound conviction of his aristocratic status leads to tragedy. He starts drinking to excess and neglecting his job. As the family fortunes decline, Tess, his daughter, is forced to beg for a position as a domestic servant with the D'Urbervilles, distant cousins who have retained their upper-class status. She is seduced by Alec D'Urberville, the son of the house, and becomes pregnant.

Because this is a Thomas Hardy novel, matters go downhill from there. On the bright side, at least Tess's child does not become a Dark Wizard bent on the conquest of the magical world.

In both the Gaunt and the Durbeyfield families, the head of the family attends more to his supposed noble blood than to making sure his family is fed. In each case, the daughter of the house is both the most admirable member of the family and the one who suffers most from her father's actions.

The Malignant Ministry

The previous sections of the chapter have discussed how the Industrial Revolution facilitated the great expansion of the Muggle middle classes, principally because of the opportunities it gave for creating wealth. We should now consider how far it is reasonable to regard magical society as capitalist in any real sense. In a market economy, competition is an important factor that keeps costs down and encourages innovation. What magical society shows is a society where there appears to be only one of everything: one school, one hospital, one bank, and, most important, one Ministry.[23] There is no competition in many areas, and the absence of competitive market pressure means changes and improvements come slowly, if at all.

The chapter titled "Careers Advice," in *Harry Potter and the Order of the Phoenix* is, in part, a satire on how badly schools tend to handle this important area. Yet one factor that jumps off the page is the dominance of the Ministry as an employer. This is also borne out when one considers the careers of adult witches and wizards whom we see. Of the Weasleys, Arthur and Percy work for the Ministry; Charlie works with dragons, presumably in some official international capacity; Bill works for Gringotts; Fred and George set up Weasleys' Wizard Wheezes; and Molly combines being a stay-at-home mother with, in the later books, keeping an underground resistance organization fed and supplied. Nymphadora Tonks and Alastor "Mad-Eye" Moody are both Aurors, while Kingsley Shacklebolt is such a senior Ministry official that he is tasked with guarding the Muggle Prime Minister.

Furthermore, although Hogwarts is (officially) independent of the Ministry, wizarding examinations are administered by Ministry officials, and students can be expelled from Hogwarts on the Ministry's order.[24] Werewolves such as Remus Lupin can be rendered unemployable by Ministry decree. International sport is directly regulated by the Ministry. Commerce is controlled by Ministry rules on the thickness of cauldron bottoms and lists of tradable magical artifacts.

The magical world does not seem to be good at giving people options. This seems likely to be a factor in the rise of Dark Lords. Without constitutional or other peaceful means of changing society, people who become marginalized are likely to be forced into violent conflict with their society. We see this with the two werewolves, Lupin and Fenrir Greyback; Lupin struggles constantly with having his options repeatedly restricted because of his condition. Greyback embraces his outlaw status.

Anyone such as Gellert Grindelwald or Voldemort will find a constant stream of potential supporters among those whom magical society treats as outcasts.

Conclusion

Class has always been a key element in British humor, from Shakespeare's "rude mechanicals" in A *Midsummer Night's Dream* to the social-climbing Eltons in Jane Austen's *Emma*, and through Jeeves and Wooster to Monty Python. Python's "Four Yorkshireman" sketch is a classic example of inverse class snobbery, in which a group of successful businessmen compete with one another to describe the hardships of their childhoods.

Rowling's Harry Potter novels are squarely within this tradition. As indicated earlier, however, the ways in which the magical and the Muggle worlds parallel and diverge from each other over issues of class is also an important theme of the book. In many ways, Harry's treatment by the Dursleys, which allows him to perceive life from a low rung on the class ladder, gives him insights that eventually allow him to defeat Voldemort. For example, the

Dursleys treat him like a servant—or a house-elf. As a result, his treatment of house-elves such as Dobby or Kreacher is marked by his understanding and empathy. Hermione Granger, by contrast, tries to improve the lives of house-elves without bothering to ask them what they really want: the classic mistake of any would-be ally who is not a member of the group he or she is trying to assist.

One purpose of fiction is to cast new lights on real life. Characters such as Stan Shunpike, the Dursleys, the Gaunts, Mundungus Fletcher, and the obsequious shopkeeper Mr. Borgin, who grovels to the wealthy Malfoys to their faces and sneers at them once the shop door has closed behind them, offer some real insights into modern Muggle class issues and concerns.

Notes

1. Dr James P. Kay, *The Moral and Physical Condition of the Working Classes Employed in the Cotton Manufacture in Manchester in 1832* (Dublin: Irish University Press, 1972).

2. Regrettably, the profound role played by the railroads in the shaping of the American West and their impact, in particular, on the First Nations is outside the scope of this chapter.

3. *Quidditch through the Ages*, pp. 32–38, identifies league-standard Quidditch teams located almost entirely in remote rural areas throughout the United Kingdom.

4. Ralph Waldo Emerson, "The Young American," delivered to the Mercantile Library Association, Boston, February 7, 1844, later collected in *Nature; Addresses, and Lectures*. (Boston: James Munroe and Company, 1849).

5. Friedrich Engels, *The Condition of the Working Class in England*, ed. Victor Kiernan (London: Penguin, 1987)

6. All book quotes are taken from the British editions by J. K. Rowling as follows: *Philosopher's Stone*, London; Bloomsbury, 1997; *Chamber of Secrets*, London; Bloomsbury, 1998; *Prisoner of Azkaban*, London; Bloomsbury, 1999; *Order of the Phoenix*, London; Bloomsbury, 2003; *Half-Blood Prince*, London: Bloomsbury,2005; *Deathly Hallows*, London; Bloomsbury, 2007; *Quidditch through the Ages*, London; Bloomsbury, 2001.

7. No comparison is intended in terms of ideologies.

8. Meaning a private income from investments in government securities. Four percent remained the standard interest rate for a long period. For example, Jane Austen characters are often described as having "a fortune of ten thousand pounds" ($15,999). This represents an annual income of £400 ($612).

9. Roger Highfield, *The Science of Harry Potter: How Magic Really Works* (London: Penguin, 2003), examines possible solutions and barriers to replicating magic using technology.

10. Broomsticks are attested to from as early as 962 C.E. (*QTTA*, 2).

11. On August 11, 1968, the *Oliver Cromwell's* journey from Liverpool to Carlisle concluded 138 years of steam-powered passenger transport in the United Kingdom.

12. His real name was Theophrastus Philippus Aureolus Bombastus von Hohenheim, which would have been a bit long for a chocolate frog card. Roy Porter, *The Greatest Benefit to Mankind* (HarperCollins, London, 1997), 201–205, details his career and influence on medical history.

13. C. P. Snow's phrase to describe the inner circles who controlled the country. C.P. Snow *Corridors of Power* (London: Macmillan, 1964).

14. *Self Help*, Project Gutenberg text, 17, www.gutenberg.org/catalog/world/readfile?fk_files=37550&pageno=17.

15. "England Your England," collected in *Selected Essays* (London: Penguin, 1957), 89.

16. This department is a fitting location, because the only sustained efforts at technological innovation we see are in Quidditch broomstick development. Judging by GB Patent 1426698 (Photon Push-Pull Radiation Detector for Use in Chromatically Selective Cat Flap Control and 1000 Megaton Earth-Orbital Peace-Keeping Bomb), ludicrous patents are far from a magical specialty; see *OOTP*, 119.

17. Lysenko worked on crop breeding. In that field, his claims were the equivalent of asserting that any son of Mad-Eye Moody would be born with a false eye and a stump.

18. Flora Thompson, *Lark Rise to Candleford* (London: Penguin Modern Classics 1973), 344.

19. Pamela Horn, *Rise and Fall of the Victorian Servant* (Dublin: Gill and Macmillan, 1975), 27. This figure refers to a broader occupational category than the class of "servants" discussed in chapter 6, since it also includes those employed in hotels and other commercial establishments.

20. Thompson, *Lark Rise to Candleford*, 155–172.

21. Including the current incumbent, nineteen UK prime ministers attended Eton College.

22. The year 1066, the date of the Battle of Hastings, which initiated the Norman Conquest of England and Wales, seems to be roughly contemporaneous with the date of the founding of Hogwarts.

23. Except pubs, this being a British series after all. Hogsmeade alone has two, the Hog's Head and the Three Broomsticks.

24. During *Order of the Phoenix*, the Ministry tries, unsuccessfully, to expand its control over Hogwarts, and after Voldemort's accession in *Deathly Hallows*, it largely achieves this.

Hairy Snout, Human Heart?

Werewolves in Harry Potter's World and in European History

Eveline Brugger

"Which of you can tell me how we distinguish between the werewolf and the true wolf?" said Snape.

—*Prisoner of Azkaban*, 171[1]

The idea of humans transforming into animals is one of the oldest myths of humanity and can be found all over the globe. In the magical world of Harry Potter, there are three different ways for a human to turn into an animal: through Transfiguration, by becoming an Animagus, or by being infected with lycanthropy. A person who's transfigured into an animal by a witch or a wizard truly becomes that animal, thus losing his or her humanity until the spell is reversed. Turning oneself into an animal while keeping one's human mind is difficult and dangerous, and the few wizards and witches who accomplish it have to be officially registered as Animagi with the Improper Use of Magic Office.

This cautious approach already indicates that the whole topic of human-animal transformation is considered risky by wizards, but the caution that Harry's world shows toward Animagi pales in comparison to its reaction toward those who have been afflicted with the third condition: the werewolves. As described in *Fantastic Beasts*:

> The werewolf is found worldwide, although it is believed to have originated in northern Europe. Humans turn into werewolves only when bitten. There is no known cure, although recent developments in potion making have, to a great deal, alleviated the worst symptoms. Once a month, at the full moon, the otherwise sane and normal wizard or Muggle afflicted transforms into a murderous beast. Almost uniquely among fantastic creatures, the werewolf actively seeks humans in preference to any other kind of prey. (*FB*, 41f)

This characterization of werewolves is pretty consistent with their image in today's pop culture—with a few notable exceptions, the werewolves we encounter in gothic novels and horror movies mostly fit this description. Yet the development of today's werewolf image warrants closer inspection, especially when it comes to the precarious link between lycanthropy and witchcraft.

Werewolves: A History

> The distinctive features of the wolf are unbridled cruelty,
> bestial ferocity, and ravening hunger. His strength, his cunning,
> his speed were regarded as abnormal, almost eerie qualities,
> he had something of the demon, of hell. He is the symbol of
> Night and Winter, of Stress and Storm, the dark and mysterious
> harbinger of Death.
>   —Montague Summers, *The Werewolf* [2]

Of all European predators, the wolf probably has the most ambiguous reputation. Although positive wolf myths (such as the legend of the two founders of Rome being suckled by a she-wolf) aren't hard to find, wolves also appear as threatening and dangerous, often downright malevolent creatures in European folklore. In the long run, it was the image of the "big bad" wolf that prevailed, right down to Grimm's fairy tales. Wolves presented a very real danger for livestock, and sometimes humans reinforced the negative stereotype. Christianity added its own contribution, because the wolf is used as a symbol for greed and destruction several times in the bible, in both the Old and the New Testaments. The latter especially focuses on the wolf as the enemy of flocks, juxtaposing it with Christ, the Good Shepherd.[3]

Yet what about the idea of humans turning into wolves? Both Greek and Roman authors mentioned such transformations, sometimes through magic, other times through divine interference.[4] Norse mythology, in which the wolf was strongly linked with the chief god Odin, was familiar with the concept as well. Although the belief in wolf-men (or wolf-gods) didn't disappear with the arrival of Christianity, it was now "officially" declared superstition.[5] Early medieval church authorities condemned the belief not only in werewolves, but in animal metamorphosis in general, and those who admitted to believing in these transformations had to do penance.[6] Such measures prove that folk belief in werewolves still existed and was widespread enough to warrant the attention of the church, but the sources don't contain much information on the belief itself, which means we don't know what these werewolves from early medieval folklore looked like.

It is through French literature that we first get a more detailed look at the European werewolf during the High Middle Ages. In the twelfth and thirteenth centuries, several authors wrote works of literature based on French folk tales in which men-wolves played a central part. Marie de France's *Bisclavret* is the most renowned work among them, but they all share a common theme: men who turn into wolves don't do it on their own accord. In most cases, they are the victims of some kind of spell or curse that can eventually be lifted so that they become human again. In their wolf shape, some of them are murderous beasts, while others are tame and kind, but once the involuntary transformation is undone, they revert back to their human nature.[7]

These stories of animal transformations all touched on the same theological problem as the folk belief in werewolves: according to the teachings of the church, it was not possible for humans to turn into animals. St. Augustine of Hippo, perhaps the most influential of the early Church Fathers, had already stated in the fifth century that the devil or his minions did not possess the power to cause the actual transformation of a human into a wolf. Instead, according to Augustine, people who believed themselves to be werewolves had merely dreamed the experience, although their dream-selves might—through demonic influence—actually manifest in the vis-·ible realm. This approach remained the church's official position until the Late Middle Ages, although several medical authorities argued that lycanthropy was an illness caused by an imbalance of the bodily humors that left patients with the illusion that they turned into wolves.[8]

From the fifteenth century onward, the werewolf disappeared for about 250 years as a literary trope. Instead, it now made appearances in court documents: lycanthropy began to be regarded as a facet of witchcraft and was persecuted as such.

The *Malleus Maleficarum*, the "Hammer of Witches" (published in 1486), which was to become the "handbook" of witch hunters, was the clearest and most influential expression of the fundamental change not only in the attitude toward magic and witchcraft in general, but also toward lycanthropy.[9] While early medieval doctrine had assigned the belief in werewolves firmly to the realm of superstition, if not heresy, the *Malleus Maleficarum* asserted that the devil created the illusion of witches changing into the shapes of wolves so that they could wreak all kinds of havoc. A little more than a century later, Henry Boguet, who presided over a number of werewolf trials in Burgundy (France), claimed in his demonological treatise *Discours execrable des sorciers* that the devil made a witch fall asleep and then went around in wolf shape himself to carry out the witch's wishes.[10] The most radical paradigm shift in how werewolves were seen, however, was based on the writings of the highly regarded scholar, political thinker, and jurist Jean Bodin. In his *Démonomanie des sorciers* (published in 1586),

Bodin abandoned all claims of illusions or devilish trickeries and tried to prove that—contrary to the teachings of St. Augustine— animal transformation was indeed possible and that werewolves were real. According to Bodin, werewolves were humans who used magic to turn themselves into murderous beasts in the devil's service.[11]

A pact with the devil, which constituted one of the necessary conditions of witchcraft, was now also regarded as the basis for the werewolf transformation. Although Bodin's belief in the physical reality of werewolves was by no means universally accepted, the idea that werewolves constituted a rather specific subdomain of witchcraft took hold and led to several "waves" of werewolf persecutions, although these were limited to specific regions.[12] The regions where people were tried for the crime of lycanthropy were usually rural, thinly populated areas in which wolf attacks were a realistic danger for people and livestock alike.

The first known werewolf trials were conducted in Franche-Comté, a province in Eastern France, in the sixteenth century. Most of the accused were from the lower classes, often foreigners or social outcasts who were believed to have harmed humans—often children—or livestock while in their wolf shape. In the seventeenth century, the number of werewolf trials began to dwindle in the area; folk belief in werewolves still existed, but when such matters went to court, the charge was usually changed into one of witchcraft.[13] In the neighboring territory of Lorraine, which saw about four hundred witch trials in the decades around 1600, werewolf activity was mentioned only briefly during some of the trials, but it was never a focus of attention as in Franche-Comté, where several dozen werewolf trials were held between 1520 and 1670.[14]

One of the other few regions where werewolf trials were held in significant number were the alpine parts of today's Austria, especially Styria, Carinthia, and the archbishopric of Salzburg, from the mid-seventeenth to the early eighteenth century. The accused, again mostly beggars and other members of the lowest classes in society, confessed to wolf transformations by means of magical salves and to the use of harmful magic. Aside from becoming wolves themselves, several of them also confessed to *Wolfsbannerei*, the controlling of real wolves via magical means. Again, the concepts of lycanthropy and witchcraft were closely linked, with *Wolfsbannerei* forming a kind of "missing link" between these two crimes. Between 1630 and 1725, forty-six cases are documented; about 50 percent of the accused were executed.[15]

Even rather isolated cases sometimes became (in)famous, as the trial of Peter Stump, "The Werewolf of Bedburg" (near Cologne in Germany), in 1589 proves. He doesn't fit the usual profile of lycanthropy suspects, because he was a wealthy farmer. It has been assumed that Stump, a Protestant convert, got caught up in the religious struggle between Catholic and Protestant factions in Cologne. Under torture, he confessed to the frequent use of harmful magic and said that the devil had given him a magical belt that allowed him to turn into a wolf. In wolf shape, he allegedly killed and ate humans, preferably children and pregnant women; he also confessed to rape and incest with his sister and his daughter. Pamphlets depicting Stump's trial and gruesome execution (he was put to the wheel, had his flesh torn from his body with red-hot pincers, and had his limbs broken before he was beheaded and his body burned) were published not only in Germany, but also in England, Denmark, and the Netherlands. They made Peter Stump's case the most well-known werewolf trial in Europe, even though the original court records have been lost.[16]

Werewolves and Witchcraft

[Fenrir Greyback] regards it as his mission in life to bite and to contaminate as many people as possible; he wants to create enough werewolves to overcome the wizards.

　—*Half-Blood Prince*, 334

"And I'm not a very popular dinner guest with most of the community," said Lupin. "It's an occupational hazard of being a werewolf."

　—*Order of the Phoenix*, 94

In the world of Harry Potter, werewolves and magical folks aren't on the best of terms. Werewolves are feared and shunned by witches and wizards. Even though they're clearly humans by birth and live in human shape except for the time of the full moon, werewolves are considered half-breeds or part-humans by most wizards. There is a Werewolf Registry and a Werewolf Capture Unit in the Beast Division of the Department for the Regulation and Control of Magical Creatures at the Ministry, and although there is also an office for Werewolf Support Services in the Being Division (*FB*, xiii), we don't see much support for werewolves from wizarding authorities during the course of the series. The anti-werewolf legislation passed by the Ministry makes it almost impossible for werewolves to find employment and generally pushes them toward the fringes of wizarding society. In return, Fenrir Greyback and his pack of followers wage their own war against the magical community, albeit in the service of Lord Voldemort, who is himself a wizard.

As we have seen, the hostility between magical folk and werewolves in the Harry Potter universe stands in stark contrast to the Muggle concept of lycanthropy as a subbranch of witchcraft, as it was developed during the witch trials of the Early Modern period.[17] Muggle folk belief saw things differently sometimes: there were groups such as the famous Benandanti in sixteenth- to seventeenth-century northern Italy, a fertility cult whose members believed that their spirits took on animal shape to fight against evil witches. In Early Modern Lithuania, folklore had werewolves fight on the side of good against witches.[18] Still, as far as the authorities—both secular and religious—were concerned, the different varieties of lycanthropes were actually guilty of witchcraft themselves.

If we rely on one of the most common stereotypes concerning historical witches and witchcraft, that is, the idea that it was mostly women who were persecuted as witches, we could assume that alleged werewolves constituted the male counterparts to the female victims of witch persecutions, and this assumption has indeed often been made. The term *werewolf* itself seems to indicate a relation to the male gender: the different variations of the old Germanic word *wer(e)* mean "man"—in the sense of "male human," as opposed to the more general meaning that the word *man* can have in English. Can we therefore assume that the werewolf was a way to bring men into the female realm of witchcraft? Are witch and werewolf the "real" magical pairing, corresponding to witch and wizard in the world of Harry Potter?

However tempting—and widespread—this assumption may be, it is historically inaccurate. First, contrary to popular belief, the accusation of witchcraft was by no means limited to women, as Birgit Wiedl has already described in detail in chapter 5 in this volume, "Why the Statute of Secrecy? Real Historical Oppression of Witches and Wizards." Second, although medieval werewolf literature is centered around male protagonists, the persecution of "real" werewolves during the Early Modern period included both genders. While more men than women were accused during the course of the earliest persecutions, the number of female victims approached that of the males during the later stages.[19] It is interesting to note that although the definition of werewolves in the Harry Potter universe includes both genders, because anyone could get bitten, the werewolf characters we actually get to see in the course of the Harry Potter series are all male, thus remaining faithful to the literary stereotype.

Speaking of getting bitten: although the idea of lycanthropy as a kind of contagious disease is prevalent in modern pop culture, it was by no means the most common concept during the period of the werewolf trials, when the accused were interrogated in detail about the ways in which they had turned themselves into wolves. After all, an involuntary infection would not have fit that period's notion of a deliberate pact with the devil. Instead, the method that is mentioned most frequently is the use of magic ointments, potions, or salves—quite a contrast to the Wolfsbane Potion that renders werewolves harmless in the world of Harry Potter. Belts and girdles made of wolf skin also played a role. These go back to folk beliefs about methods of werewolf transformations that included the wearing of wolf skins—which, in turn, led to the motif that a werewolf can't change back into human form if he can't put his clothes back on.[20]

That Time of the Month: Werewolves and the Moon

"[Snape]'ll be delighted," said Lupin coolly. "He assigned that essay hoping someone would realize what my symptoms meant . . . Did you check the lunar chart and realize that I was always ill at the full moon? Or did you realize that the boggart changed into the moon when it saw me?"

—*Prisoner of Azkaban*, 346

It is interesting to note that one of the most popular elements of modern werewolf lore, the moon, doesn't play a prominent role either in pre-modern werewolf literature or in the werewolf persecutions. In the Harry Potter universe, the full moon is crucial for the transformation, and most other modern werewolf stories also mention the influence of the moon in some form.

In classical and medieval literature, most werewolves remain in their wolf shapes for prolonged periods of time—days, weeks, sometimes even years. Early Modern werewolf trials usually went with the assumption that the transformation could happen whenever the werewolf-witch in question chose, although nighttime transformations were frequently mentioned—which stands to reason, not only because darkness was considered the natural realm of demonic evil, but also because the wolf was known as a nocturnal predator.

There are a few isolated discussions of lunar influence, though: in the early thirteenth century, Gervase of Tilbury stated in his *Otia Imperialia* that the werewolf transformation took place during specific phases of the moon, although he mentions the new moon, not the full moon. One of the classical werewolf tales, included by the Roman author Petronius in his *Cena Trimalchionis* (ch. 62), describes a werewolf transforming by the light of the full moon but makes no specific connection between these two events.[21] The immediate connection between werewolves and the moon is a result of werewolf fiction, a genre that was rediscovered when the persecutions of "real" werewolves came to an end; this fiction became popular during the nineteenth century and still has a lot of appeal today.[22]

Generally, modern werewolf tales (whether books or movies) come in many varieties. Most of these firmly belong in the horror genre, although there are other, more sophisticated takes as well. Some of these werewolves turn into full-fledged wolves, others into some kind of wolf-human hybrid (which often was a technical necessity in movies during the pre-CGI era). In addition, we now also encounter wolves that turn into humans, instead of the other way around. The actual transformation can be painful (as it is in the Harry Potter books) but rather unproblematic as well; in Terry Pratchett's Discworld series, the female werewolf Angua describes it as a "full body sneeze."

What most modern fictional werewolves have in common is the fact that they are extremely hard to kill—not only because of the wolf strength that was already ascribed to their pre-modern predecessors, but also because of new features that were introduced more recently, such as the idea that werewolves are "allergic" to silver and can only be killed with silver bullets. Although it is a very old concept that silver has apotropaic qualities (possesses the power to ward off evil), it's not part of historical werewolf folklore and wasn't introduced into werewolf fiction until the twentieth century.[23]

While the most common way to become a werewolf in modern werewolf fiction is still by being bitten by one, another element from the werewolf folklore of old turns up again there, too: the concept of lycanthropy as a hereditary condition. In the Harry Potter series, the question is left unresolved: Lupin worries that his unborn child will be affected because his "kind don't usually breed," although it eventually turns out that his son is not a werewolf (*DH*, 213). Many other werewolf stories do go down that route, sometimes to the extent that werewolves are regarded as something akin to a separate species.[24] The concept that the children of a werewolf can and will inherit lycanthropy stems from late medieval folklore, where it was usually regarded as an affliction that would be passed down from father to son.[25] Teddy Lupin therefore dodged a bullet, whether it was silver or not.

Lupin versus Greyback: A Study in Contrasts

Professor Lupin, who appears in the third book, is one of my
favorite characters. He's a damaged person, literally and metaphorically. I think it's important for children to know that adults,
too, have their problems, that they struggle. His being a werewolf
is a metaphor for people's reactions to illness and disability.

   —J. K. Rowling[26]

Fenrir Greyback is, perhaps, the most savage werewolf alive
today. [. . .] Voldemort has promised him prey in return for his
services. Greyback specializes in children. [. . .] Voldemort has
threatened to unleash him upon people's sons and daughters;
it is a threat that usually produces good results.

   —Half-Blood Prince, 334–335

Between the two of them, Remus Lupin and Fenrir Greyback represent the entire range of werewolf characterizations, not only in the
Harry Potter universe, but in modern werewolf fiction in general.
Friendly, gentle Professor Lupin is a staunch supporter of Harry
and Albus Dumbledore, and the hardship he has to endure because
of his condition—which isn't his fault, given that he was bitten at a
very young age—indeed worked well as the metaphor that Rowling
mentioned in the quoted interview in 2002. The metaphor no longer applied, however, once the character of Greyback was introduced in the sixth volume (published in 2005): although we don't
know how Greyback originally became a werewolf, it is made very
clear that instead of struggling against his condition, as Lupin does,
he actively embraces his monstrous nature, even cherishes it to the
point where he acts wolflike even in his human shape.

    While Lupin's condition—and the reaction it causes among the
majority of the wizarding population—indeed resembles a dangerous, contagious illness (AIDS immediately springs to mind, given
the social shunning that HIV-positive patients often encounter),
Greyback doesn't fit that particular pattern. Actually, if one takes
both Lupin and Greyback into account, one can't help drawing
the conclusion that the most fitting "real" analogy to lycanthropy,

as J. K. Rowling presents it, would be pedophilia: although sexual attraction toward children is generally considered perverse in today's Western society, it is not in itself a crime as long as the person afflicted by it doesn't act based on that attraction. Yet even if a person manage to keep a tight grip on his or her pedophilic urges, he or she will undoubtedly face a severe social backlash in the form of fear and revulsion if his or her inclinations become public knowledge. It is absolutely certain that such a person would not be allowed to work with children—just as Professor Lupin lost his job as a teacher at Hogwarts when parents learned that he was a werewolf. All of the other anti-werewolf measures mentioned in the Harry Potter books, from forced registration to the near impossibility to find a job, fit that analogy remarkably well, too.

> Fenrir Greyback grinned, showing pointed teeth. Blood trickled down his chin and he licked his lips slowly, obscenely.
>
> "But you know how much I like kids, Dumbledore."
>
> "Am I to take it that you are attacking even without the full moon now? This is most unusual . . . you have developed a taste for human flesh that cannot be satisfied once a month?"
>
> "That's right," said Greyback. "Shocks you, that, does it, Dumbledore? Frightens you?"
>
> "Well, I cannot pretend it does not disgust me a little," said Dumbledore. (*HBP*, 593)

Greyback can be seen as analogous to a pedophile who actively pursues his or her inclinations—an analogy that works especially well, given Greyback's taste for children, which is explicitly mentioned several times and the fear he causes among wizarding parents. Besides, the concept of the werewolf as a killer of children and as a sexual predator (although not necessarily in combination) was an integral part of older werewolf folklore, as well as one of the standard accusations in werewolf trials.[27]

Other than working well as a present-day metaphor, Lupin and Greyback also reflect—whether intentionally or merely by coincidence—the medieval versus the Early Modern approach toward werewolves: Lupin, one of the most positive characters in the entire series, is clearly a victim who deserves sympathy and needs medical attention in the form of Wolfsbane Potion, just as medieval authors depicted werewolves as the victims of curses, and natural philosophers from the same period considered lycanthropy a physical and/or mental illness.[28] Greyback, on the other hand, is a criminal who—even though he may not have become a werewolf out of his own free will—is responsible for his crimes because he willingly gives up his humanity in favor of his nature as a monster, just like those accused of lycanthropy during the Early Modern period, who were believed to have made a pact with the devil out of their own choosing.

As is so often the case with characters from the Harry Potter books, Lupin's and Greyback's names already give away both their wolf nature and their moral quality. Remus Lupin, whose parents were obviously clairvoyant (because he wouldn't be bitten and turned until he was a small boy), bears the name of one of the two legendary founders of Rome, Romulus and Remus, who were nursed by a she-wolf. Remus was later killed by his brother, Romulus, which might be a hint at Lupin's status as a victim throughout the books, right up to his death, which he met without being granted so much as an onstage death scene in the final installment of the Harry Potter series.[29] His last name is obviously derived from the Latin word for wolf, *lupus*, and is therefore telling without being outright ominous.

Fenrir Greyback is another matter entirely: while his last name is a more general allusion to his wolfish nature, because "gray" is one of the most frequent descriptive terms used in folkloristic monikers for wolves, his first name is one of many variations of the *Fenrisúlfr*, the great wolf from Norse mythology, who is a thoroughly sinister character.[30] Brother to Hel, the goddess of the Underworld, and to the Midgard Serpent that circles the world of men, Fenris plays a key role in the Norse Doom of the Gods. We don't know whether Greyback chose Fenrir as his nom de guerre once he became a werewolf or whether his first name is another case of parental second sight, but it's certainly more than fitting for the Big Bad Wolf of the Harry Potter series.

Notes

1. All book quotes are taken from the American editions by J. K. Rowling as follows: *Prisoner of Azkaban*, New York: A.A. Levine Books, 1999; *Order of the Phoenix*, New York: A.A. Levine Books, 2003; *Half-Blood Prince*, New York: A.A. Levine Books, 2005; *Deathly Hallows*, New York: A.A. Levine Books, 2007; *Fantastic Beasts*, New York: A.A. Levine Books, 2001.

2. Montague Summers, *The Werewolf* (London: K. Paul, Trench, Trubner, 1933), 65.

3. See, for example, John 10:12: "He who is a hired hand, and not a shepherd, who is not the owner of the sheep, sees the wolf coming, and leaves the sheep and flees, and the wolf snatches them and scatters them."

4. Keith Roberts, "Eine Werwolf-Formel. Eine kleine Kulturgeschichte des Werwolfs," in *Dämonen, Monster, Fabelwesen. Mittelalter Mythen 2*, ed. Ulrich Müller and Werner Wunderlich (St. Gallen: UVK Fachverlag für Wissenschaft und Studium, 1999), 565–567.

5. Utz Anhalt, "Der Werwolf. Ausgewählte Aspekte einer Figur der europäischen Mythengeschichte unter besonderer Berücksichtigung der Tollwut," MA thesis, Universität Hannover, 1999, 12–15.

6. Rolf Schulte, *Man as Witch: Male Witches in Central Europe*, trans. from the German by Linda Froome-Döring, Palgrave Historical Studies in Witchcraft and Magic (New York: Palgrave Macmillan, 2009), 18f.

7. Ibid., 20.

8. Roberts, "Eine Werwolf-Formel," 567f.

9. Adam Douglas, *The Beast Within: A History of the Werewolf* (London: Chapmans, 1992), 160. On the topic of the *Malleus Maleficarum* and its influence, see chapter 5 in this volume, "Why the Statute of Secrecy? Real Historical Oppression of Witches and Wizards," by Birgit Wiedl.

10. Roberts, "Eine Werwolf-Formel," 573f.

11. Schulte, *Man as Witch*, 22.

12. Nicole Jacques-Lefèvre, "Such an Impure, Cruel, and Savage Beast . . . Images of the Werewolf in Demonological Works," in *Werewolves, Witches, and Wandering Spirits. Traditional Belief and Folklore in Early Modern Europe*, ed. Kathryn A. Edwards (Kirksville, MO: Truman State University Press, 2002), 184.

13. Schulte, *Man as Witch*, 23–32.

14. Robin Briggs, "Dangerous Spirits: Shapeshifting, Apparitions, and Fantasy in Lorraine Witchcraft Trials," in *Werewolves, Witches, and Wandering Spirits. Traditional Belief and Folklore in Early Modern Europe*, 6; Schulte, *Man as Witch*, 32, note 84.

15. Martin Scheutz, "Bettler—Werwolf—Galeerensträfling. Die Lungauer "Werwölfe" des Jahres 1717/18 und ihr Prozess," *Salzburg Archiv* 27 (2001): 221–268.

16. Elmar M. Lorey, "Zum Fall Peter Stump," www.elmar-lorey.de/werwolf/Stump.htm.

17. Elmar M. Lorey, "Wie der Werwolf unter die Hexen kam. Zur Genese des Werwolfprozesses," www.elmar-lorey.de/werwolf/genesetext.htm, chap. 2.

18. It has been speculated that these benign werewolves might have been remnants of shamanic practices, although the matter remains a point of debate. See Carlo Ginzburg, *The Night Battles: Witchcraft and Agrarian Cults in the Sixteenth and Seventeenth Centuries* (Baltimore: John Hopkins University Press, 1983); Elmar M. Lorey, "Das Werwolfstereotyp als instabile Variante im Hexenprozeß. *Gefragt, wie oft er sich des Jahrß zum Wehrwolf gemacht*," *Nassauische Annalen* 112 (2001): 135–176, www.elmar-lorey.de/Stereotyp.htm, chap. 4; and Christoph Daxelmüller, "Der Werwolf. Ein Paradigma zur Geschichte der kulturellen Wahrnehmung," *Zeitschrift für Volkskunde* (1986): 203–208.

19. Schulte, *Man as Witch*, 32, 99.

20. Roberts, "Eine Werwolf-Formel," 578f.

21. Ibid., 577f.

22. Elmar M. Lorey, "Besichtigung der Restbestände. Was nach Ende der Hexenprozesse im 20. Jahrhundert schließlich vom Werwolf übrig blieb in Volkserzählung, Literatur und Film," www.elmar-lorey.de/werwolf/Literatur.htm, chap. 2.

23. Hanns Bächtold-Stäubli, ed., *Handwörterbuch des deutschen Aberglaubens*, vol. 8 (Berlin: de Gruyter 1937), 1–3; Roberts, "Eine Werwolf-Formel," 578.

24. For example, the aforementioned werewolf Angua from Terry Pratchett's Discworld series belongs to an entire clan of werewolves.

25. Schulte, *Man as Witch*, 21.

26. Lindsay Fraser, "Harry Potter—Harry and Me," *Scotsman*, November 2002, www.accio-quote.org/articles/2002/1102-fraser-scotsman.html.

27. Lorey, *Werwolfstereotyp*, chap. 3.6.

28. Roberts, "Eine Werwolf-Formel," 573f.

29. Rowling has stated that Lupin was originally meant to survive but then was killed off when she decided to spare Arthur Weasley the same fate. See "Rowling: I Wanted to Kill Parents," today.msnbc.msn.com/id/20026225/, July 29, 2007.

30. Hanns Bächtold-Stäubli, ed., *Handwörterbuch des deutschen Aberglaubens*, vol. 9 (Berlin: de Gruyter 1941), 717.

Hermione Raised Her Hand Again

Wizards Writing History

Anne Rubenstein

"I was wondering if you could tell us anything about the Chamber of Secrets," said Hermione in a clear voice. [. . .]

Professor Binns blinked. "My subject is History of Magic," he said in his dry, wheezy voice. "I deal with *facts*, Miss Granger, not myths and legends." He cleared his throat with a small noise like chalk snapping and continued, "In September of that year, a delegation of Sardinian sorcerers—"

He stuttered to a halt. Herminone's hand was waving in the air again . . .

"Please, sir, don't legends always have a basis in fact?"

Professor Binns was looking at her in such amazement, Harry was sure no student had ever interrupted him before, alive or dead.

"Well," said Professor Binns slowly, "yes, one could argue that, I suppose." He peered at Hermione as though he had never seen a student properly before.

—*Chamber of Secrets*, 149[1]

The word *history* has at least three meanings.

First, "history" can refer to the entire past. The word can mean the sum of everything that ever happened: the Louisiana Purchase, the brand of cereal you ate for breakfast last Tuesday, everything. Sometimes this is limited to the period of time since humans started writing, so that everything before that is "pre-history." Sometimes the word "history" means all events that ever happened, large and small. Either way, when we use the word "history" this way, it means the entire past, without regard for the importance of any particular event, without any effort at explaining the past, and without any sense that the past is connected to the present.

Second, the word "history" can refer to the stories we hear about noteworthy events in the past and the important people who made those events happen. Such stories can be found in history textbooks, on TV documentaries, in movies set in the past, on plaques on the walls of old buildings, on statues commemorating important events, on postage stamps, and in all sorts of other places. This kind of history often is "the official story": a smooth, uncomplicated explanation for why the world is the way it is, leaving out the parts that might confuse the listeners or embarrass the tellers. It is this kind of history that, as the cliché goes, is "written by the victors."

Sometimes, when historians use the word "history," we mean it in one of those two ways. Yet other times when historians say "history," we mean something very different. The word "history," used in this third way, points to the work that historians do, the active process of asking a question about the past and using firsthand information from the past to answer that question. When historians talk about "primary sources," they mean documents that contain firsthand information from some place and time about which the historian is asking questions. The use of primary sources—which can be, for example, a diary, a newspaper article, a phone bill, a photograph, or a birth certificate—to understand the past is one of the most important parts of doing historical research in this third sense of the word.

Every so often, the third meaning of "history" bumps up against the second meaning of "history." A historian who asks just the right question and uncovers just the right evidence to answer the question and interprets the evidence in just the right way can end up challenging what everyone believed to be the settled story of the past. And once in a while, changing the official story of the past changes the present as well.

The wizarding world has its own official story, which can be glimpsed in the seven Harry Potter novels, the film versions of the novels, and the three associated books written by J. K. Rowling. Wizards' official history is recorded in textbooks such as Bathilda Bagshot's *A History of Magic*, the children's book *The Tales of Beedle the Bard*, and the reference books *Quidditch through the Ages* and *Hogwarts, A History*.[2] Statues and sculptures in the halls of Hogwarts and the atrium of the Ministry of Magic, too, help tell the story of the past in the magical world. Texts such as articles in the *Quibbler*, Gilderoy Lockhart's memoirs, Sirius Black's Wanted poster, and the blurbs on the backs of chocolate frog cards repeat simplified (and not always trustworthy) stories about the past of the wizarding world.

There are three central themes in the official story of the magical world's past: the story that wizards and witches tell one another and their children in textbooks and other versions of their official story. First, there is the story of how Muggles hunted witches and wizards, who eventually decided to remove themselves peacefully from the Muggle world. Second, there is the story of how witches and wizards persuaded or forced other magical beings—goblins, giants, centaurs, and house-elves—to accept an inferior status and even (in some cases) to serve them. This is the story told by the golden statue in the center of the Ministry of Magic that Harry sees in *Order of the Phoenix*, which shows the "lesser" magical beings staring up adoringly at the wizard and the witch. Third, there is the story of conflicts among wizards and witches: first, the war against Gellert Grindelwald and his followers, followed by the first war against Lord Voldemort and the Death Eaters. The official story, at the opening of the Harry Potter series, is that all of these conflicts are in the past, that the good guys have won, and that all is well and will continue to be well in the future.

Old-School History: Binns, Bagshot, and Other Nineteenth-Century Historians

Magical historians record that story and pass it on to younger wizards and witches. Two of them appear in the Harry Potter books and movies: Professor Binns and Bathilda Bagshot. In many ways, Bagshot and (especially) Binns resemble ordinary Muggle historians. In the nonmagical world, professional historians usually work at colleges and universities; the careers of Muggle historians frequently combine teaching history students with engaging in archival research and writing books and articles about history. So Professor Binns—in some ways, at least—is a typical professional historian, with a teaching job.

Historians like to complain about the "dead white men" who are so often the heroes of official history—presidents, prime ministers, generals, and judges. Two hundred years ago, Jane Austen put the same complaint into the mouth of the heroine of her novel *Northanger Abbey*: "History . . . tells me nothing that does not either vex or weary me. The quarrels of popes and kings, with wars and pestilences in every page; the men all so good for nothing, and hardly any women at all—it is very tiresome."[3] Rowling tells a good joke about this when she makes Professor Binns himself a dead white man. History at the Hogwarts School of Witchcraft and Wizardry is taught by a ghost: "Professor Binns had been very old indeed when he had fallen asleep in front of the staff room fire and got up the next morning to teach, leaving his body behind him." (SS, 133)

Binns is a terrible teacher. He "droned on and on"; "It was amazing how he could make even bloody and vicious goblin revolts sound . . . boring." (SS, 133 and GOF, 392) Students have trouble staying awake in his classes. Binns forgets Seamus Finnigan's and Parvati Patil's names after they have been attending his classes for three years, calling them "O'Flaherty" and "Miss Pennyfeather." (COS, 151–152) Even in Harry's fifth year at Hogwarts, Binns thinks his last name is "Perkins" instead of Potter (OOTP, 318). In fact—and this may be what makes him so bad at teaching—he often seems to forget that the students are there at all, because he is interested only in what he is teaching, not in the people he is teaching it to.

Yet as bad as he is as a teacher, Professor Binns is not a terrible historian, in some ways—just a very old-fashioned one. Like most historians, he specializes in a particular topic. Nothing interests Professor Binns as much as the Goblin Rebellions and the Goblin Wars of the seventeenth and eighteenth centuries, and the History of Magic classes that he teaches focus on them. His greatest concern is accuracy: in addition to admonishing Hermione that he deals in facts, "not myths and legends," he discourages wild speculation by insisting that his students must pay attention only to "*history*, to solid, believable, verifiable *fact!*" (*COS*, 152)

Peter Novick, a scholar who studies the historical profession, dates the high point of this "cult" of "the scientific fact" among historians in the English-speaking world to "the late nineteenth and early twentieth centuries."[4] That makes sense for Binns, because he would have been trained as a historian around then. Present-day historians in the Muggle world, for the most part, understand their work differently: they use *facts* about the past as the basis for *interpretations* of the past. Historians disagree about where fact ends and interpretation begins; they argue about what kinds of facts matter most; they have a range of methods for organizing and understanding the facts they gather and strongly held opinions about which of those methods works best. Yet almost all real-life, living historians would disagree with Professor Binns when he declares that only facts matter, because we know that the facts do not simply speak for themselves.

Bathilda Bagshot, the other professional historian who appears in the Harry Potter books, is the author of the textbook that Binns assigns to his students, A *History of Magic*. Her career appears to have been very different from that of Professor Binns and even less like a typical Muggle historian's career. Unlike most Muggle historians and Professor Binns, she does not seem to have had a job, other than writing her book, and she does not appear to have spent much time in the company of other historians. Most historians in the nonmagical world are employed by an institution such as a university, a college, an archive, or a library. (Less often, historians

work for museums, government offices, or nonprofit organizations.)
They conduct their research, for the most part, in specialized libraries and archives, and they rarely publish the results of their research
without extensive processes of consultation with fellow historians.

Real-world historians meet often, in formal conferences and
seminars and less formal reading groups and workshops, in order to
hear about their peers' research and help one another think more
clearly about what they have discovered. So their workplaces and
their work practices usually keep Muggle historians in regular contact with many other scholars. Even though most historical books
and articles have only one author, a whole community of teachers,
students, colleagues, editors, and friends are likely to have helped
the author figure out what questions to ask about the past and how
best to find the answers to those questions. Yet Bathilda Bagshot
seems to have lived most of her life alone in a cottage in the village
of Godric's Hollow, without much ongoing contact with her professional peers. This makes her a very unusual historian.

Bathilda Bagshot helped raise her great-nephew, who grew up
to be the evil wizard Grindelwald, and she comes to a bad end at
the hands of the Death Eaters. So she played an active role in the
violent conflicts and the political debates that shook up the magical world in her lifetime. Yet in her writing, she seems to have tried
to avoid taking sides by staying far away from controversial current
events: A *History of Magic* concludes around 1900 and does not
refer to anything that happened in the twentieth century at all.

This, too, is an old-fashioned approach to the study of history.
Historians who explicitly link the past to current events are sometimes called "present-minded." A hundred years ago, historians tried
hard *not* to be present-minded but instead to study "the past for its
own sake." They went so far as to pretend not to care—or even to
know—about present-day consequences of the historical events they
were describing and analyzing.[5] Nowadays, historians, by and large,
study the relationship between the present and the past. They may
argue fiercely about exactly what that relationship between past
and present is, but very few are so old-fashioned that they claim the
relation between the present and the past does not or should not
matter to us. Like Professor Binns, but in a different way, Bathilda

Bagshot embodies a set of ideas about what history is and how history should be studied that was popular many decades ago but that now is generally seen as outmoded.

Hermione, a History: The Trio Goes Right to the Source(s)

All the same, Hermione found Bagshot's A *History of Magic* useful enough that she carried it along with her when she joined Harry and Ron Weasley in their quest to find the Horcruxes, in *Deathly Hallows*. Hermione is not as impressed by some of the other history texts she reads. At first, she quotes from *Hogwarts, A History* at every opportunity. Yet by her fourth year, although she is still citing the book frequently, she reads it more skeptically. She says, "with her usual air of impatience . . . 'It's all in *Hogwarts, A History*. Though, of course, that book's not *entirely* reliable. A Revised *History of Hogwarts* would be more accurate. Or A *Highly Biased and* Selective *History of Hogwarts, Which Glosses Over the Nastier Aspects of the School.*'" (GOF, 238)

Hermione has learned that she cannot trust the official history of the magical world to answer her questions about the relationship between the world she sees and the past she reads about—in this case, her questions about the enslavement of house-elves. And from the first Harry Potter book to the last, Harry, Ron, and Hermione have to find out what happened in the past in order to solve their problems in the present.

Solving the present-day problems in each of the Harry Potter books usually depends on understanding the past differently. In order to overcome Voldemort's supporters and eventually to defeat Voldemort himself, the three Hogwarts students have to know some aspect of the official history of the wizarding world, to figure out what questions to ask about the official history, to locate the evidence of what happened in the past that will allow them to understand what's incomplete or wrong about the official history, and to revise the story they have been given into one that fits the facts they have uncovered. In other words, they have to move from learning "history" in the second sense of the word to researching "history" in the third sense of the word. Harry, Ron, and especially Hermione have to learn to act like historians themselves.

The Trio usually start with the official history in some form as they try to figure out the past. Sometimes this is the story that they seem always to have known, a story that they were told so often they can no longer remember the first time they heard it. At the very beginning of *Sorcerer's Stone*, for example, Harry already knows that he lives with his aunt and uncle, the Dursleys, because his own parents died when he was very young—which is true. But he believes that they died in a car crash—which is, of course, not true at all. Similarly, in *Deathly Hallows*, Ron (like all children raised in the wizarding world) knows the fairy tales originally composed by Beedle the Bard and is surprised to discover that Hermione and Harry, who grew up among Muggles, do not. As it turns out, Ron has never read the original fairy tales; he knows them because his mother told versions of them to all of her children, changing details to make them "a bit spookier" or simply because her own memory of the stories might have been imperfect (*DH*, 336).

Yet sometimes Harry, Hermione, and Ron have to do a little research even to find out what the official story is. They consult books such as *Hogwarts, A History*, and they ask questions of their teachers. For instance, in *Chamber of Secrets*, Hermione interrupts Professor Binns's "deadly dull lecture on the International Warlock Convention of 1289" with a question about the Chamber of Secrets, and she keeps asking until he finally tells as much as he knows about the story of Salazar Slytherin's thousand-year-old plan to rid Hogwarts of Muggle-borns (*COS*, 148–149). In *Sorcerer's Stone*, Harry "had questions to ask, hundreds of them," when Rubeus Hagrid finally rescues him from the Dursleys, and he learns a more truthful (though still very incomplete) story about his family's place in the wizarding world by asking some of those questions (*SS*, 57).

Harry, Ron, and Hermione cannot settle for the official history, the story they have already been told. Over and over again, they turn to primary sources—firsthand evidence from the past—to uncover a truer version of the stories they think they already know. Take the solution to the mystery posed in the first Harry Potter book, for instance: What is the Sorcerer's Stone (aka the Philosopher's Stone), who has it, and who is trying to take it? Carefully reading the back of Professor Albus Dumbledore's chocolate frog card shows Harry that the Headmaster had known and worked with Nicholas Flamel; Harry, Hermione, and Ron have been searching for Flamel because Herminone's research in the library has connected his name to the Sorcerer's Stone, and putting these two facts together suggests to the three friends that the Sorcerer's Stone must have been hidden at Hogwarts, by Dumbledore.

Of course, Hermione, Ron, and Harry have an advantage over ordinary historians, because magic offers many kinds of primary sources that the nonmagical world lacks. Muggle historians often interview people about events in the past, a process that is usually called oral history. But sometimes people lie, and even when they intend to tell the complete truth, perceptions of the pasts differ, historians misunderstand what the people they are speaking to are telling them, and memories change over time. So oral histories are difficult sources for ordinary historians to use—although they are often very valuable ones, too. Pensieved memories have some similar limitations as a source: they, too, come from a specific person's point of view. Yet memories preserved in a Pensieve do not change over time, and it seems impossible to directly lie to a Pensieve without leaving the memory fogged up and clearly altered (as with the memory that Professor Horace Slughorn originally offered to Dumbledore in *Half-Blood Prince*). So Harry can use memories preserved in a Pensieve as a historical source, as he does in the chapter "Snape's Worst Memory," in *Order of the Phoenix*. This causes him, once again, to reevaluate the story he thought he knew about his parents: now he can see them—especially his father—neither as perfect heroes nor as careless drunks, but as human. His parents, he learns, combined bravery and selflessness with moments of stupidity and heartlessness, as most people do.

Harry rethinks the story he knows about his parents as he accumulates more evidence, and different kinds of evidence, from various points of view. He goes through a similar process with his godfather, Sirius Black, whom he first learns about from a Most Wanted poster, then from Arthur Weasley, then from Professor Lupin, then from Professor Snape, and finally from Black himself. Each new piece of evidence offers a new version of Black's story that adds to the last, so that Harry's view of him changes completely from the beginning of *Prisoner of Azkaban* to the end. Yet each new piece of evidence also requires careful listening or reading on Harry's part and sometimes careful discussion with his friends before he can decide how the pieces of the puzzle fit together.

Historians in the real world work hard at interpreting the documentary evidence they uncover. Even seemingly simple, trustworthy documents—newspaper articles, for example—cannot be taken at face value. In the magical world, we discover, this is just as true. Journalist Rita Skeeter quotes the people she interviews accurately enough, with her Quick-Quotes Quill (and, in the case of her interview of Bathilda Bagshot, her willingness to use Veritaserum). But the tricky questions Skeeter asks, and the slant that the Quick-Quill's literary style gives to the descriptions it writes, reveal that Rita is willing to stretch and bend the facts to reach the conclusion she wants to reach, and that the Quick-Quill helps her to do this. Accuracy in citation is not always enough; historians, whether Muggle or magical, have to interpret the documents they study very carefully. Historians must understand the opinions and the positions of the people who produced the documents, they must know who the authors of the primary sources hoped to speak to with these documents, and they must know what point the authors of the documents were hoping to make.

Even written records produced by governments can be surprisingly unclear, inaccurate, biased, or otherwise difficult for historians to understand. Seemingly simple documents, such as national census records, are shaped by contemporary political arguments (for instance, "who decides what counts as a marriage?") and more subtle hidden assumptions (for instance, "every married couple shares the same last name" or "everyone has an address"). Historians have to know the context in which the government documents were produced, in order to understand them fully and interpret them accurately.

Sorting the Sources

Similarly, in the wizarding world, the records kept by long-standing institutions such as Hogwarts, the Wizengamot, and the Ministry of Magic also require care. The songs of the Sorting Hat and the prophecies stored in the Ministry, for example, are full of useful information, but no matter how obvious they might seem to be, they turn out to be full of ambiguities. Was Sibyll Trelawney's prophecy really about Harry, or might it be about Neville Longbottom? There is nothing in the document itself—in this case, within the fragile glass sphere that contains the captured prophecy—that can resolve that ambiguity. Instead, a historical researcher, such as Hermione, must take into consideration all of the circumstances in which the prophecy was produced, in order to arrive at a tentative interpretation of this difficult historical document.

Treated with that kind of care, even the least trustworthy sources can yield valuable information. Tom Riddle's diary, for instance, in *Chamber of Secrets*, is a terrifying example of a bad historical source: it actively works not only to confuse its readers, but to manipulate them into committing crimes and even to kill them. The diary leaves Harry in a state of deep confusion over his own character and identity—Slytherin or Gryffindor? Yet the diary also reveals the true identity of Lord Voldemort, a crucial piece of information that all of the characters who fight the Death Eaters will need to know in the months and the years that follow this historical revelation.

Good historians often come up with different, even contradictory, interpretations of difficult primary sources. Harry, Hermione, and Ron work through similar disagreements as well. For instance, when Harry ends up with a used Potions textbook in *Half-Blood Prince*, he believes the handwritten advice he finds in the margins to be simply a piece of luck, the luck he needs to help him pass a difficult class. Hermione, however, is less trusting of the written word, and Ginny Weasley—for very good reason, because she learned from Riddle's diary about the damage an old book could cause—is more suspicious still. They have to be convinced that Harry's helpful find truly is "just a textbook," rather than a trap set by Voldemort and his followers (*HBP*, 183). Both of these interpretations turn out to be wrong: the Potions textbook that once belonged to the Half-blood Prince is neither a trap nor a mere schoolbook. Instead, it is valuable as a document of Severus Snape's own early years at Hogwarts.

The world of the Harry Potter books and movies shows us how Ron, Harry, and especially Hermione turn into historians. It offers fans the chance to think like historians, too. We can read some of the same documents that Hermione and her friends read. Some of these documents are embedded in the novels, such as the page of an old letter from Harry's mother to Sirius that Harry finds in Grimmauld Place and Elphias Doge's obituary for Dumbledore in *Deathly Hallows* or the Educational Decrees that Argus Filch puts up all over Hogwarts in *Order of the Phoenix* or the words to the Sorting Hat's songs. Others were published separately, such as the textbooks *Fantastic Beasts and Where to Find Them* and *Quidditch through the Ages* and the children's book *The Tales of Beedle the Bard*.

Potter fans love to debate the meanings of these documents, just as they argue over the meanings of the novels and the movies. For Harry, Ron, and Hermione, learning to act like historians was a matter of survival. The readers who love them, too, learn about doing history, in that third sense of the word. Yet we also learn that doing historical research—finding and interpreting the evidence of the past in order to make sense of the present—can be a lot of fun.

Notes

1. All book quotes are taken from the American editions by J. K. Rowling as follows: *Sorcerer's Stone*, A.A. Levine Books, 1998; *Chamber of Secrets*, New York: Scholastic, 2000; *Prisoner of Azkaban*, New York: A.A. Levine Books, 1999; *Goblet of Fire*, New York: A.A. Levine Books, 2000; *Order of the Phoenix*, New York: A.A. Levine Books, 2003; *Half-Blood Prince*, New York: A.A. Levine Books, 2005; *Deathly Hallows*, New York: A.A. Levine Books, 2007.

2. Hermione talks about several other history texts in the very first chapter in which she appears: "I got a few extra books for background reading . . . *Modern Magical History*,

and *The Rise and Fall of the Dark Arts* and *Great Wizarding Events of the Twentieth Century.*" (SS, 106) The wizarding world appears to have a strong interest in its own history and a thriving publishing industry. Yet none of these books receive a second mention.

3. Jane Austen, *Northanger Abbey* (London: Penguin Classics, 2003), 104.

4. Peter Novick, *That Noble Dream: The "Objectivity Question" and the American Historical Profession*, 4th ed. (Cambridge, UK: Cambridge University Press, 1988), 31.

5. Ibid., 272.

The Hogwarts Faculty

Ruth Abrams is a freelance writer, an editor, and an enthusiastic researcher; she holds a doctorate from Brandeis University, where she wrote about the role of Jewish women in European feminism from 1880 to 1920. She has wide-ranging experience as a Jewish educator, from teaching Judaic studies at the University of Massachusetts at Amherst in the late 1990s to managing the Web site www.interfaithfamily.com. Nevertheless, no one expected her to write about the Spanish Inquisition.

Eveline Brugger is a lecturer at the University of Vienna, Austria, and an instructor at the Viennese Institute for Economic Promotion. She specializes in medieval Central European history and archival sciences. She may have spent more time with dusty old books than any Hogwarts student, with the possible exception of Hermione Granger, and she maintains that Madam Pince has the right idea when it comes to dealing with readers who don't treat her babies with the care they deserve.

Don Keck DuPree has taught at Sewanee (University of the South), Rutgers University in New Jersey, and Centenary College of Louisiana. He currently practices theoretical and practical alchemy at Pace Academy, the Hogwarts of Atlanta. His students spend nearly as much time with alchemical tomes as they do with Chaucer, Shakespeare, and Dickens. He maintains open links to the Invisible College and other European practitioners of the magical arts.

M. G. DuPree teaches Latin at the Westminster Schools in Atlanta, Georgia. She has been a devoted linguist ever since she discovered that the more languages you know, the more you can curse without anyone knowing what you are saying; this is a knowledge she applies with some frequency to recalcitrant students. She is of the opinion the Unforgivable Curses have just been misunderstood and is working on the development of the Imperio atomizer mist personal body spray.

Alexandra Gillespie is an associate professor at the University of Toronto. She has written a book and articles and edited collections of essays on medieval manuscripts and early printing. Professor Gillespie is currently working on a catalogue of all extant copies of *The Invisible Book of Invisibility*.

Susan Hall is a UK lawyer and partner at Cobbetts, LLP, based in Manchester, England. In addition to publishing numerous articles on intellectual property and information technology, she has managed to conjure articles on legal aspects of Harry Potter into publications ranging from the *Law Society Gazette* to the *Journal of Intellectual Property Law and Practice*. A long-time defender of Richard III against the historical calumnies perpetrated by That Man Shakespeare, she is currently collaborating with Sir Nicholas de Mimsey-Porpington (d. 1492) on a major work concerning the Princes in the Tower, which will contain groundbreaking new eyewitness evidence and a damning indictment of staff morale and training standards at the Tower of London.

Janice Liedl is an associate professor of history at Laurentian University in Sudbury, Ontario. She has published in Tudor and Stuart English history, as well as on the question of memory in history. She hopes that her research will someday reverse the last bits of Gilderoy Lockhart's fiendish Obliviating Charm, which stole her memory of life in the wizarding world.

Grace Loiacono recently completed a graduate degree in Library Science at Pratt Institute. She plans to work in the Hogwarts Library and is currently developing spells to protect the books from being despoiled. An energetic Quidditch fan, she enthusiastically supports her House team.

Laura Loiacono is a graduate student in English. After several falls, she is waging a campaign against changing staircases. She enjoys sugar quills and butterbeer and can often be found in the Room of Requirement, reading and enjoying much-needed solitude.

Nancy R. Reagin is a professor of history and women's and gender studies at Pace University in New York; she's published several books and a number of articles in modern German history. Horrified by Professor Binns's teaching methods, she has recently collaborated with a wizarding colleague to author *Pensieves, Spells, and Charms in the Teaching of the History of Magic: A Modest Proposal* (Obscurus Books, 2010). She frequently spends a good deal more than she ought at Flourish and Blotts.

Anne Rubenstein is an associate professor of history at York University in Toronto. She is the author of *Bad Language, Naked Ladies, and Other Threats to the Nation: A Political History of Comic Books in Mexico*, as well as numerous articles in twentieth-century Mexican cultural and gender history and many collaborations on edited volumes and journals. Her current research focuses on movie audiences and fans in Mexico and elsewhere. This research would be much easier if only she had a Pensieve and some Veritaserum

Birgit Wiedl is a lecturer at the University of Salzburg in Austria. She is a trained archivist and a historian with a particular fondness for the Middle Ages and the Early Modern period. She has therefore not only seen her fair share of manuscripts that only reluctantly reveal their secrets, but would simply die to get her hands on a nifty Time-Turner. She would give it much more than just three turns.

Index

Notable Magical Words of Our Time

Page numbers in *italics* refer to illustrations.